AF335531

Repairing IBM PCs and Compatibles
An Illustrated Guide

Michael F. Hordeski

Windcrest®/McGraw-Hill

FIRST EDITION
FIRST PRINTING

© 1992 by **Windcrest Books**, an imprint of TAB Books.
TAB Books is a division of McGraw-Hill, Inc.
The name "Windcrest" is a registered trademark of TAB Books.

Printed in the United States of America. All rights reserved. The publisher takes
no responsibility for the use of any of the materials or methods described in this
book, nor for the products thereof.

Library of Congress Cataloging-in-Publication Data

Hordeski, Michael F.
    Repairing IBM PCs and compatibles : an illustrated guide / by
Michael F. Hordeski.
      p.   cm.
    Includes index.
    ISBN 0-8306-3900-4 (hard)   ISBN 0-8306-3899-7 (pbk.)
    1. IBM Personal Computer—Maintenance and repair.   2. IBM-
compatible computers—Maintenance and repair. I. Title.
    TK7889.I26H67 1992
    621.39′16—dc20   91-39662
                                     CIP

TAB Books offers software for sale. For information and a catalog, please
contact TAB Software Department, Blue Ridge Summit, PA 17294-0850.

Acquisitions Editor: Roland S. Phelps
Book Editor: Andrew Yoder
Director of Production: Katherine G. Brown
Book Design: Jaclyn J. Boone
Cover: Sandra Blair Design and Brent Blair Photography,
  Harrisburg, PA.   EL1

Contents

Acknowledgments

Many thanks to Dee, who did many of the illustrations in addition to typing, proofreading, and correcting.

Introduction

The better you understand how PCs are designed and how they work, the easier it is to discover when they are not working correctly. If you use, manage, maintain, or repair PCs, you will find this book helpful.

The architecture of the IBM-PC families and compatible computers is explained. Common buzzwords and acronyms are defined and effective troubleshooting techniques are detailed.

Nontechnical and novice personnel can become knowledgeable and lose their fear of PCs. More experienced users can improve upon their knowledge. With this new understanding, you will be able to identify and solve problems quicker and easier. You will also be able to make informed decisions regarding your PC's performance and functionality.

The book focuses on what can go wrong with a PC and how to fix it. You will learn about the most cost-effective approaches to maintenance, troubleshooting, and repair. The many ways a PC can fail, how to detect those failures, and how to make the appropriate repairs are also covered.

It is important to understand the problem of data disasters as well as the inner workings of hard disk drives. Failures in a PC's data storage are often critical because these failures often indicate a loss of data.

Many of these failures are not hardware faults; they are often correctable data defects. This book presents techniques for diagnosing and treating both kinds of failure.

This book should make you more technically proficient. It provides a good working knowledge of how PCs are built and how they function. You will gain in-depth information and practical tips about how critical hardware and software elements can malfunction.

You will learn how to use diagnostic programs for troubleshooting. You can find memory faults using only DOS, but this task is much easier with commercial diagnostic software. Also, hard disks can be fixed before problems occur and techniques can be used to recover data that DOS cannot read. These diagnostic skills are available using today's state-of-the-art programs.

You will find how to test processors, memory, hard disks, mouse units, networks and power supplies without special equipment. If you learn how to maintain your system, you can reduce downtime and the cost of being down. Because most computer malfunctions are not defective components, it is easy to make these repairs. These simple repairs can be a lifesaver. You can learn how to diagnose computer problems, then decide when you can repair it yourself, or when you should use an outside service. In many cases, all that is required are your fingers. You should know how to aid technicians, when they are needed, with diagnoses that will save time, money, and quickly get you operating again.

Anyone who works with an IBM PC/XT/AT or compatible system should find the book helpful. If you are an end user, you can save hours of time by taking care of simple problems on your own. If you are a data-center staff member who supports end users, you can learn valuable tips that will constantly help you with your job. If you are responsible for repairs, you will be able to make intelligent decisions.

This book has many illustrations and was specifically developed to be a valuable on-the-job reference. You should find it helpful when faced with making upgrading choices, diagnosing and maintaining systems, and making repairs.

1

The IBM PC architecture

The IBM PC computer

The IBM PC computer shown in Fig. 1-1 has a modular design. It uses an 8088 16-bit processor. The computer's PC-DOS allows you to use software packages available from a wide range of independent suppliers.

The PC's system functions are shown in the block diagram of Fig. 1-2. The 8088 processor controls the disk drive's reading and writing of data, while the 8088 processor controls the monitor, the keyboard, the communications connectors, and all options that are added to the system.

The original PC has 16 to 64K of main memory. One byte represents one character position. This memory can be expanded to 256K with the addition of a memory extension option. The computer also comes with a disk drive that holds 180 or 360K of auxiliary memory on single- or double-sided 5$\frac{1}{4}$-inch diskettes. A second disk drive brings the total auxiliary memory to 720K.

The PC's design makes it easy to install, comfortable to operate, and easy to repair. The system is designed to operate by minimizing conditions that might lead to strain and fatigue. It is also flexible so that you have the freedom to adapt it to your needs.

The 3-component structure of the computer allows you to place the components in many locations. You can use a floor stand to hold the system unit and keep your work surface free. The components are relatively light, compact, and portable. The keyboard comes with a 6-foot cord that you can place anywhere—even on your lap.

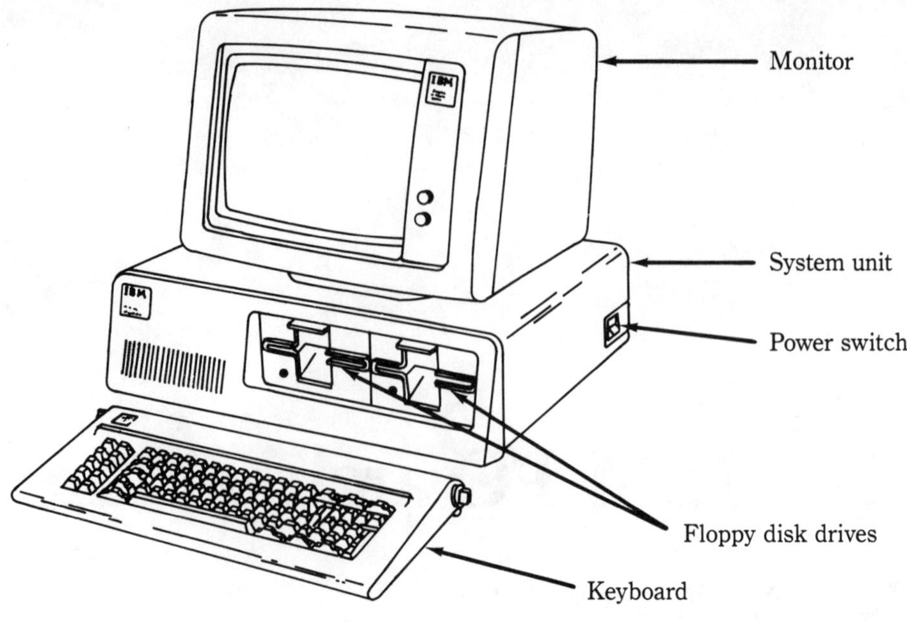

1-1   An IBM personal computer.

The monitor

The PC computer's monitor contains a video screen (Fig. 1-3) that has a diagonal dimension of 30.5 cm (12 inches). You should not touch the screen because fingerprints show up easily.

The monitor supplies video information. The video control system resides on the video adapter board inside the system unit. Adjustments on the monitor's back or side let you adjust the screen's brightness and contrast levels as you would on a television set.

The keyboard

The PC computer uses a low-profile keyboard that has 84 keys (Fig. 1-4). The standard keys at the center and left provide the uppercase and lowercase alphabets, numbers, and punctuation. To the right of these keys are the basic editor keys: Insert, Delete, End, Home, Print Screen, Page Down, Page Up, Number Lock, and the cursor arrow keys. On the same side is the numeric keypad.

On the left side of the keyboard are the special function keys for different types of applications: word processing, electronic mail, accounting, and spreadsheets.

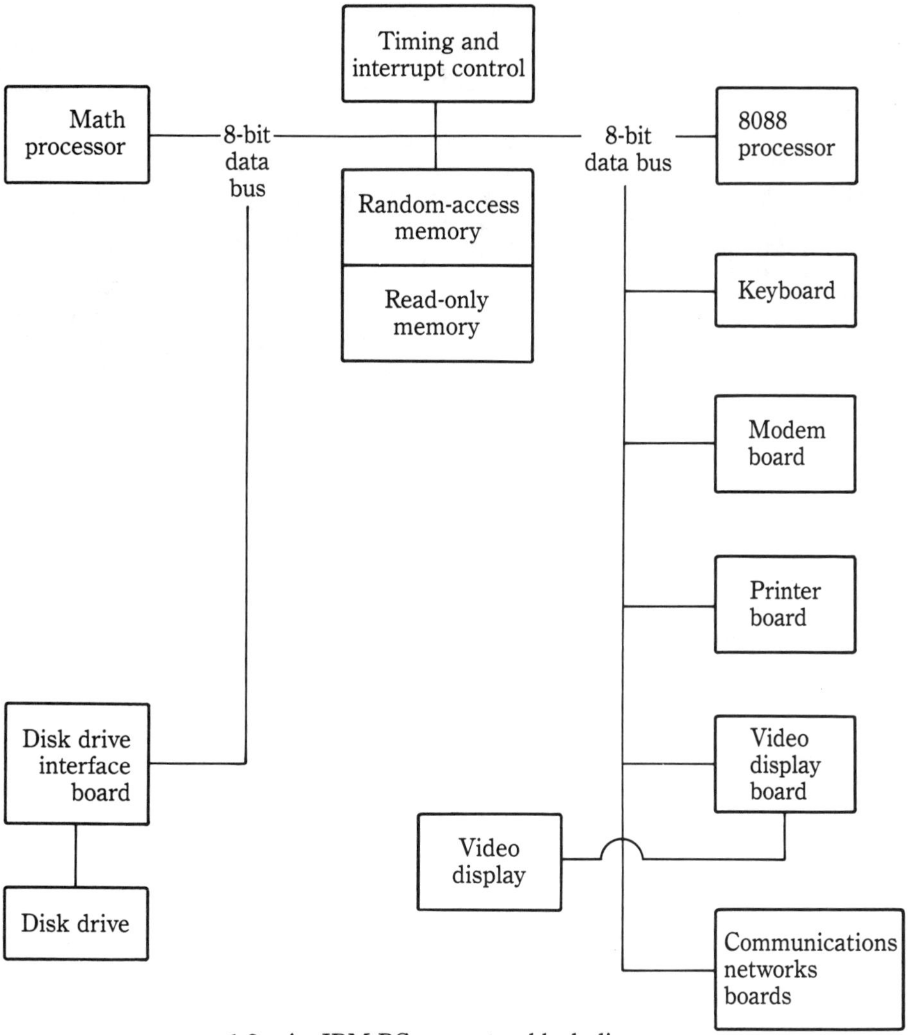

1-2 An IBM PC computer, block diagram.

1-3 An IBM PC computer monitor.

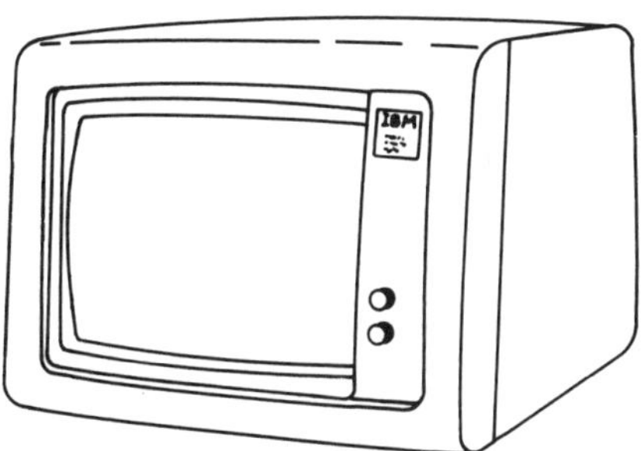

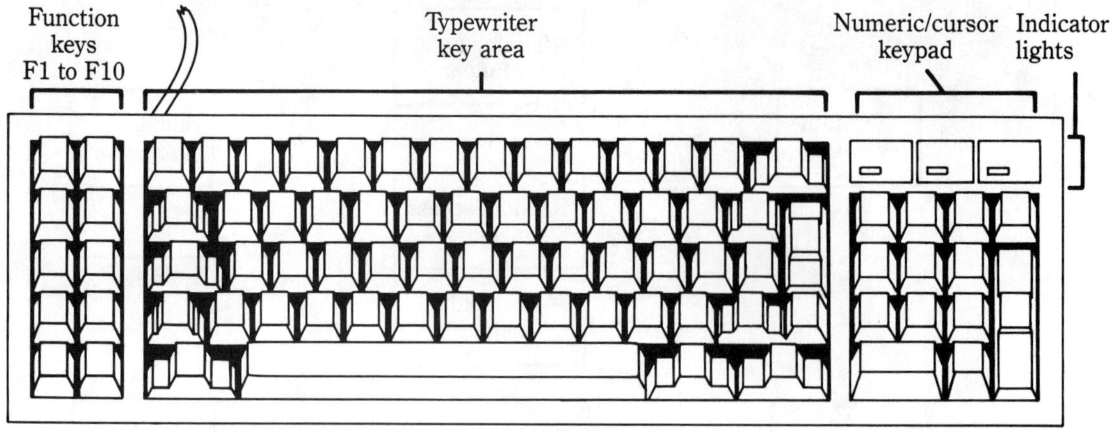

1-4 A PC keyboard.

The keyboard has the following features:

- A low profile that allows access to the disk drives in the system unit, if you would want to place the two components on the same table or desk.

- Keyclicks sound as the keys are pressed. You can often adjust the keyclick volume or turn it off.

- A keyboard tone generator that produces a margin bell. The tone volume can also be adjusted.

- Auto-repeat of all keys on the main keypad array, the numeric keypad, and the function keys (including Space, Del Char, and Tab).

The keys are arranged in an electrical matrix, which is scanned for keys that are pressed. A single-chip, 8-bit processor detects whenever a key is pressed and transmits the event to the system module.

A click sounds when a key is pressed. You might be able to turn the keyclick feature on or off or adjust its volume through a Set-Up feature. Many keyboards have lights that can be turned on and off by the system. These lights are assigned specific functions during normal system operation—an example would be the caps key lock.

The floppy-disk drive

The PC computer family uses a compact disk subsystem that consists of a disk-controller board (Fig. 1-5) and a floppy-disk drive (Fig. 1-6), which controls the diskettes on a single spindle. These disks or diskettes provide mass storage, data exchange, and file backup capabilities. The early disk-

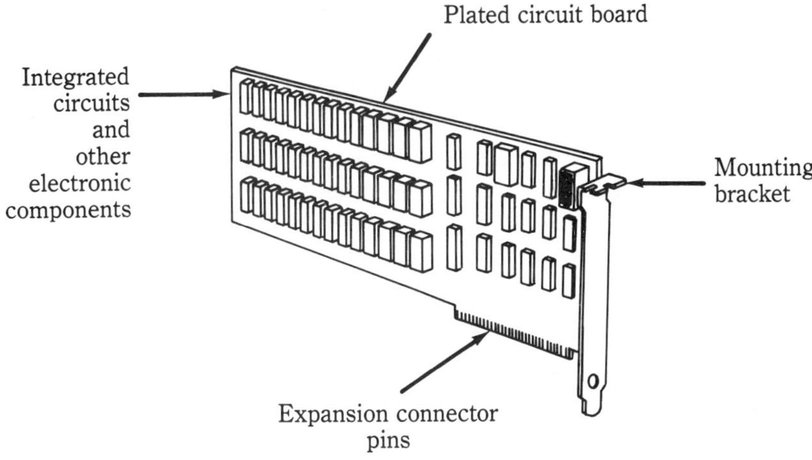

1-5 A typical disk controller board.

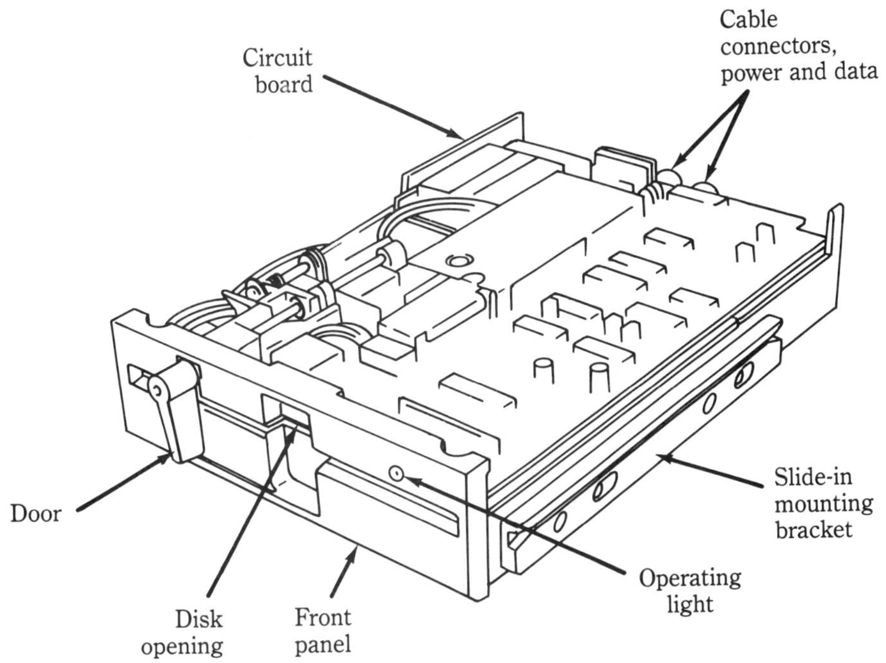

1-6 An IBM floppy disk drive.

ettes stored 180 to 360,000 bytes of information. Later, this number was expanded to 1,200,000 bytes.

Disk storage capacity is usually expressed in terms of *kilobytes* and *megabytes* (a 30M hard drive, for example, or a 360K floppy disk). Items stored on disk are not directly accessed by the CPU, a disk controller is used to connect the disk to the CPU. The controller can be a separate expansion board or it can be part of the main system board.

The disk drive has a single spindle that is turned by the drive motor. The drive accesses the diskettes with a single-head carriage assembly (if it is single-sided) or with a dual-head assembly (if it is double-sided). In either case, the assembly is moved by one stepper motor/lead screw combination.

The disk drive has two sensors that detect when a diskette is installed in it. These sensors also look for the notch on the side of the diskette's protective cover to see if the diskette is write protected. If this notch is covered, the disk drive cannot write on the diskette.

PC evolution

The original PC-DOS IBM personal computer uses an Intel 8088 microprocessor at 4.77 MHz. The memory is 256K to 640K of RAM and 40K of ROM. The storage is on one or two 5¼" floppy-disk drives.

The PC offered five expansion slots and an optional expansion unit to accommodate eight additional boards. For additional storage capacity, up to two 10M hard-disk drives are offered.

IBM PC/XT

The XT IBM personal computer uses an Intel 8088 CPU at 4.77 MHz. The memory is 128K to 640K of RAM with 40K of ROM. The storage is with one or two 5¼" 360K floppy-disk drives, or one 5¼" 360K floppy-disk drive and one 10M hard-disk drive.

The PC/XT includes eight expansion slots with one floppy-disk drive and one hard-disk drive. An optional expansion unit allows the availability of eight additional slots. For increased storage capacity, a 10M hard-disk drive and one 180K or 360K floppy-disk drive can be installed.

IBM PC/AT

The AT IBM personal computer AT uses an Intel 80286 CPU at 6 MHz. The memory ranges from 256K to 3M RAM. The storage is with one 1.2M floppy-disk drive with a 20M hard-disk drive.

The system offers seven available I/O expansion slots for additional peripherals. The original AT's memory can be expanded to 3M RAM and the storage capacity can be increased to accommodate a 40M hard-disk drive.

Typical MS-DOS compatibles

Typical MS-DOS compatibles include the AT&T Personal Computer 6300, which use an Intel 8086 CPU at 8 MHz. The memory is 128K to 640K of

RAM for the floppy version, 256K to 640K of RAM for the 10M hard-disk version, and 512K to 640K RAM for the 20M hard-disk version. The storage is with two 5¼" 360K floppy-disk drives, or one 5¼" 360K floppy and one 10M or 20M hard-disk drive. The unit can accommodate an optional 8087 math coprocessor. The floppy-disk system has seven available expansion slots and six available slots are on the hard-disk system. A 16/8-bit data-bus converter is also available for communications-interface capability.

ComPaq

The ComPaq Deskpro (Model 4) uses the 8086 CPU at 4.77 or 8 MHz. The memory is 128K to 640K of RAM with 8K of ROM. The storage is with one 5¼" 360 floppy-disk drive and one 10M hard-disk drive.

The Model 4 includes a 10M tape-backup system, and the storage capacity can be expanded to accommodate a 30M hard-disk drive. The system has a slot for an optional 8087 math coprocessor and includes one parallel and one serial port, and has four available expansion slots. A switchable clock speed is used for greater software compatibility.

The Compaq Deskpro 286 (Model 2) uses an 80206 CPU at 6 or 8 MHz. The memory is 512K to 8.2M of RAM with 8K of ROM. The storage is with one 3½" 1.2M disk drive and one 30M hard-disk drive. The storage capacity can be expanded to accommodate up to a 70M hard-disk drive. A 10M tape-backup system is also available.

The system has a slot for an optional 80287 math processor and includes four available expansion slots. The Model 2 has one parallel and one serial port. A switchable clock speed is used for software compatibility.

Corona

The Corona ATP-6-QD from Corona Data Systems uses an 80286 CPU at 6 MHz. The memory ranges from 512K to 16M RAM. The storage is one 5¼" 360K floppy-disk drive and one 3½" 1.2M disk drive.

The Corona ATP-6-QD system can accommodate an optional Intel 80287 math processor and the unit includes five expansion slots. Also included are one serial and one parallel port. The Corona ATP-6-Q20 is standard with one 1.2M floppy, one 20M hard-disk drive and one hard-disk controller.

Ericsson

The Ericsson Personal Computer Model S02 from Ericsson Information Systems uses an 8088 CPU at 4.77 MHz. Memory is 256K to 640K of RAM with 8K of ROM. The storage is with two 5¼" 360K floppy-disk drives.

The Ericsson Personal Computer has a socket for an optional Intel 8087 math coprocessor. It has five IBM bus-compatible expansion slots, and one serial and one parallel port.

Hewlett-Packard

The Touchscreen II from Hewlett-Packard uses an 8088 CPU at 8 MHz. The memory is 256K to 640K of RAM. The storage is with two 3^1/$_2$″ 710K disk drives, or one 3^1/$_2$″ 710K disk drive and one 10M, 20M, or 40M hard-disk drive.

This upgraded version of the HP-150 has touch-screen features. The standard system has four available expansion slots and four serial ports. For more storage capacity, a 10M, 20M, or 40M hard-disk drive can be added.

ITT

The ITT Xtra XP from ITT Information Systems uses an 80286 CPU at 4.77 or 6 MHz. The memory is with 512K to 1.6M of RAM and 64K of ROM. Standard storage is with one 5^1/$_4$″ 360K floppy-disk drive and one 10M or 20M hard disk.

The ITT Xtra XP can accommodate an optional Intel 80287 math coprocessor. The memory can be expanded to 1.6M. The XP has four available expansion slots after monitor hookup (three on the hard-disk version) and one parallel and one serial port. A switchable clock speed is used for applications software compatibility.

Kaypro

The Kaypro 286i (Model A) uses an 80286 microprocessor at 6 MHz. The memory is 512K to 15M of RAM and 32K of ROM. The storage is with one 5^1/$_4$″ 1.2M floppy-disk drive.

The 286i is a clone of IBM's AT. The Kaypro 286i uses a socket for an 80287 math coprocessor. The system memory can be expanded up to 15M RAM with additional boards. The system has seven expansion slots.

The Model B has one floppy and one 10M hard-disk drive, five expansion slots, one serial and two parallel ports, and an RGB interface for a PC/AT-compatible monitor.

Leading Edge

The Leading Edge Model D uses an 8088 CPU at 4.77 MHz. The memory ranges from 256K to 640K of RAM. The storage is with two 5^1/$_4$″ 360 floppy-disk drives, or with one floppy and one 10M hard drive.

The Model D has four available IBM-compatible expansion slots. The system can accommodate an optional 8087 math coprocessor. Also included are one parallel and one serial port.

NCR

The NCR PC6 used an 8088-2 CPU at 4.77 or 8 MHz. The standard memory is 256K or 512K to 640K of RAM and 40K of ROM. The storage is with two 5¼" 360K floppy-disk drives; or one 360K floppy and one 20M hard disk; or one 360K floppy, one 20M hard disk, and one 10M streaming-tape backup. The unit has six available expansion slots (five on the hard-disk versions), one RS232 and one parallel port.

The PC8 used an 80286 microprocessor at 6 MHz. The memory is 256K to 4M of RAM and 40K of ROM. The standard storage is one 5¼" 1.2M floppy-disk drive. The unit has six available expansion slots, and the system's storage capacity can include a 40M hard-disk drive. The PC8 enhanced version is standard with 512K RAM, five expansion slots, a 1.2M floppy and 20M hard-disk drive, and one serial and one parallel port.

Tandy

The Tandy 1200 HD uses an 8088 CPU at 4.77 MHz. The memory is 256K to 640K of RAM. The storage is with one internal 5¼" 360K floppy-disk drive and a 10M hard-disk drive. The motherboard on the Tandy 1200 HD can accommodate an Intel 8087 math coprocessor. Five IBM-compatible expansion slots (four after optional monitor hookup) are furnished. The unit can be furnished with an external 35M hard-disk drive. One parallel port is standard.

TeleVideo

The TeleVideo AT (Model I) uses the 80286 CPU at 6 or 8 MHz. The memory is 256K to 15M of RAM and 32K of ROM. The standard storage is with one 5¼" 1.2M floppy-disk drive. The TeleVideo AT has eight expansion slots for additional peripherals, and can accommodate an optional 80287 math coprocessor. The memory can be expanded to 15M with the addition of optional memory boards. The system's storage capacity can be expanded to 40M. One serial and one parallel port are standard.

Wang

The Wang PC-PK6 used the 8086 microprocessor at 8 MHz. Memory can range from 128K to 640K of RAM. The standard storage is with one 5¼" 360K floppy-disk drive and one 10M hard drive. The system has four available expansion slots, an RS-232C port, and a parallel port.

Zenith

The Zenith Z-200 Advanced PC uses the 80286 CPU at 6 MHz. The memory is 512K to 16M. The storage is with one 5¼" 1.2M floppy-disk drive with or without a 20M hard drive. The computer has seven expansion slots and a slot for an 80287 math coprocessor.

A bit of history

In the mid-1980s, many computer makers released PC and XT versions to undermine IBM's stronghold in the personal-computer market. Although many manufacturers were still following the traditional lead of the computer giant in developing PC and XT compatible systems, IBM made an end-run maneuver and released its AT, which expanded its line into a second generation of microcomputers.

Several manufacturers then released AT clones in attempts to battle IBM for a part in this new market. Early sales of AT compatibles were primarily from the following systems: Compaq Computer's Deskpro 286, Corona DataSystems' Corona ATP, Texas Instruments' Business Pro, TeleVideo Systems Inc.'s TeleVideo AT, and Kaypro Corp.'s Kaypro 286i.

IBM released the AT as a higher-end system in August 1984. By March 1985, about 10% of IBM's microcomputer unit shipments were derived from the AT. By July 1985, about 110,000 ATs were in use.

The manufacturers of compatible systems included upgrades in clock-speed and disk storage to promote their systems. With its more sophisticated features, the AT and its clones had a greater appeal to a larger cross section of users for business applications. Typical of this trend were enhanced versions that allowed users to expand the hard-disk storage capacity to 60M or greater.

At the beginning of 1985, combined sales of the AT and compatibles averaged around 15,000 and 20,000 units per month. For the first seven months of the year, IBM had about 80% of the AT marketplace, but competition slowly began to erode IBM's lead. The total units sold for 1985 amounted to about 700,000 units, of which IBM had about 70%. The use of Intel's 80286 microprocessor chip allows the AT faster data processing than its predecessors in the PC-compatible arena that rely on the 8088 processor.

Although most of the compatibles are clones of the IBM desktop machines, some manufacturers, such as Corona Data Systems and Compaq, began offering portable XT and AT-compatible machines. Most of the portables use the same circuitry, but the size of the circuit boards has been reduced to provide units that can easily be transported. These portable PCs are generally not hardware compatible and are not covered in this book. Tables 1-1, 1-2, and 1-3 list the various PC types (IBM, XT, and AT compatibles) that are covered in this book, along with their basic characteristics. Table 1-4 summarizes other essential characteristics of the PC, XT, and AT family.

Table 1-1. IBM personal computers PC & AT

Processor	MHz	Memory	Storage
IBM personal 8088 computer	4.77	256K to 640K RAM; 40K ROM	One or two 5¼″ floppy disks
IBM personal 8088 computer XT	4.77	256K to 640K RAM; 40K ROM	One 5¼″ floppy disk. One 10M hard disk
IBM personal 80286 computer AT	6	256K to 3M	1.25M floppy disk. One 20M hard disk

Table 1-2. Typical XT-compatible computers

Company	Processor	MHz	Memory	Storage
Athena Canon	8086	4.77	256K to 512K RAM; 16K ROM	Two 360K 5¼″ floppy disks
AT&T personal computer	8086	8	128K to 640K	One 360K 5¼″ floppy and one 10M hard disk; two 360K floppies and a 10M hard drive.
BIOS	8088	10	640K	360K floppy drive 40M hard drive
Commodore PC	8088	4.77	PC XT 640K	2-360K 5¼″ floppies
DTK Data	8088	4.77/10	640K	360K, 20M
Epson Equity I Plus	8088	8	640K	360K
Ericsson personal computer Model S02	8088	4.77	256K to 640K RAM; 8K ROM	Two 360K 5¼″ floppy disks
Headstart II	8088	10	640K	5¼″ and 3½″ floppy drives. 360K and 720K
ITT Xtra	8088	4.8	128K to 640K RAM; 320K ROM	One 360K disk
Leading Edge personal color computer	8088-2	7.16 4.77	256K to 640K RAM; 20K ROM	Two 360K 5¼″ floppies or one floppy and one 10M hard disk
NCR PC4	8088	4.77	128K to 640K RAM; 8K ROM	Two 360K 5¼″ floppies or one 360K floppy and one 10M hard disk
Tandy 1000	8088	4.77	128K to 640K	One 360K 5¼″ floppy disk
Z-150 Zenith Data	8088	4.77	320K to 720K RAM; 32K ROM	Two 5¼″ 320K/360K floppies or one floppy and a 10M hard disk

Table 1-3.   Typical AT-compatible computers

	Processor	MHz	Memory	Storage
AGI/Everex 1700C	80286	12	1M RAM	1.2M, 40M
AST Premium drive	80286	6/12	512K RAM	1.2M floppy 1.2M, 40M
Compaq E Model 1	80286	12	1M RAM	1.2M
DTK Tech 1260	80286	8/12	640K RAM	1.2M, 20M
Epson Equity II Plus	80286	12	640K RAM	1.2M, 40M
Leading Edge D2	80286	8/12	640K RAM	1.2M, 50M
Packard Bell PB-286	80286	8/12	640K RAM	1.2M, 40M

Table 1-4.   PC family characteristics

DOS versions	Compatibles generally use the latest release of MS-DOS. IBM machines use some version of PC-DOS.
BIOS manufacturer and release date	This refers to the brand name and revision date of the BIOS (Basic Input/Output System) firmware chip. Early chips might not be completely software compatible.
Processor type	The type of main processor used in the PC determines the relative performance of the machine.
Intel 8088	Used in the IBM PC, XT and most turbo compatibles.
Intel 8086	This chip is usually found in higher performance XT-type machines, such as the AT&T PC 6300.
NEC V20/V30	These chips are clones of the Intel 8088 and 8086 chips. They operate faster than the Intel versions. These chips are found in some compatibles or they are installed to improve performance.
Intel 80188/80186	These processors are later versions of the 8088 and 8086 chips. They are similar functionally to the earlier processors but they can process instructions faster and run at a faster clock rate. These processors are often found on early accelerator boards.
Intel 80286	Machines using this processor are generally AT class PCs. The IBM PC/AT uses the 80286 chip and most PC compatibles of the 286 class use the 80286 processor.
Bus type	In addition to the processor type, several possible bus types will affect the relative performance of the machine.
XT bus	This refers to an 8-bit bus like that found in an IBM PC or XT. This bus is used in machines with an 8088, 8086, V20, or V30 processor.
AT bus	This refers to the 16-bit bus that is used in the IBM AT or compatibles.

2
System components

The system unit

The system unit, shown in Fig. 2-1, contains the power supply, the system board, disk drives, a fan, and the system power switch. This unit can be placed horizontally on a disk or vertically in a floor stand. Placing the system unit in a floor stand decreases the amount of desk space needed by the personal computer. The floor stand also keeps the unit fixed and allows proper airflow.

The components of the system unit are designed to make installation of options and maintenance of components easy. The system unit's cover is secured by screws at the rear of the system box (Fig. 2-2). The disk drives and power supply can be removed by disconnecting their cables and removing their mounting screws.

The system chassis slides out the back of the system unit (Fig. 2-3 to 2-10). This module has connectors in it for mounting the disk controller, memory extension options, and other options. The connectors for the peripheral devices are at the back of the system unit, as shown in Fig. 2-2.

The system module

The system chassis, located inside the system unit, is made up of electrical components and circuits. Its major components are the microprocessor, memory chips, power supply, and related hardware. Mounted on the system chassis is the drive controller board (Fig. 2-11), which controls reading and writing on the disk drives. The system chassis has connectors for mounting memory extension options and other expansion-board options.

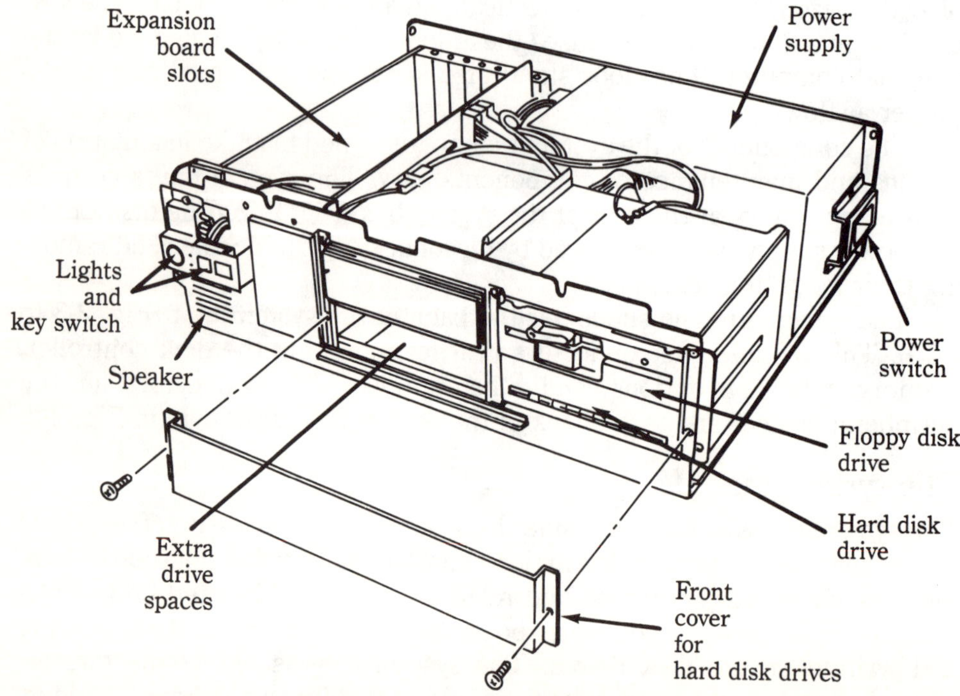

2-1   An AT-type system unit.

Closeup of expansion board connector
slots. Keyboard connector is the round
connector on the lower left side. Monitor
connectors can be seen in slot 1.

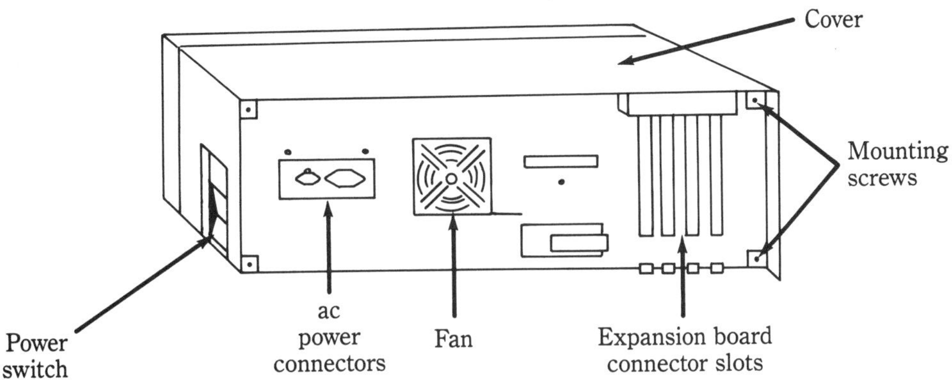

2-2 The rear views of the system unit.

You could expand the system's memory by adding a memory extension
board. The system chassis also has a ROM section, which contains diagnostic tests and a bootstrap program for power up.

The microprocessor controls the monitor, keyboard, and printer (if connected). It also controls any additional options that might be added to the
system unit.

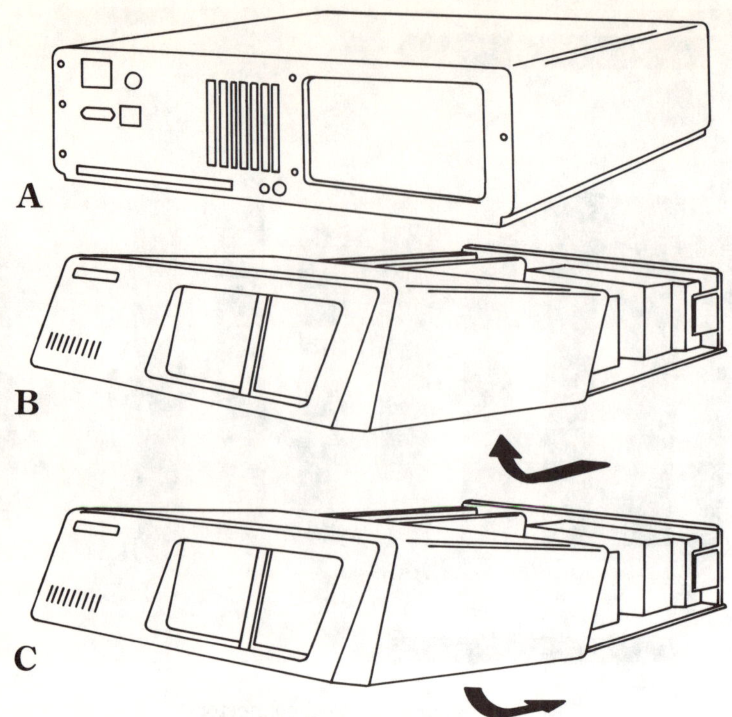

2-3   (A) The Columbia Desk Top is similar to many XT clones. First, remove the screws at the rear, (B) then slide the cover off and lift up. (C) To replace, slide the cover down and back. Then, replace the screws at the rear.

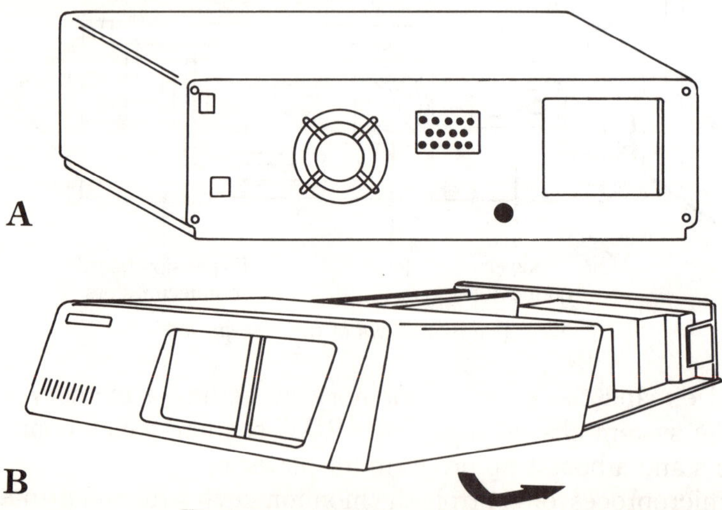

2-4   (A) The Tandy 1200 has screws at the rear that must be removed (like many clones).
(B) To replace, slide the cover down and back, then replace the cover holding screws.

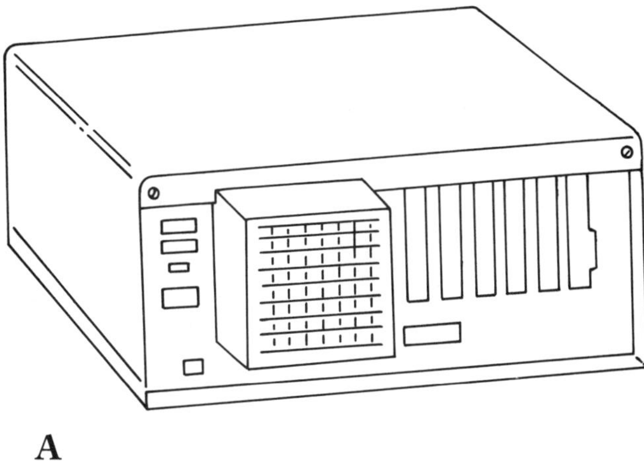

A

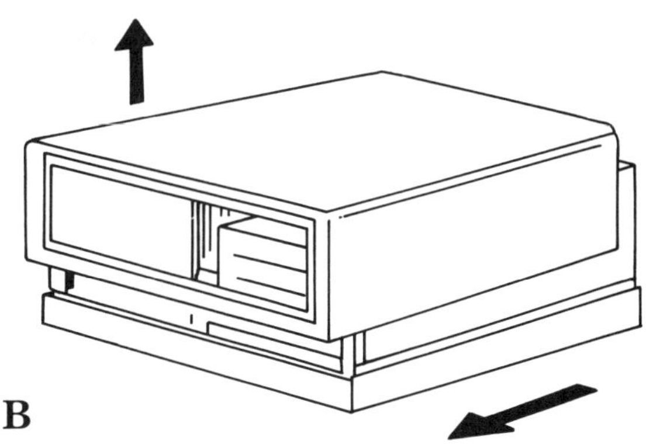

B

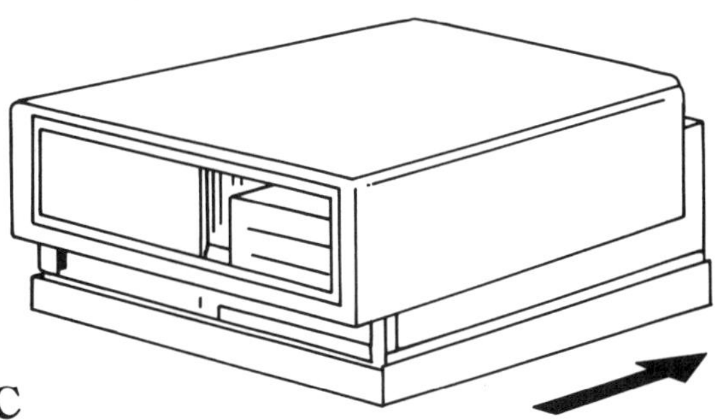

C

2-5 (A) To remove the cover from the AT&T 6300, remove the screws from the back of the computer. (B) Slide the cover forward to release it and lift off. (C) To replace the cover, place it on the chassis and slide back. Then, replace the screws at the rear.

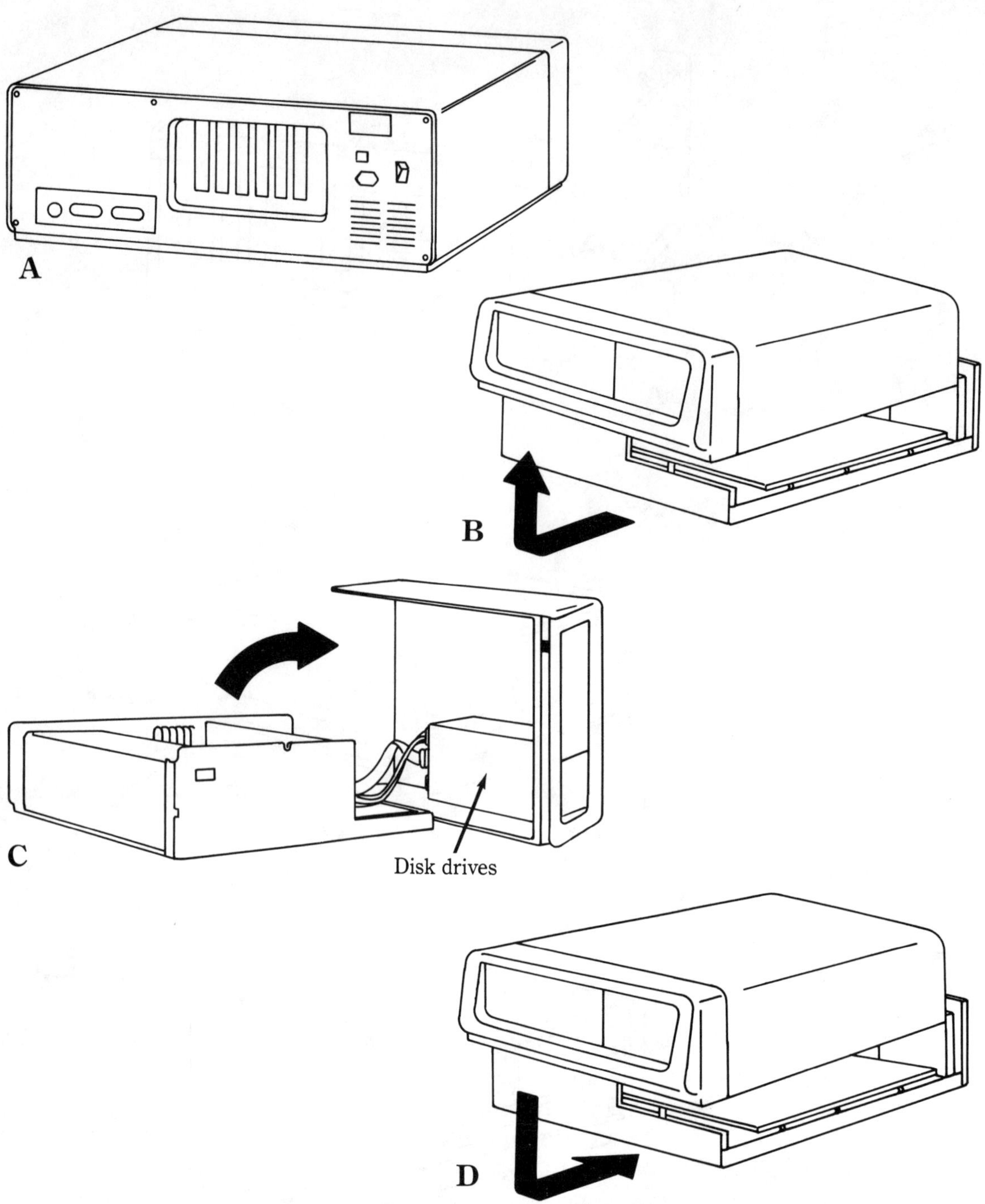

2-6 (A) The ADDs PC also has its cover screws at the rear. First, remove these. (B) Then, slide the cover back slightly and lift up carefully. The disk drive cables are attached to the cover. (C) Slide the cover on its side when it is clear of the chassis. (D) To replace, lift the cover onto the chassis and push it back.

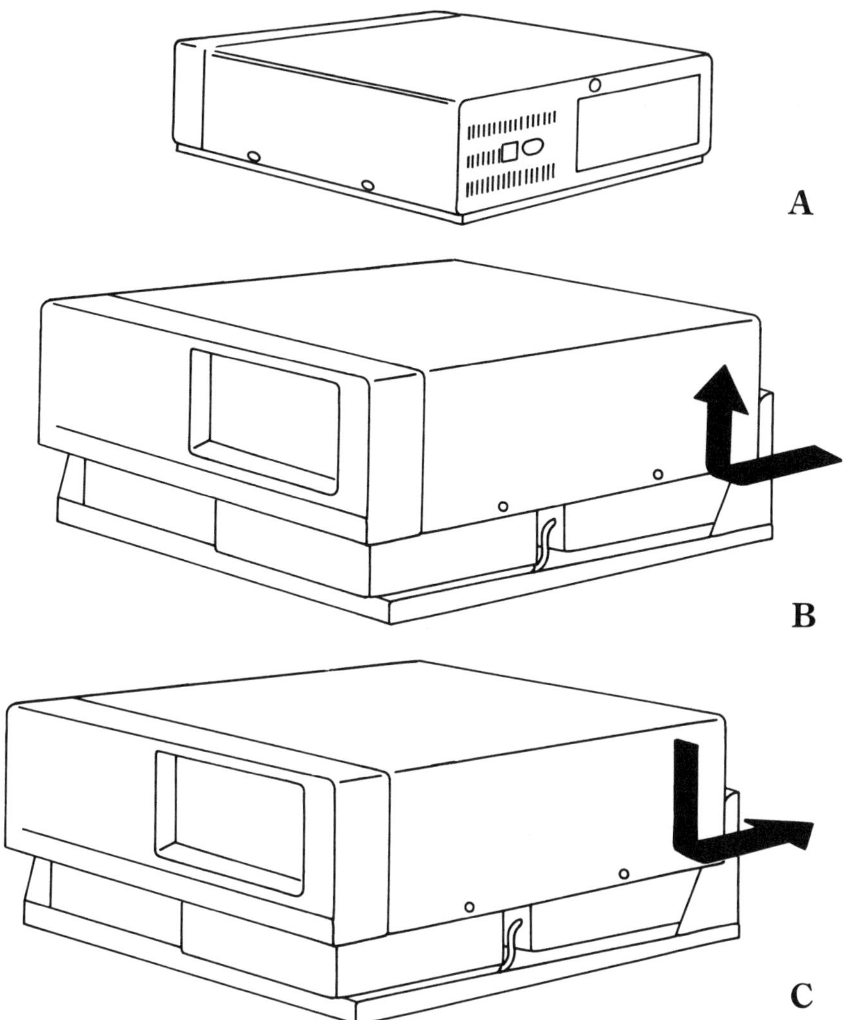

2-7 (A) The Leading Edge computer has some of its cover-holding screws on the sides. Remove the five screws. (B) Slide the cover forward and up to remove it. (C) To replace the cover, slide it back on the chassis and replace the cover-holding screws.

ROM and RAM *ROM (Read-Only Memory)* and *RAM (Random-Access Memory)* provide the unit's basic electronic memory. ROM and RAM are alike in some ways and different in others. Both are fabricated on computer chips and both are measured in terms of kilobytes (K) or megabytes (M).

A ROM chip is a read-only so that you can read its contents, but not change them. The information is permanently burned into the chip. The ROM chips contain the fixed instructions that allow the PC to boot-up following the application of power and to instructions that are related to the specific hardware for that machine.

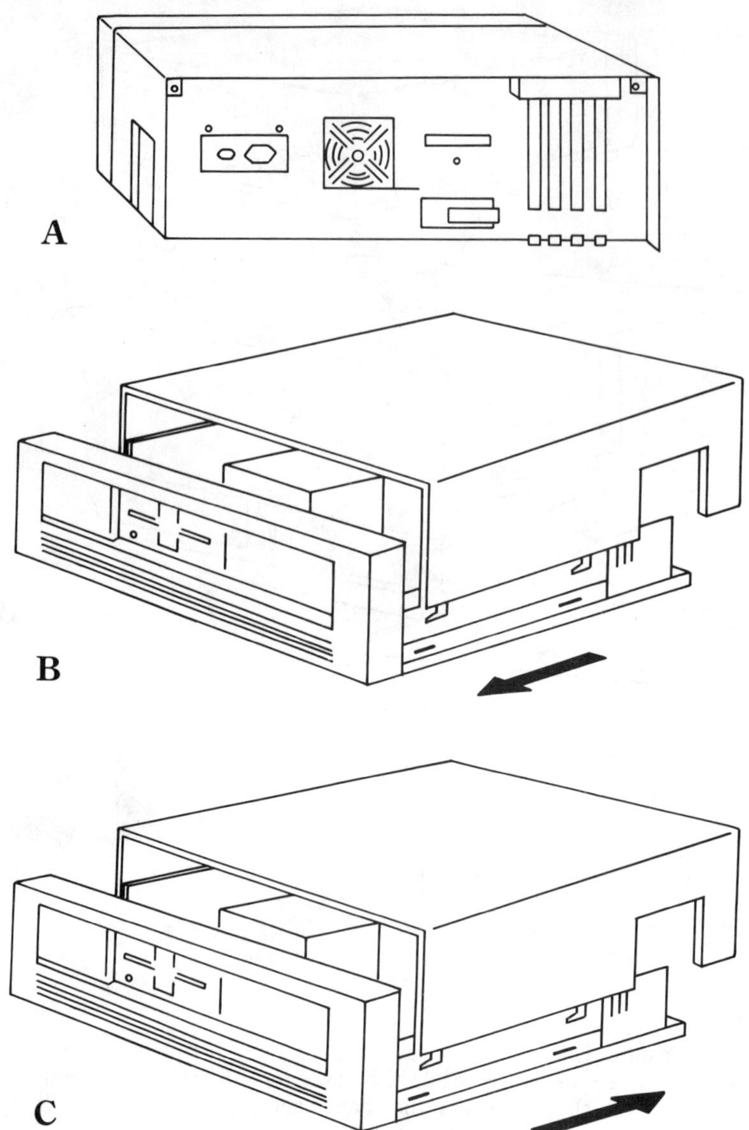

2-8 (A) The Texas Instruments professional computer has two cover holding screws at the rear. You must remove these first. (B) Slide the cover back until it is released and lift it off. (C) To replace the cover, lift it on the chassis, put the metal tabs on the cover into the slots, and slide forward. Then, replace the screws.

A RAM chip is reusable. RAM provides the temporary storage that the computer needs to process program instructions and data. The RAM chips hold the data and program instructions only while you work with them. When power is turned off, the RAM chips lose their contents.

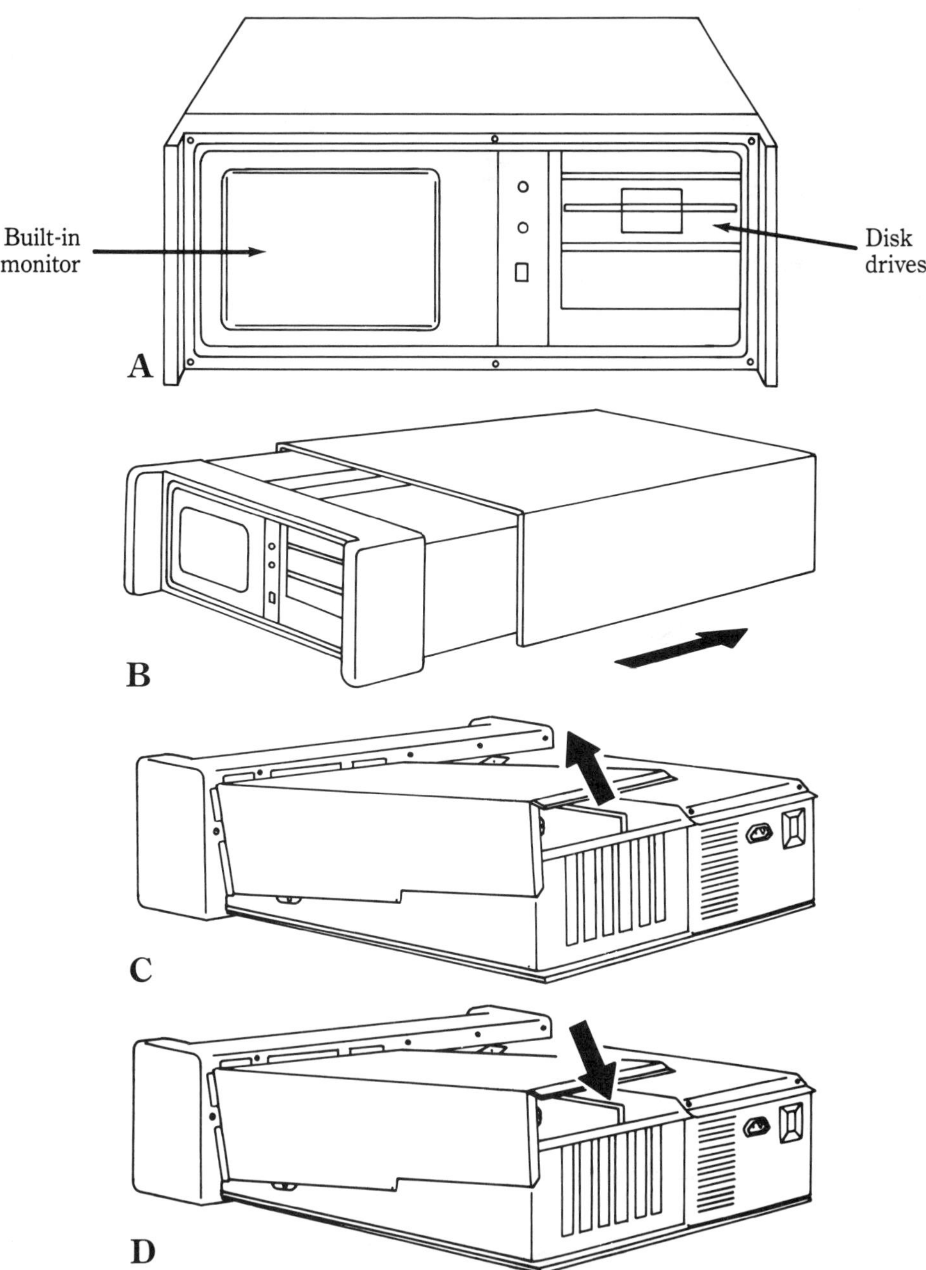

2-9 (A) The IBM portable personal computer has a built-in monitor, but its cover removal is similar to most desktop systems. (B) To remove the cover from the IBM portable personal computer, remove the screws from the back of the computer, and slide the cover back and up. (C) Remove the screws from the shield on the right side of the computer to get at the expansion slots. (D) To replace the cover on the IBM portable personal computer, replace the shield and shield screws. (E) Slide the cover on and replace the cover screws.

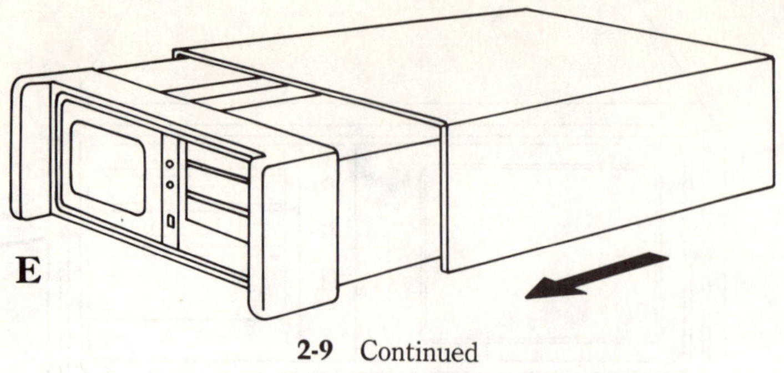

2-9 Continued

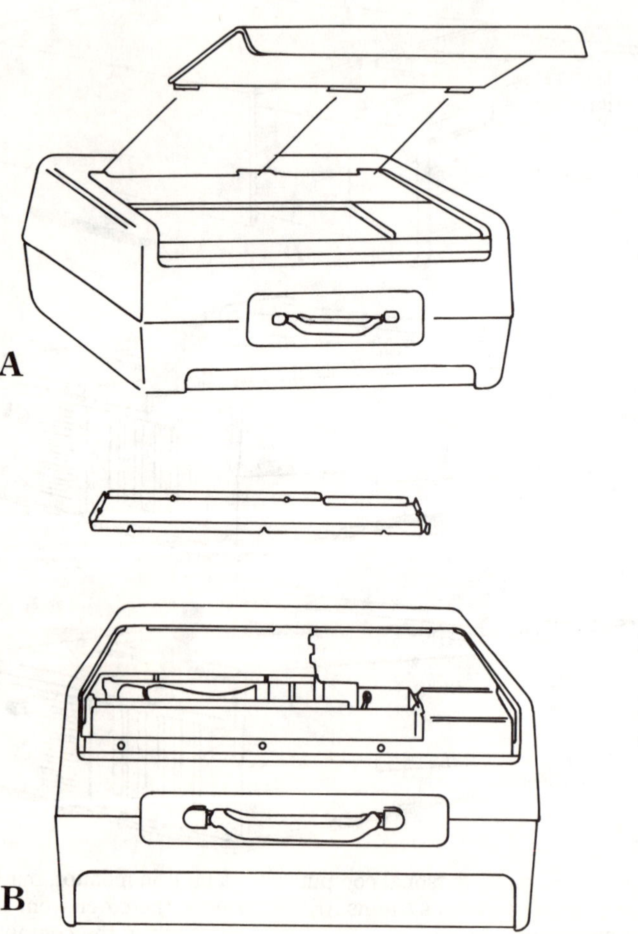

2-10 (A) The Compaq portable computer has a lid that opens by pushing inward on the cover and then lifting up. When you close the cover, insert the tabs on the cover into the slots on the back and push down until the cover snaps closed. (B) A metal cover must be removed to get at the expansion slots. Seven screws hold the cover.

A

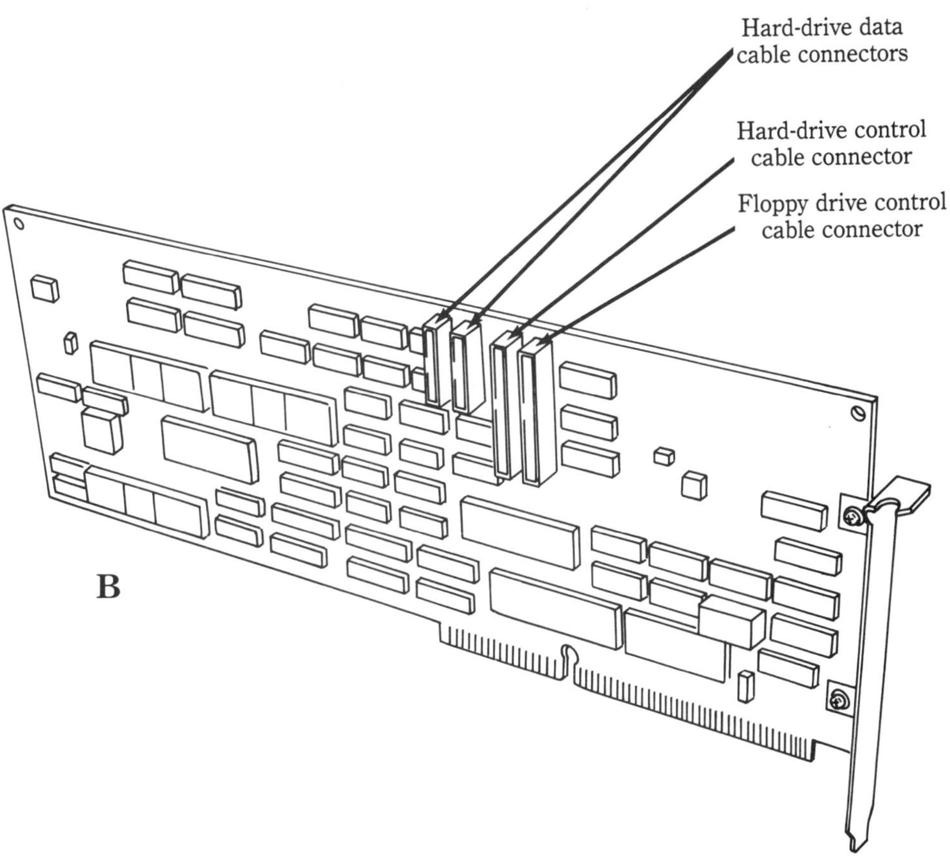

B

2-11 (A) This hard disk controller is used in XT computers. (B) The floppy and hard disk
controller used AT computers.

RAM disks One program included on the DOS diskette (version 3.1 or later) can be used to create a RAM disk in your extended memory. A RAM disk behaves like an extra floppy- or hard-disk drive installed in the system. However, because no disk is actually mechanically attached, access time is extremely fast.

Crystals The crystal provides the timing for all computer functions. Suppose your computer comes with a 20-MHz crystal. Because computers generally run at half of their crystal speed, the computer will run at 10 MHz. If the crystal is dead, the rest of the circuitry will not operate and you might have to change the crystal. You might be able to even change to a faster crystal, such as 24 MHz. Switching to this particular crystal speeds the system up to 12 MHz.

The crystal looks like a little tin pellet on two wires (Fig. 2-12). One side is usually attached to the system board by an adhesive pad. To change crystals, pull the old crystal loose from the adhesive pad and slide it off of the holder. Then, install the new crystal on the holder, with the printing side face up, and stick it down on the adhesive pad.

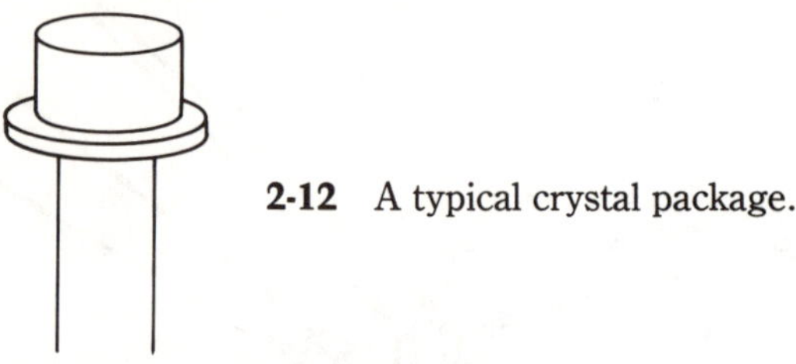

2-12 A typical crystal package.

Memory, I/O and multifunction cards The AT, for example, is capable of addressing a maximum of 16 megabytes of memory. You might have add-in memory cards that occupy the expansion slots of the unit to upgrade the memory to this limit. If you use your personal computer with a printer, a modem, or another external device, you will use a serial or parallel port (depending on the device). These ports also come with add-in cards. Because many users are interested in both of these options, and because the number of expansion slots inside each computer is limited, some manufacturers offer multifunction cards, which combine additional memory with serial and/or parallel ports, and offer additional features on a single card. As with all add-in cards, the card must be designed to run on the system clock speed.

Other possible peripherals that you might have in your personal computer include an internal or external modem, a mouse, a light pen, or more floppy- or hard-disk drives.

The AT system uses a 16-bit bus. However, in many units, a few of the expansion slots are designed to accommodate an 8-bit card. The left-rear section of the system chassis houses the expansion slots.

Expansion slots The expansion slots hold the other circuit boards (the terms *board* and *card* are used interchangeably) that operate the system. In most AT systems, the expansion slots are located in the left-rear section of the system box (Fig. 2-13). Each slot has a rectangular hole in the

2-13 (A) Expansion slots are located in the left rear section of the AT system box. (B) A close-up of expansion slot area showing connectors on system board and metal covers at rear of system chassis. Five long (16 bit) and one short (8 bit) slot connectors are available.

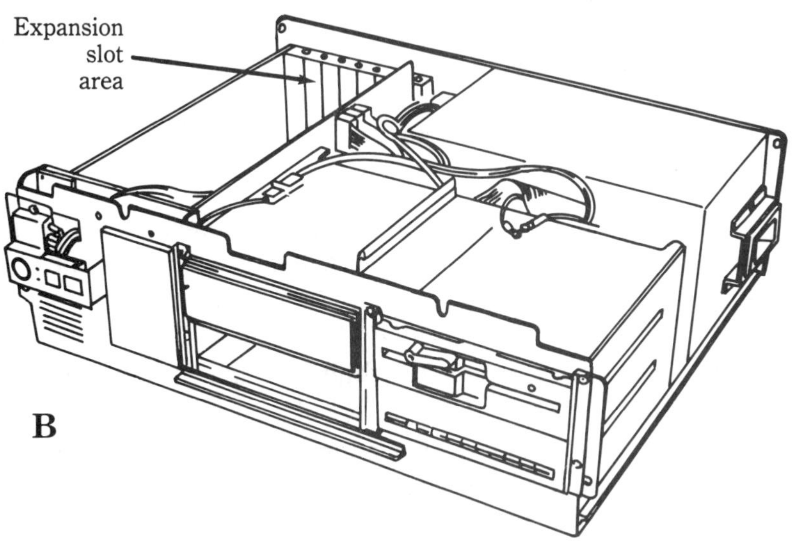

back of the chassis. These are covered by narrow metal plates, called *slot covers*, when the slot is empty and by the endplate of the expansion card when the slot is occupied.

When a card is installed in an expansion slot, the slot cover is removed and the board is inserted into the data bus connector. The slot cover screw is used to secure the endplate of the card to the back of the chassis.

It is possible to install an 8-bit card in an 8-bit slot because some eight-bit cards are physically compatible with a 16-bit slot. The difference is in the bottom edge of the card next to the 8-bit connector pins. If a wide cut-out is on the card next to the 8-bit tab connector, or if the edge goes straight out from the tab, it is physically compatible.

If the edge of the card dips down again next to the 8-bit tab connector, it is physically incompatible. You cannot install this card in a 16-bit slot because this part will interfere with the second connector on the system board.

The endplate of the expansion card provides space for a rear connector so that a monitor or a printer can be plugged into the card. The endplate bracket also anchors the card to the system chassis and completes the metallic shield to minimize the entry of electromagnetic interference.

Short cards are less than half the length of standard boards. Short cards were designed for the PC-XT and compatibles, which have one or more expansion slots behind the left-hand disk drive, where only about half of the usual space is available. These short slots work the same as long slots, but they require a card that fits physically into a small space.

The 286 computers have no short slots. But, you can use short cards in the 286. They are all 8-bit cards and require the same criteria (speed, configurability, and physical compatibility with 16-bit slots) that are required to use any 8-bit card. To install an expansion card with a 16-bit bus, you must use a 16-bit slot. Some, but not all, 8-bit cards will run in a 16-bit slot.

The primary source of information when replacing peripheral cards is the operation's manual that accompanies each product. However, a few general rules apply:

1. Always remember that circuit boards are very sensitive to static electricity. One discharge can permanently damage some electronic chips. You should rid your hands of static electricity by touching the system chassis every time before touching a circuit board.

2. Do not eat, drink, or smoke while you are working over an open computer.

3. Remember to screw down the endplate brackets of your cards and keep slot covers in place over every unused slot. This measure minimizes the possible entry of radio interference.

4. Cards that attach to ribbon cables, such as drive-controller cards, should generally be installed to the right of cards without cables. Thus, the cables are not in the way of other expansion slots.

5. Be careful not to let metal parts (such as screws) get loose in the computer. If you drop a screw on the system board, you must find it and remove it before you can apply power to the computer or it might cause a damaging short-circuit.

The actual replacement of cards in your expansion slots is simple. Choose an empty slot and remove the screw holding the slot cover to the back of the chassis. Slide the card into place so that its tab(s) meet the grooves in the expansion slot (Fig. 2-14). The endplate of the card should be in the same place that the slot cover just occupied. When the tab meets the groove, press carefully on the top edge of the card. The tab will snap into place.

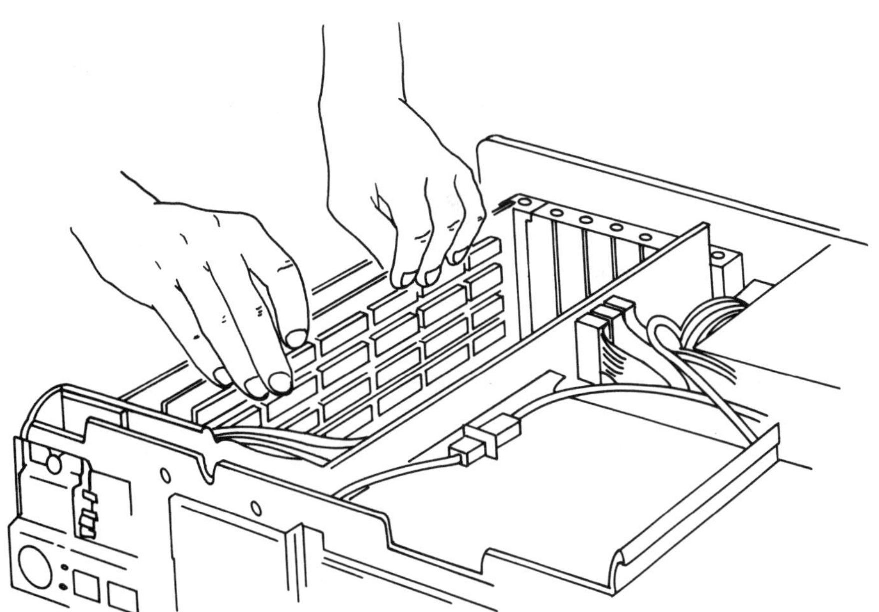

2-14 Replacing a card in an expansion slot.

The PC bus The original PC used a clock of 4.77 MHz with the Intel 8088 microprocessor. The expansion board connections are essentially the same as found on the microprocessor pins. Besides the 8-bit bidirectional data bus and the 20 address lines, there are 6 interrupt lines, 3 sets of Direct-Memory-Access control lines and a number of data-control and status lines. The 62 pins, which make up the IBM PC bus, are divided into two rows (A1 through A31 and B1 through B31) in the expansion slot edge connectors.

The IBM PC is a single-board computer that is commonly called the *motherboard* or *system board*. The processor, some of the I/O circuits, and memory, reside on this board with the five edge connectors for expansion boards. Data is transferred on the PC bus over the dataline pins (A2 through A9). Addresses for bus transfers are specified on the 20 address pins (A12 through A31). The 8-bit version of the Intel 8086 16-bit processor was used in the PC and XT. This simplifies the bus by reducing the number of lines required and avoids the problem of byte transfers in 16-bit systems.

The PC used the 8088 processor in the so-called *maximum mode*, which requires an Intel 8288 bus controller. The 8288 control signals are brought out to the bus, so the two signals ALE (Address Latch Enable) and AEN (Address Enable) are on the bus. For pins B28 and A11, ALE indicates that a valid address is on the bus address lines and AEN signals if the processor or the DMA controller is driving the bus during a DMA transaction. Other 8288 signals that can also be found on the bus include:

I/O Read (IOR)	B14	I/O Write (IOW)	B13
Memory Read (MEMR)	B12	Memory Write (MENW)	B11

A bus handshake line, I/O CH RDY (A10), can be used to increase the current bus cycle. This line can only be asserted for a few microseconds so that the dynamic memory is always refreshed. RAM refresh in the PC is handled by one channel of the system DMA controller, which requires the bus.

The 6 interrupt pins (B21 through B25 and B4) are connected to an interrupt controller on the main board, which automatically generates vectors for interrupt servicing. The no interrupt-acknowledge signal is on the PC bus.

The three pairs of DMA handshake lines include the DRQ1-3 lines (B-18, B-6, and B-16 pins), which are used for DMA requests and $\overline{\text{DACK}}$1-3 (B-17, B-26, and B-15 pins), which are used as the acknowledge lines. $\overline{\text{DACK}}$0 (pin B-19) is used to refresh dynamic RAM boards, which can be plugged into the bus. T/C (B-27) is used to indicate when the correct number of DMA bus cycles have occurred during a DMA transfer. OSC (B-30) is used for a 14.31818-MHz clock and CLK (B-20) is the 4.77-MHz clock, which runs the processor. RESET DRV (B2) is a reset signal for all cards on the bus. The power supplies available to the bus cards include +5 V (B-3), −5 V (B-5), +12 V (B-9), and −12 V (B-7). The three ground pins are B-1, B-10, and B-31.

Bus cycles require four clock cycles (840 ns). DNA cycles take five clock cycles (1.05 μs). The cycles are controlled by an 8288 bus controller that runs at 4.77 MHz. The bus card has a metal plate attached to one end. This plate is used as both a card guide for the back of the card and a support for I/O connectors, which can be attached to the card.

Although it never evolved into an actual industry standard, the IBM PC bus became the most popular microprocessor backplane bus ever introduced. Thousands of boards from hundreds of companies have been designed to plug into the PC bus.

The PC/AT bus

The AT is a full 16-bit computer based on the INTEL 80286 microprocessor (Fig. 2-15). The 80286 uses a 16-bit data bus, but the AT expansion bus has a wider data path, more interrupt lines, and more DMA signals. Like the PC bus, the AT bus signals resemble the microprocessor signals, on which the computer is based. In order to maintain compatibility with expansion boards designed for the PC, the original 62-pin connector and pin definitions remained the same. A second connector with 36 pins was added to carry the additional signals. The second connector is in front of the 62-pin connector, because some older boards designed for the IBM PC will physically interfere with the AT expansion connector.

2-15 A typical AT clone.

Because an actual standard board size and shape was never developed for the PC expansion boards, some manufacturers used the available space by dropping the bottom edge of the board just in front of the PC's edge connector.

Most of the signals on the AT's 62-pin connector retain the same names they had on the PC's bus, but a few signals have new names, but similar functions. For example, $\overline{\text{DACK0}}$ 4K0 on the PC was renamed $\overline{\text{REFRESH}}$ for the AT bus. B-8 on the PC bus was not used, it became 0WS (zero-wait state), which allows an expansion board to signal that it does not require the main to insert wait states in the bus cycle. The $\overline{\text{MEM CS16}}$ (D-1) and $\overline{\text{I/O CS16}}$ (D-2) signals allow an expansion board to indicate that it can accept a 16-bit, 1-wait-state transfer. These signals are added on the 36-pin connector.

Some of the address lines (C-2 through C-8) on the 36-pin connector partially replicate the addresses on the 62-pin connector. Unlike the PC's original address lines, the AT's 36-pin address lines are not latched on the computer's motherboard. Expansion boards that use these lines must latch the address values on the falling edge of the ALE signal.

Since the introduction of the original AT, the clock speeds of compatible computers have increased to over 20 MHz as Intel and other microprocessor vendors have improved their manufacturing processes. The manufacturers of compatible computers have adopted the AT bus for their 80286-based machines. Chip manufacturers, such as Chips and Technologies and Western Digital, have developed ICs that reduce the motherboard size. In addition to machines based on the 80286 microprocessor, several 80386-based machines also use the AT bus, which adds extensions for 32-bit memory boards. However, vendors of 80386-based computers use different techniques for extending the AT bus to 32 bits so that memory boards for these computers are not compatible.

Some vendors offer extensions to the AT bus. AST Research offers an AT bus extension, called *Smartslot*, which adds an additional 8 pins to the bus. These pins allow multiple processors on several expansion cards to share the bus using an arbitration scheme. A central arbiter for all Smartslot cards grants the bus to one of the requesting cards.

The IEEE created the P996 bus committee to study the feasibility of standardizing the AT bus, but before the committee could produce a standard, IBM introduced its PS/2 line of personal computers that use a completely different, incompatible bus.

Power supply

The *power supply* is the shielded cube in the right-rear section of the chassis. In the 286 AT compatible, it is likely to be a 190- to 200-W power supply, which means that you will probably never need to augment it with an extra power supply. The unit's power-on switch is usually part of the power supply, as are the internal cables that are designed to be connected to the drives (Fig. 2-16). A switch on many units lets you select 220 V operation if you need to use the unit outside the United States. If you need more power cables for additional drives, you can get an inexpensive Y power cable that will connect to one of the cables and split its output in two. You should not use more than one Y cable per system because it is possible to overload the power supply.

The power supply inside the system unit provides power for the system board, adapters, diskette drives(s), hard disk drive(s), monitor, and keyboard. The power supply is designed to operate the maximum number of drives that can be added inside the system unit. IBM AT-compatible computers have a total output of 175 to 200 W. A 115/230 Vac-selectable switch is usually located at the rear of the power-supply enclosure.

Supply characteristics The power supply is typically designed to operate at a frequency of either 60 $\pm$3 Hz or 50 $\pm$2 Hz at 100 to 130 Vac with 5.0 A, or at 220 to 260 Vac with 2.5 A. The voltage can be selected by a switch at the rear of the power supply. The input requirements then become:

ac input voltage: 100 to 130 V/200 to 260 V selectable.

Output The power supply provides +5, −5, +12, and −12 Vdc. Table 2-1 shows typical load current and regulation tolerance for a 200-W supply. The power supply is a switching oscillator type with the functional blocks shown in Fig. 2-17. Testing starts by checking the regulator outputs. If these are all dead or low, check the fuse or circuit breaker and the rectifier circuits. The problem could be a faulty diode or capacitor.

Table 2-1. Typical power supply output characteristics

Output	Load	Tolerance	Ripple
+5 V	20 A	+/−2%	50 mV
+12 V	7.3 A	+/−5%	100 mV
−5 V	0.3 A	+/−10%	100 mV
−12 V	0.3 A	+/−10%	100 mV

If only one output is dead or low, the problem is probably in the regulator circuit. Check the regulator capacitors for shorts. Typically, the voltage into the regulator will be about double the output voltage. So, the -5-V regulator should have an input voltage of about −9 or −10 V, while the +5-V regulator should have an input voltage of about −9 to −10 V. These lines

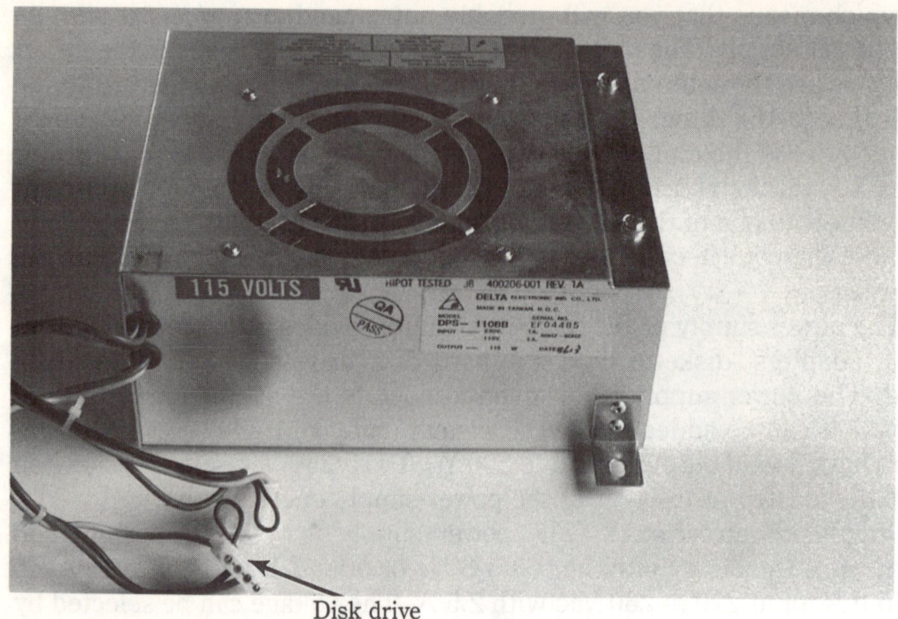

A

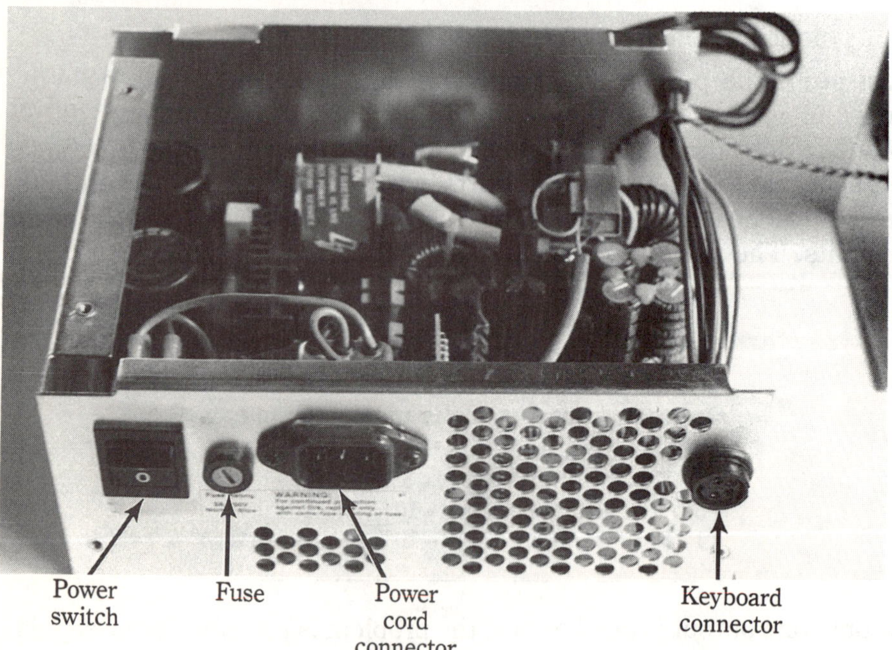

B

2-16 The disassembled power supply. (A) An XT-type power supply removed from system unit (front view).   Notice the connectors for disk drives.   (B) The rear view with top cover removed.   (C) A removed power supply circuit board.   (D) A power supply chassis with the circuit board removed.

C

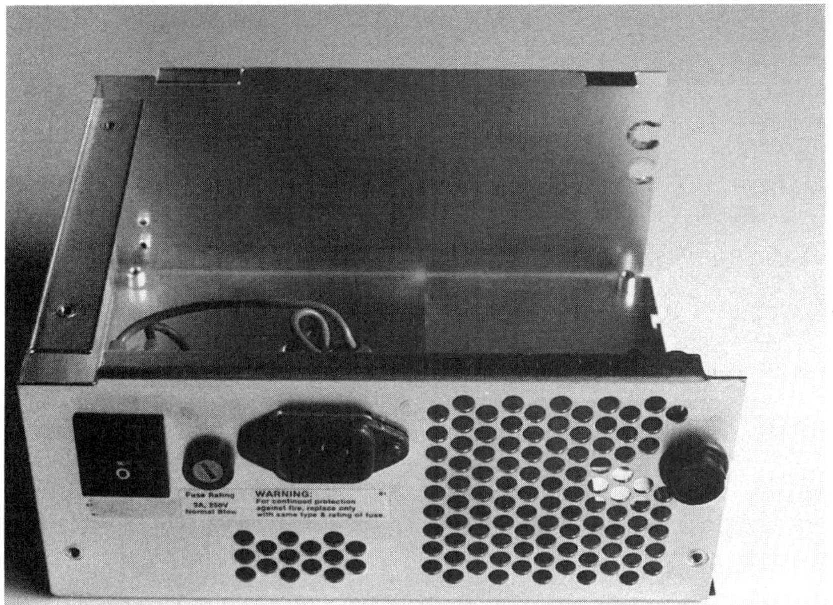

D

can be traced back if any voltages appear to be in error. You can also run resistive tests to check for shorts to ground. If you trace the problem to a major component, such as a transformer, it might be simpler and just as economical to replace the power supply. These can be purchased from most computer-supply outlets. Just make sure the replacement has the proper wattage.

Output protection If any output becomes overloaded, the power supply will switch off within about 20 ms. This action will normally prevent an overcurrent condition from damaging the power supply.

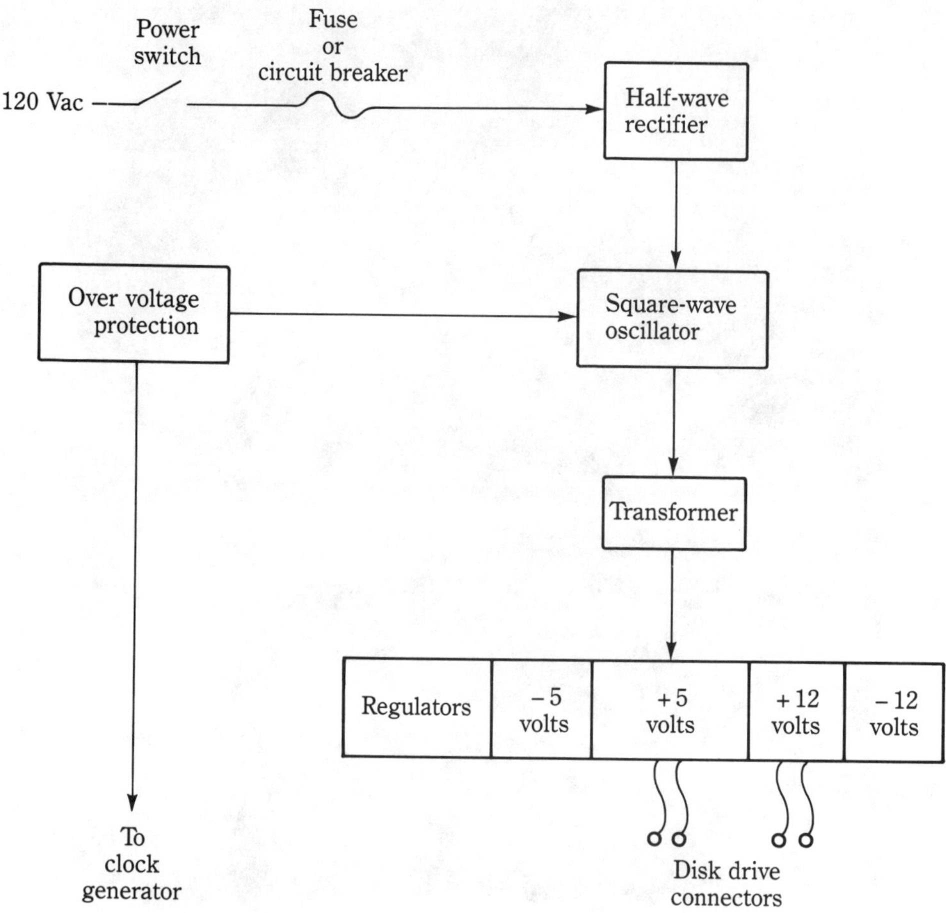

2-17   A typical switching power supply.

Video adapters

The following display adapters are used in the PC family:

1. **Monochrome Display Adapter (MDA)** This video card can display only text characters in one color.

2. **Hercules Graphics Adapter (HGA)** This popular video card is not made by IBM. Because of its popularity, it has become a defacto standard. It emulates an MDA card, but it also supports high-resolution monochrome graphics.

3. **Color Graphics Adapter (CGA)** This video card can display text and graphics in any of eight colors.

4. **Enhanced Graphics Adapter (EGA)** This video card can dis-

play text and graphics in any of 16 colors from a palette of 64. It also supports a higher resolution than CGA video cards.

5. **Multi-Color Graphics Adapter (MCGA)** This video card is a cross between a CGA and a VGA. It supports all CGA modes and can display graphics in up to 256 simultaneous colors.

6. **Video Graphics Adapter (VGA)** This video card can display text and graphics in any of 256 colors from a palette of 262,144. It also supports a higher resolution than CGA, EGA, or MCGA video cards.

3
The system unit

The system unit contains the main PC board, called the *system board*, and the metal shield that contains the power supply and the disk drives. The system board contains chips to handle RAM, support chips to produce clock signals, a set of chips for the ROM programs, and I/O chips to connect the computer to the peripherals.

The IBM PC system board contains about 100 chips, as well as the connectors for the expansion boards. Each short connector or slot will accept 62 connection pins. The slots are wired in parallel. They form the output bus for the 62-pin PC boards that will plug into the slots.

The internal program selects the correct expansion board—even though they are all wired in parallel. These cards add the peripherals to the computer. For example, the disk-controller card connects the disk drives to the system board. A video adapter and a printer card are needed to connect the monitor and printer to the system board. Other cards are available to expand the computer for other options. For example, a modem could be used with additional disk drives, additional memory, printers, and other peripherals with the proper card.

RAM configurations

The 8088 and 8086 chips can only recognize addresses up to 1M of memory. Out of this 1M, DOS can access addresses from 0K to 640K for RAM. This 640K total RAM is the convention for working memory. The remaining 384K is used for system functions, such as for video and ROM instruc-

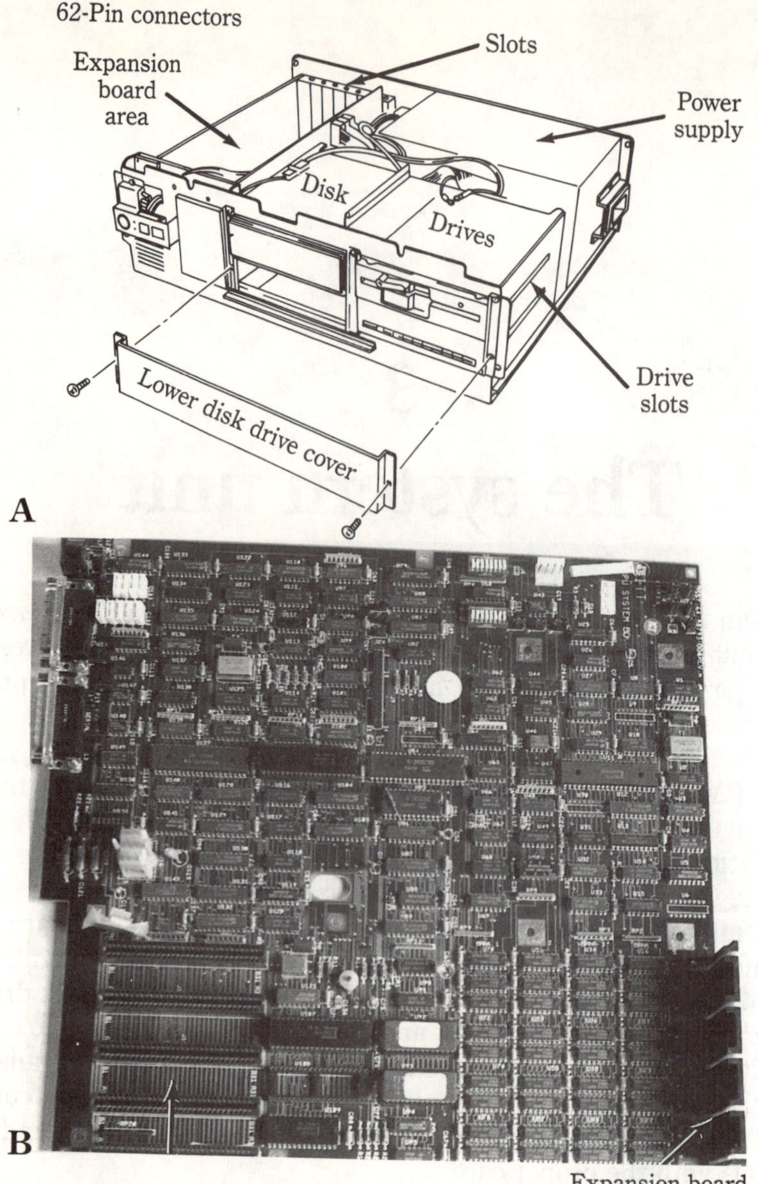

3-1   (A) An AT system unit (cover removed). (B) An XT system board.

tions. The 1M limit goes back to PC and XT computers that used the 8088 microprocessor chip; the 8088 can access 1M of addresses.

The AT used the 80286 microprocessor chip, which can access 16M of memory (16,777,216 storage addresses). The 386s can access 4 gigabytes, or more than 4 billion addresses. None of this extra storage space exists as far as DOS is concerned.

Although a 286 system can access 16M, it can only contain 1M of RAM. Even this memory is more than DOS can access. DOS can only access 1M; out of that 1M, DOS can only use 640K of RAM to run a program.

Two types of memory, *expanded memory* and *extended memory*, go beyond DOS's limits. Both of these types use RAM beyond DOS's 640K limit. Expanded memory has no corresponding physical memory addresses. Expanded memory was originally developed to get around the physical memory constraints of the XT. On an XT no addresses are above 1M. Lotus, Intel, and Microsoft developed a standard for an add-in memory board, called the *EMS (expanded memory specification) board.*

Extended memory, in contrast, is standard in many 286 and 386 computers. Extended memory is linear; its addresses start at the 1M limit (Fig. 3-2).

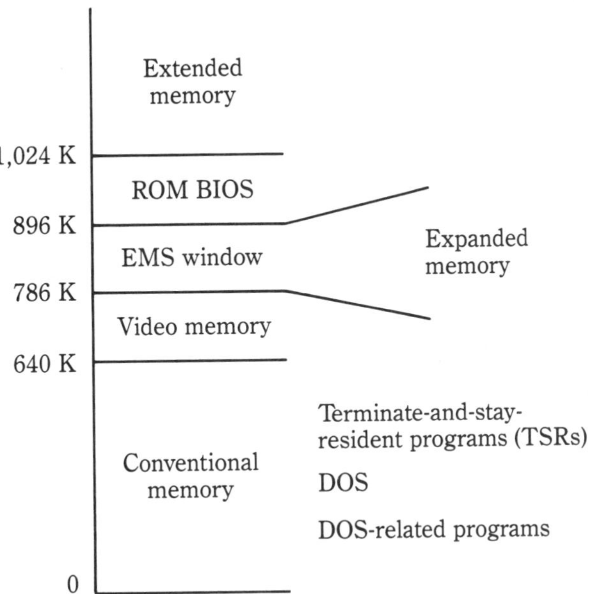

3-2 Memory map showing conventional memory, expanded memory and extended memory.

System RAM

The typical 286-compatible system comes with 512K to 1M RAM on the system board. This amount can be upgraded to 640K or to 1M, depending on the space available on the system board. In addition to its system-board RAM, the 286 unit can hold up to 16M of extended memory on add-in cards. DOS is able to support up to 640K of user-addressable base memory.

If you add RAM chips to a 1M 286 board, you will get a total of 1,024K of memory. The extra 384K will become extended memory.

System-board RAM chips are often arranged in rows. These rows make up logical banks. For example, as you count from the front of the chassis, the first and third rows might make up bank 1 while the second and fourth rows make up bank 0.

Each bank must be either completely full or completely empty. You can never have one row or part of one row empty. The 286 can use 64K or 256K RAM chips. The 286 should use chips with a speed of 150 ns or faster. The RAM chip configuration of the 286 is selected by a dip switch on the system board.

Table 3-1 shows typical configurations of system board RAM and the type of chips used in bank 0 and bank 1 that provide the desired total. Figure 3-3 shows another memory arrangement where an XT memory combo board is used to upgrade from 256K on the main board. Two plug-in modules are used to increase the memory to 640K. Figure 3-4 shows a base memory map that was obtained from a diagnostic program. The conventional memory is 640K.

**Table 3-1.   Typical system board
RAM configurations**

Total RAM	Chips in bank 0	Chips in bank 1
256K	64K	64K
512K	256K	Empty
640K	256K	64K
1M	256K	256K

Suppose you wish to upgrade and your computer has a total of 18 chips per bank. You would need 18 chips, if you are adding one bank, or 36 chips, if you are pulling out the existing 256K chips and entirely populating the board with 64K chips.

Each chip has a pin 1, which is marked with a notch or a dot. If you look closely at the green PC card, beneath the empty chip socket you can usually see a printed white outline of a notched chip in the proper orientation (pin 1 toward the front of the chassis). You must install each chip in the correct orientation with all the pins fully seated in the socket.

The pins that connect each chip to its socket are easily bent. Only a little force is required to install RAM chips. If you have to press hard, you are probably bending a pin.

If you make a mistake and have to remove a chip from a socket, insert

3-3 XT memory board with plug-in memory module.

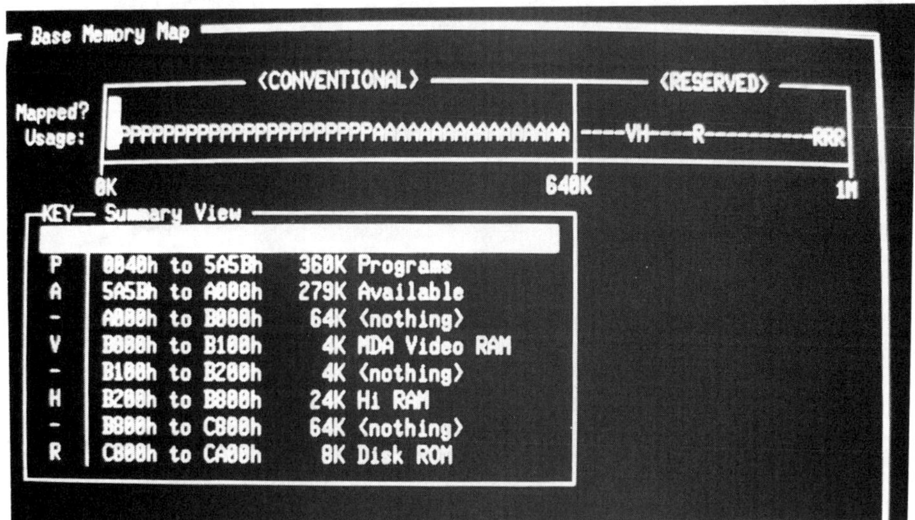

3-4 Base memory map obtained by diagnostic program. The addresses are in hexadecimal.

the tip of a small flat-blade screwdriver under one end of the chip and twist it gently. When the chip begins to loosen, move the screwdriver to the other end and loosen that side. Work gently back and forth until the chip is freed. Then, straighten the bent pin and start over.

Memory-management schemes

Memory-management hardware, such as expanded-memory boards, add memory to the system. Memory-management software does not add any chips, but it does help to more efficiently use the existing RAM. DOS was developed for 8088 and 8086 microprocessors, which cannot work directly with anything over 1M of RAM; 384K of that is set aside for system use, which leaves only 640K for programs. Two types of memory, expanded and extended, are available for programs that need more than 640K.

Expanded memory is RAM on an expansion board (Fig. 3-5). This type of memory is accessible only through a window or page frame in conventional memory. The window holds different pages of memory that are swapped (as needed) into the processor's address space. To use expanded memory, a memory board and software that follow the *expanded-memory specification (EMS)* standard are needed. EMS 4.0 allows the user to run programs and store data in up to 32M of paged RAM. It works on IBM compatibles, from XTs to 486 machines.

3-5   An expanded memory with 2M that supports the EMS standard.

Extended memory is an extension of RAM. It is not available on 8086- and 8088-based machines. It is possible to add 15M of extended RAM at the end of 1M in an 80286- or 386SX-based machine. The 386 and 486 machines can handle an additional 4,095M.

Some operating systems, such as OS/2 and Unix, can use extended memory directly, but DOS cannot. To run in extended memory, a program must contain a DOS-extender that switches the CPU between the real mode, used by DOS, and the protected mode, which can access memory beyond 1M. Three standards are used: *Extended Memory Specifications (XMS), Virtual Control Program Interface (VCPI),* and *DOS Protected-Mode Interface (DPMI).*

Extended memory is simpler to use than the EMS scheme. However, extended memory will not work in XT-class machines and is newer than EMS for 286s and 386s. However, EMS is a popular standard for all three classes. Hardware and software products can use either one or a combination of the two memory types.

Expanded memory uses existing addresses within DOS's 1M address limit that are available. Expanded memory swaps additional blocks of memory into those unused addresses by a process called *bank switching*. The expanded memory manager uses a 64K window, called a *page frame*, to access the memory located outside RAM. The page frame is located within the 1M that DOS recognizes. The page frame lets DOS access up to four blocks or pages of memory at once.

When the program needs data that is located in expanded memory, the *expanded-memory manager (EMM)* finds the page or pages that the program is looking for, and moves it into the 64K page frame so that DOS can find it.

Expanded memory is utilized by adding an EMS board or installing a software emulator. The emulator mimics an EMS board. Expanded memory can be added to an XT, AT, or a 386 machine.

Expanded memory results in more memory space for those programs that can take advantage of EMS. These memory expanders commonly take the form of an EMS 4.0 memory board. Software products emulate expanded memory by swapping sections of code using the hard drive or extended RAM to simulate EMS's paged RAM.

An example is *Above Disk*, which is primarily an EMS emulator, but it also includes utilities for borrowing 96K of EGA or VGA video memory for nongraphics programs and for relocating Novell Netware TSRs. It can be used to simulate EMS 4.0's entire 32M limit in extended memory or on a hard disk. It is one of the easiest memory managers to install. It begins by asking if this is a first-time installation and which disk and subdirectory to copy files to. Then, a configuration screen is used to show the settings for emulating EMS memory in the system. A device driver is added to the CONFIG.SYS file and a memory-resident module is added to AUTOEX-EC.BAT.

Above Disk will not work with some programs, such as Microsoft Windows/386. Protected mode only works on 286s or 386s with CPUs that are dated August 1987 and that run DOS 3.3 or later. The package comes with a Lotus 1-2-3 EMS emulator that provides memory management not available in the main program. It can provide three memory-management functions:

1. Emulating EMS.
2. Reclaiming unused video RAM.
3. Space for large 1-2-3 worksheets.

TC power supplies EMS emulation only. The installation procedure requires you to create a new hard-disk subdirectory, copy the program files, and accept the default settings before rebooting. The program adds a command line to CONFIG.SYS. It can combine extended, expanded, and hard-disk memory in any combination up to the 32M that EMS 4.0 allows. Like Above Disk, TC Power will run on an XT, but because XTs do not support extended RAM, the program uses only the machine's hard disk for EMS emulation. The disk-based emulation can provide the full 32M of EMS 4.0 memory.

Some products make room for the software application by moving TSRs and drivers out of the lower 640K and relocating them to expanded or extended memory, the hard disk, or gaps between 640K and 1M (if your system has memory in this range). The latter occurs with some 286 and 386 compatibles that have 1M on the motherboard.

Other products stretch DOS RAM to 704K or 736K, depending on the type of video card used. Monochrome and CGA cards do not use the memory addresses immediately above 640K, so a memory manager can assign the empty space to DOS. Also, some memory-management products designed for 386s convert extended memory to expanded memory. These products use the 386 chip's memory-mapping capability to substitute for the circuitry on the EMS boards. These products convert extended memory to EMS RAM and use the 386's memory-mapping features to relocate TSRs and drivers.

Extended memory

MS-DOS (Microsoft Disk Operating System) version 3.X is able to support only 640K of user-addressable base memory. In the 286, memory is linear. That means that it proceeds (theoretically, not physically) in a straight line from bit 1 through the highest bit in the memory. The memory up to the 640K point is called the *base memory*. DOS can use this memory for any purpose. Memory from the 640K point up to the 1M point is reserved for ROM. This section of memory acts as built-in permanent software so that the system can perform its most basic functions, such as starting up (also called *booting*) and testing the system during this power up.

The user does not have access to the memory in the reserved area between 640K and 1M. Above 1M, extended memory begins. DOS does not recognize extended memory, but many applications programs use it. Extended memory goes from 1M to 16M for a 286 system. If you install 1M of RAM on the system board, the first 640K goes to base memory, and the remaining 384K jumps above the reserved area for ROM to become the first 384K of extended memory.

A common application for extended memory is in a *RAM disk*. DOS version 3.1 and above usually includes a program for creating a RAM disk in extended memory. The RAM disk is electronic memory that acts like a fast disk drive. DOS treats it like an extra floppy- or hard-disk drive connected to the system. Because no physical disk is involved, the access time to and from the RAM disk depends only on the speed of the memory chips. Even though it acts like storage, a RAM disk is still volatile memory. The contents of the RAM disk must be saved to a true storage device after a computing session.

Extended memory is different from expanded memory in that only 286s and 386s can use it. Extended memory is linear; its addresses begin where the DOS limit leaves off, from 1M on up to 16M in a 286 and 4,996M in a 386. Extended memory does not require bank switching, like expanded memory does. It is all available simultaneously, instead of being limited to 64K chunks. Extended memory is necessary for multitasking (running several applications at once) and for the operating systems that can handle multitasking (OS/2 and Unix).

When 286s and 386s use extended memory, they are working in protected mode. Some software programs are written specifically for 286-and-above machines, so the program can use the extended memory. ATs and 386s can also run in real mode, the conventional 640K-RAM limit, using conventional DOS-compatible software. When running in real mode, ATs and 386s pretend to be XTs.

DOS works within a 1M limit. *Expanded memory* is memory that lies completely outside that limit, but is switched into and out of a 64K window so that DOS can work with it. Extended memory is a linear extension of that 1M and it can all be accessed directly by the CPU. Extended memory is only available with 286 and 386 computers.

Additional memory

Some 286 units come with 512K of RAM on the system board. This can be upgraded to 640K or 1M or more by installing more RAM chips on the system board. The RAM chips are located in rows on the system board. Some rows will be filled with chips and other rows will have empty sockets. The rows are divided into logical banks.

In a 16-bit system (the 286, for example) each of the logical banks contains 16 memory chips plus two organizers. An 8-bit system will use 8 memory chips plus one organizer. That way each bank can send 16 bits, one from each memory chip, onto the data bus at one time.

If empty rows of sockets are on the 286's board, you can upgrade the memory. For example, suppose you have 512K and you want to upgrade to 640K memory. This is calculated as:

1. Suppose your board has 9 sockets per row.

2. Because one chip is used for parity testing, 8 chips of actual memory are used per row.

3. 64K bits times 8 chips equals 64K bytes per row.

4. 64K bytes times 2 rows equals 128K bytes added to the system.

5. 128K bytes plus the original 512K bytes equals 640K.

If the upgrade goes to 1M of RAM, 18 256K RAM chips are needed. If you would want to downgrade the total system memory to 256K, pull two rows of existing 256K chips, and fill all four rows with 64K chips. Chips used for parity and chips used for RAM are not physically different. Any RAM chip can be the organizer if it is installed in the ninth socket of the bank.

RAM chips are available in different speeds, according to how long it takes the chip to send a bit of information to the central processing unit. Chip speeds are measured in nanoseconds (1×10^{-9} second). The lower the number of nanoseconds, the faster the chip. In the higher-performance machines, the central processing unit needs chips that can deliver information fast. The CPU cannot be kept waiting for a slow RAM chip. The recommended speed for RAM chips in most 286 machines is 150 ns. The important thing to remember about memory additions are:

1. **Capacity** For example, 64K chips were used to upgrade to 640K; 256K chips were used to upgrade to 1M.

2. **Number** Chips must be added in banks; 18 chips were added in this past section. You cannot add nine now and nine later.

3. **Speed** As discussed, 150 ns or faster are needed for most 286 systems. A smaller number of nanoseconds is a faster chip.

Some programs swap applications or TSRs in and out of the 640K working area. This lets the user switch between programs without exiting one and starting another. When tasks are switched, the program saves a snapshot of the suspended program, while the user works with the new task in the foreground. These products differ from true multitasking environments, such as those that are provided by Desqview or Microsoft Windows, which run several programs simultaneously.

System problems and solutions

A PC- or XT-class machine can use an EMS expanded-memory board that fits into an 8-bit slot. This allows improved performance for task-switching programs. A hard disk can be used for a slower, but often satisfactory solution, with a task switcher or an EMS emulator. In a 286 system, if you use hard-disk swapping without adding memory, you might find it too slow. A better solution is to combine these programs with an expanded-memory board. In a 386 system, it is best to use all the extended RAM that you can on the motherboard or in a 32-bit memory slot, instead of in a slower expansion-board slot. A 386 memory manager will allow EMS access. A task switcher can be used to make sure that all of the RAM is fully utilized.

Initial checks

When you first turn the power on, check for any indication of power. This includes the screen display, beep sounds, and disk-drive lights. If these seem to be normal, turn off power to the computer, remove the case, and unplug the power cables (on the 5150 PC, these are labeled P8, P9, P10, and P11). Then, reapply power and check plug P9 for $+5$ V on pins 4, 5, and 6, and -5 V on pin 3. Check plug P8 for $+12$ V on pin 3, and -12 V on pin 4. Check plugs P10 and P11 for $+12$ V on pin 1 and $+5$ V on pin 4. If all of these voltages are missing, check for an open fuse. The fuse is usually part of the power-supply unit.

If one or more voltages are in error, the problem is probably in the power supply or power-supply cables. If all the voltages test good at the plug pins, reconnect the power plugs to the system board. Remove all of the expansion cards, turn the power back on and recheck the voltages on the same plug pins that were tested earlier. If the voltages are still present, turn off the power and reinstall one of the expansion cards. Turn the power back on and retest the power pins for the proper voltages. If they still appear to be good, turn the power off and install another card. Turn the power on and test all voltages. If the test passes, continue on with another card. In this way, you can find the card that causes loss of some or all the voltages. The card that causes the power failure will most likely have a component or circuit-board failure.

Visually check for anything that could cause a short on that adapter card (i.e., a loose wire or a piece of loose solder). Turn the card over and shake it.

System board problems

System-board failures can be caused by the loss of the $+5$-V power or by the loss of clock pulses. An absent, jittery, or noisy clock signal can affect the rest of the system. A faulty clock signal can cause marginal operations or transient problems that can be difficult to find. This problem can require the testing of power, clock, ROM, RAM, I/O ports, interrupts, and bus-control logic.

The system board (Fig. 3-6) can be divided into two sections or functional areas. One will contain the CPU circuitry. This includes the microprocessor, the arithmetic processor (if used), the clock generator, bus controller, and buffers (Fig. 3-7). The other section contains the peripheral I/O devices, RAM, and analog circuits.

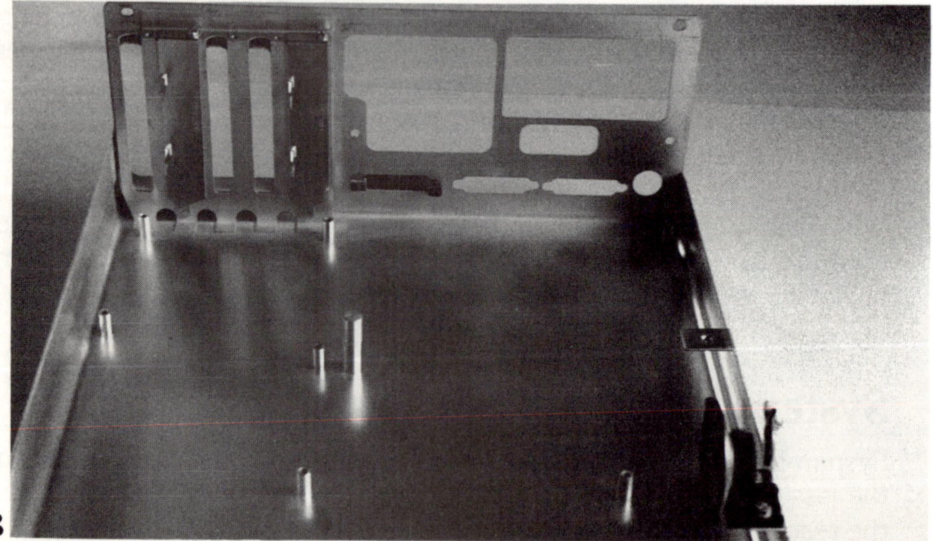

3-6   (A) An XT system board installed on system chassis. (B) A system chassis with system board removed. Notice the speaker mounted to the chassis, and the studs that are used to hold system board.

3-7 A close-up of the system board showing arithmetic processor socket.

Figure 3-8 shows the chip layout for the IBM PC system board. Figure 3-9 shows the pins for the 8088 microprocessor with normal voltage levels. Dynamic RAM is typically used in personal computers.

Dynamic RAM chips

Whenever 4K or more RAM is needed, *dynamic RAM* (*DRAM*) is used. It uses less circuit-board area, less power, and costs less than static RAM. Static RAMs use flip-flop circuits that can store a high- or low-voltage level (1 or 0 bit) and they hold this level as long as power is applied to the chip. Dynamic RAMs use the capacitance on the gates of field-effect transistors (FETs) that are connected together. The logic states are held as a charge or a noncharge in the capacitance between the FET gates and ground.

After a logic state is established, a static RAM holds the state as long as it is powered. In a dynamic RAM, the charge on the capacitors will leak off in a short time, unless it is refreshed. The dynamic bits are recharged every few milliseconds using special circuits, such as refresh counters that readdress the storage bits. Refreshing starts at the bottom row of memory and continues to the top row.

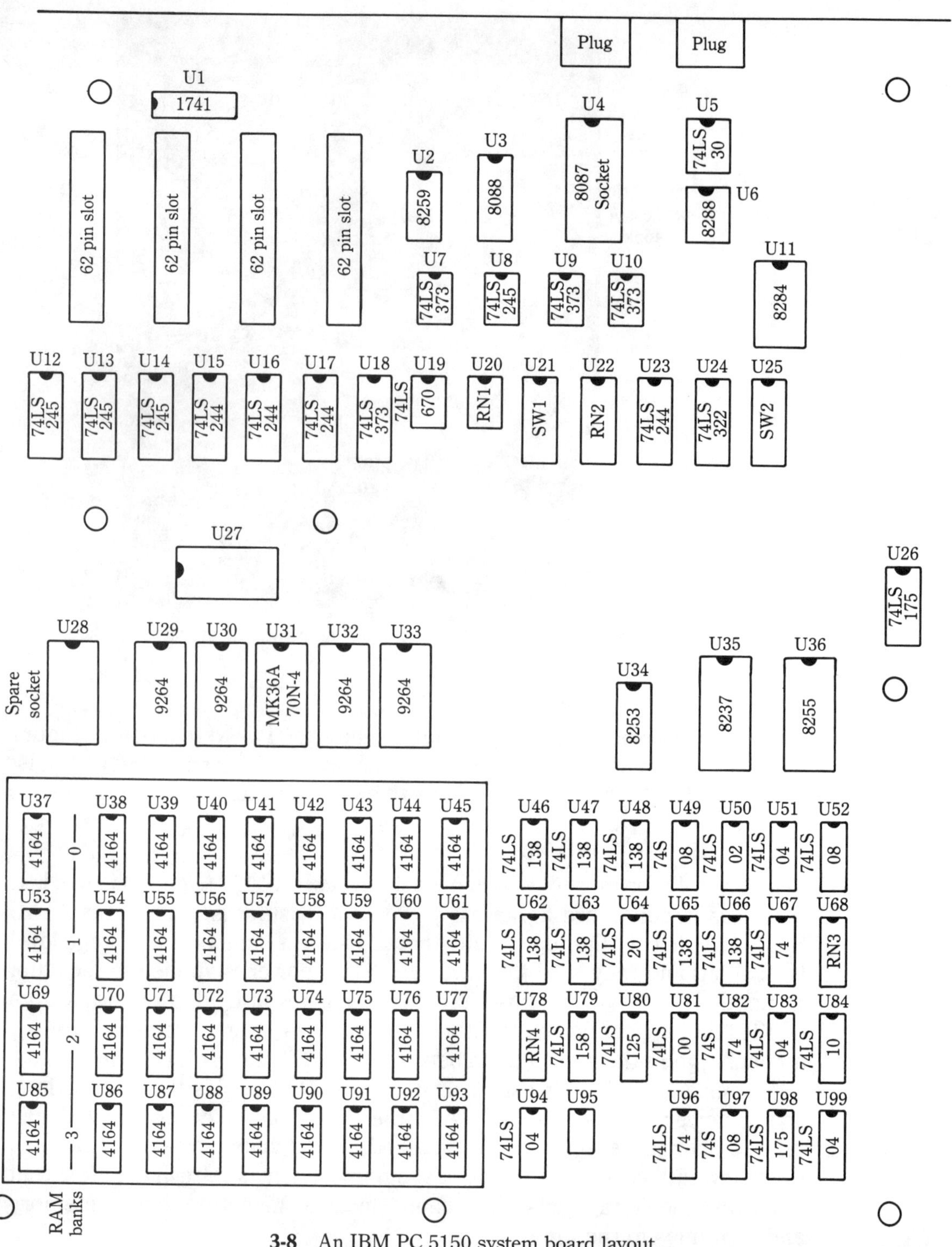

3-8   An IBM PC 5150 system board layout.

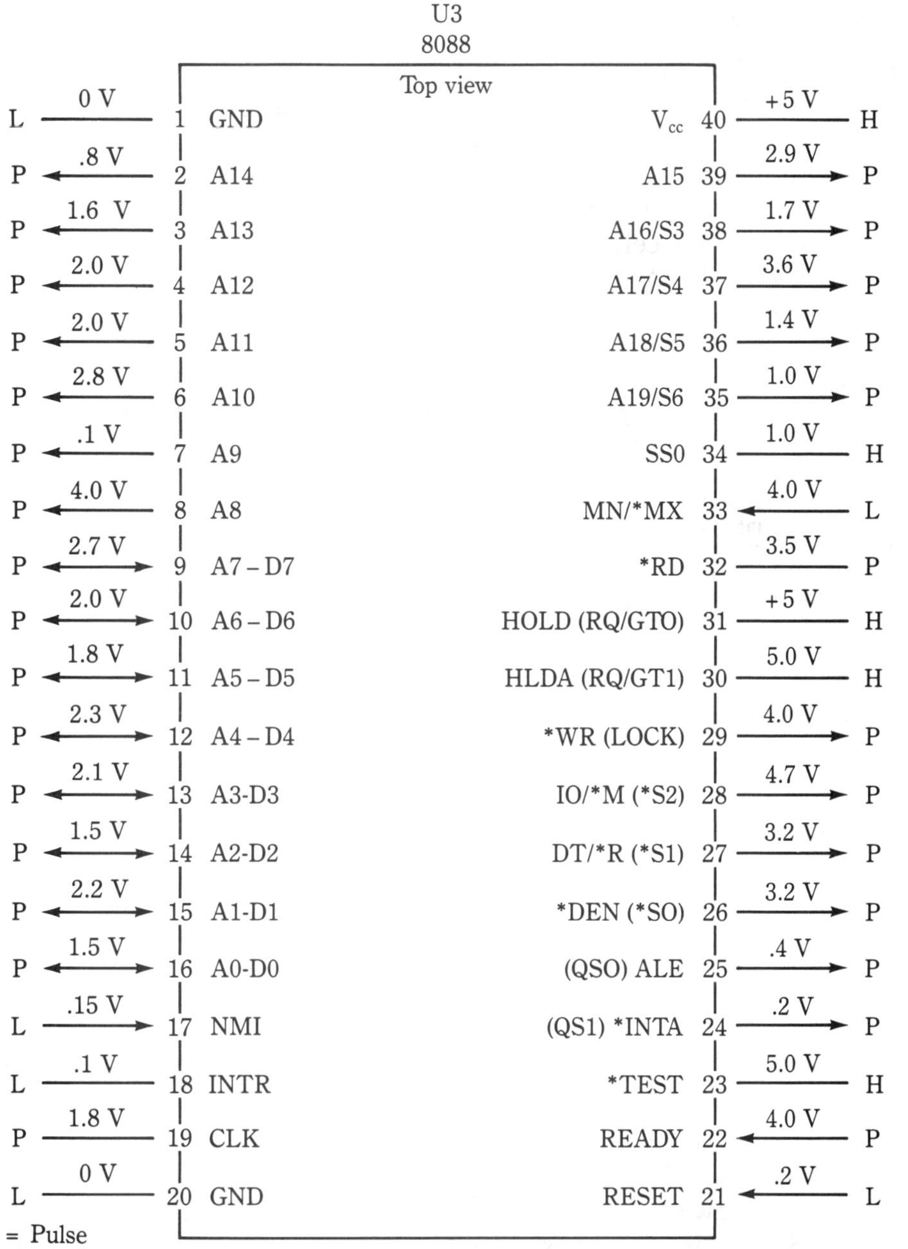

U3
8088
Top view

Left (0 V line)	Pin	Signal		Signal	Pin	Right
L — 0 V	1	GND		V_{cc}	40	+5 V — H
P ← .8 V	2	A14		A15	39	2.9 V → P
P ← 1.6 V	3	A13		A16/S3	38	1.7 V → P
P ← 2.0 V	4	A12		A17/S4	37	3.6 V → P
P ← 2.0 V	5	A11		A18/S5	36	1.4 V → P
P ← 2.8 V	6	A10		A19/S6	35	1.0 V → P
P ← .1 V	7	A9		SS0	34	1.0 V — H
P ← 4.0 V	8	A8		MN/*MX	33	4.0 V ← L
P ↔ 2.7 V	9	A7 – D7		*RD	32	3.5 V — P
P ↔ 2.0 V	10	A6 – D6		HOLD (RQ/GTO)	31	+5 V — H
P ↔ 1.8 V	11	A5 – D5		HLDA (RQ/GT1)	30	5.0 V — H
P ↔ 2.3 V	12	A4 – D4		*WR (LOCK)	29	4.0 V → P
P ↔ 2.1 V	13	A3-D3		IO/*M (*S2)	28	4.7 V → P
P ↔ 1.5 V	14	A2-D2		DT/*R (*S1)	27	3.2 V → P
P ↔ 2.2 V	15	A1-D1		*DEN (*SO)	26	3.2 V → P
P ↔ 1.5 V	16	A0-D0		(QSO) ALE	25	.4 V → P
L → .15 V	17	NMI		(QS1) *INTA	24	.2 V → P
L — .1 V	18	INTR		*TEST	23	5.0 V — H
P — 1.8 V	19	CLK		READY	22	4.0 V ← P
L — 0 V	20	GND		RESET	21	.2 V ← L

P = Pulse

Notes: Multiplexed data lines are A7 – D7 through A0 – D0, *H* indicates a steady high level and *L* indicates a steady low level. *P* indicates a pulsed condition.

Pinouts for the 8088 microprocessor used in the IBM PC and compatibles. A top view chart such as this can be used for troubleshooting the microprocessor chip.

3-9 An IBM PC 5150.

The 4116 RAM

The 4116 RAM chip was used in some early PCs (Fig. 3-10). It is a 16K chip. The actual memory matrix has 128 rows and 128 columns (Fig. 3-11). The 16 address bits are usually utilized with the two most significant bits used as the chip select. The next seven most significant bits are used to address the 128 rows. The seven least significant bits address the 128 columns. Each bit cell can be addressed by first addressing a row, then addressing a column.

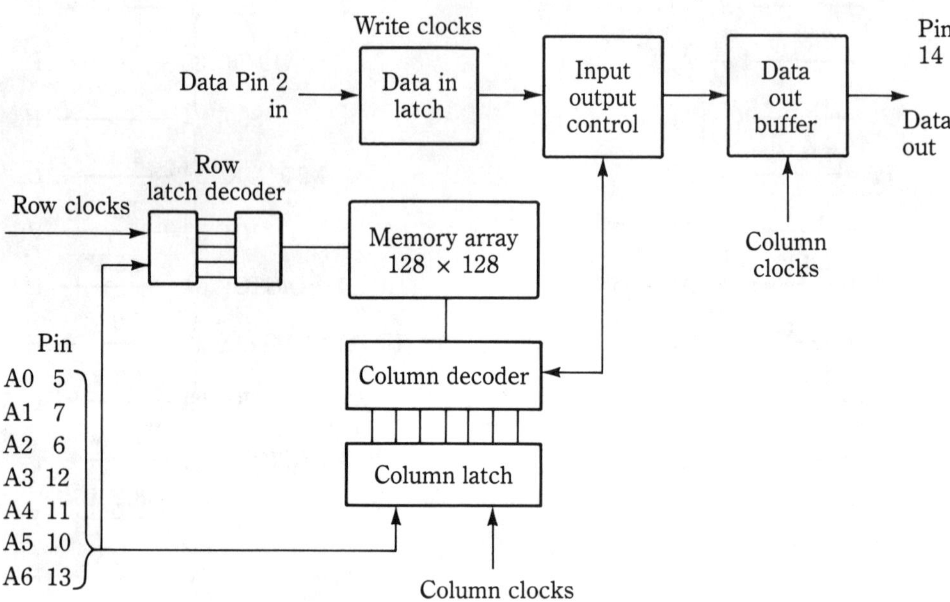

3-10 A block diagram of 4116 RAM.

The 4116 chip is used in groups of eight that are wired in parallel (Fig. 3-12). Each byte is spread over the eight chips, with one bit in a corresponding location in all eight chips. The array of eight chips provides a total of 16,384 total bytes (16K). The eight chips are usually numbered 0 through 7.

The top view of the chip is shown in Fig. 3-13. Both TTL logic circuits and MOS logic circuits are used on this chip. The TTL circuits are used for input and output functions, while the MOS circuits are used in the memory matrix to store the logic states. The TTL circuits are powered with $+5$ V at pin 9 and -5 V at pin 1. The MOS circuits are $+12$ V at pin 8 and the ground is pin 16.

The seven address lines are A6 through A0. These lines are in parallel with all of the address lines for the rest of the chips in the 16K array.

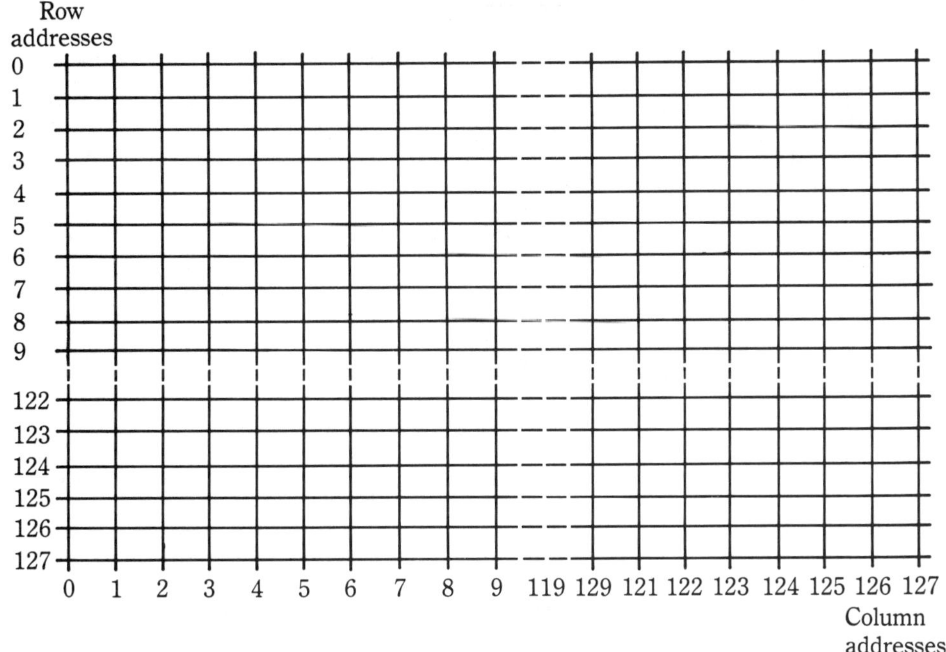

3-11   The 4116 16K RAM chip has a memory matrix of 128 rows and 128 columns of bit locations.

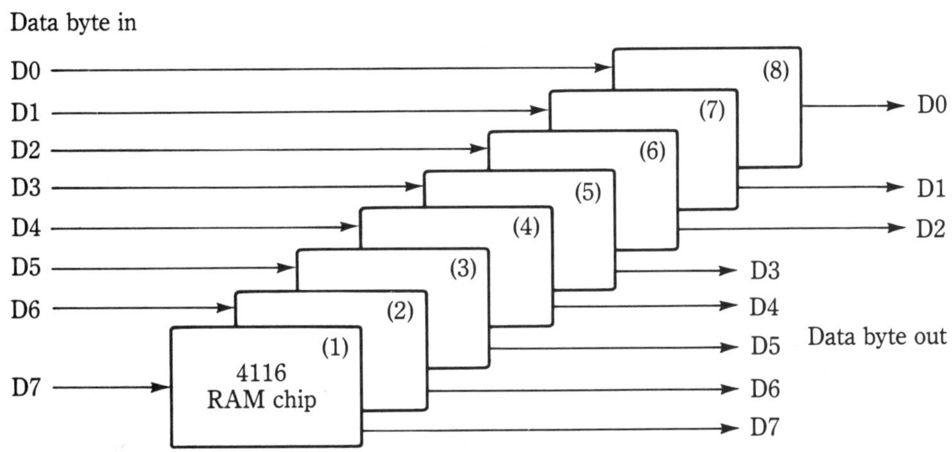

3-12   To make a byte, eight chips are used.

Because a total of 14 address bits are needed to address the memory matrix (seven bits for the 128 rows and seven bits for the 128 columns), a multiplexing scheme is used.

Two signals are used in the multiplexing technique. Pin 4 (Fig. 3-14) uses an input called *RAS (Row Address Strobe)* and pin 15 uses another

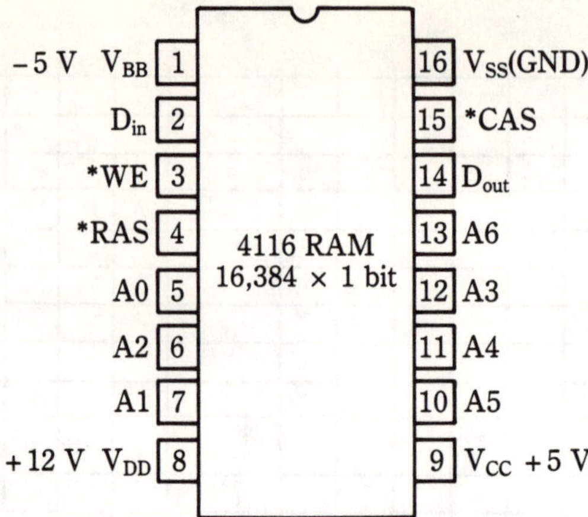

3-13   The 4116 RAM chip with 16K individual bits. It uses a 16-pin dual-in-line package (DIP).

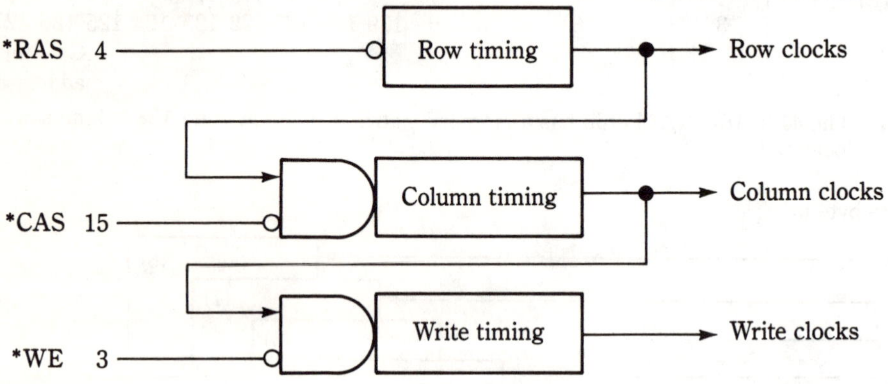

3-14   These three timing signals are applied to each 4116 RAM at pins 4, 15, and 3.

input called *CAS (Column Address Strobe)*. Multiplex chips receive the 14 address bits and separate them into two sets of bits (Fig. 3-15). They then send the two sets alternately to the array. The multiplexer does this operation in time sync with the RAS and CAS signals. The pin called *WE (Write Enable)* works the read/write function. The contents of the eight bits are either read out or loaded with data. Multiplexing saves seven pins on the chip. Only two data pins are used on a chip: Data In (which is pin 2) and Data Out (which is pin 14).

RAM chip evolution

The 16K 4116 RAM chip has been replaced by other denser chips. The 64K 4164 uses the same 16-pin chip as the 4116. The 4164 uses a 256-×-

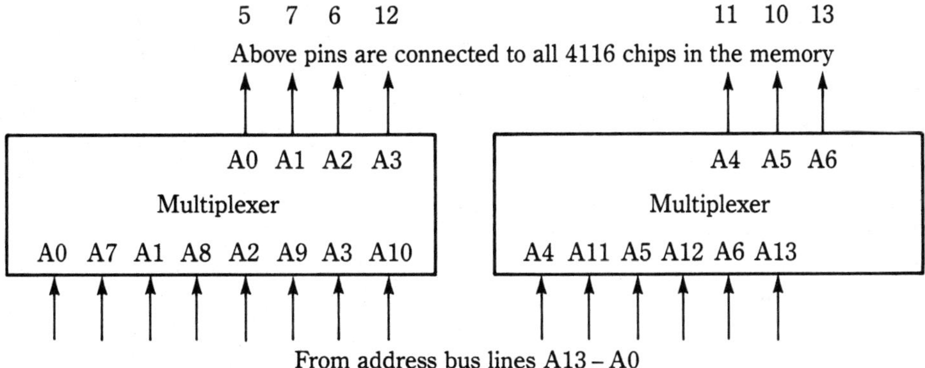

3-15 The multiplexer chips receive 14 bits from the address bus. During the 4116 RAS time, they send seven bits (A6-A0) to the 4116s. During the 4116 CAS time, they send the other seven bits A13-A7 to the RAM chips.

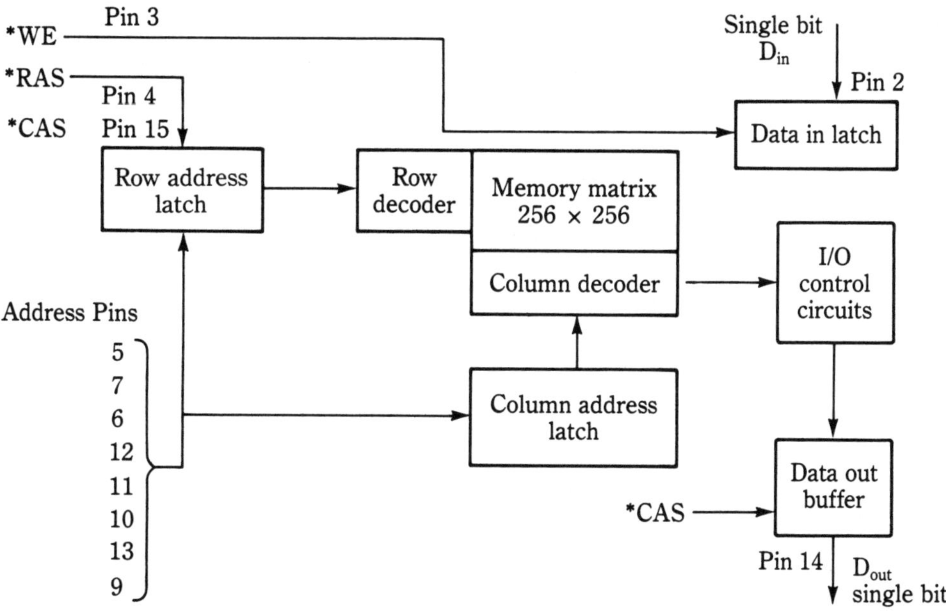

3-16 In the 4164 memory chip, the eight-row and eight-column address bits alternately enter through the eight address pins. RAS is used to strobe the row address into a latch and CAS will strobe the column address into another latch.

256 bit cell matrix (Fig. 3-16) and has only two power pins (8 and 16), while four power inputs (1, 8, 9, and 160) are used in the 4116. Pin 1 is not connected and pin 9 is used as an additional address pin (A7) for the 64K bits.

The 41256 chip, shown in Fig. 3-17, has 262,144 bit cells. This four-fold density increase is achieved by doubling the numbers of rows and

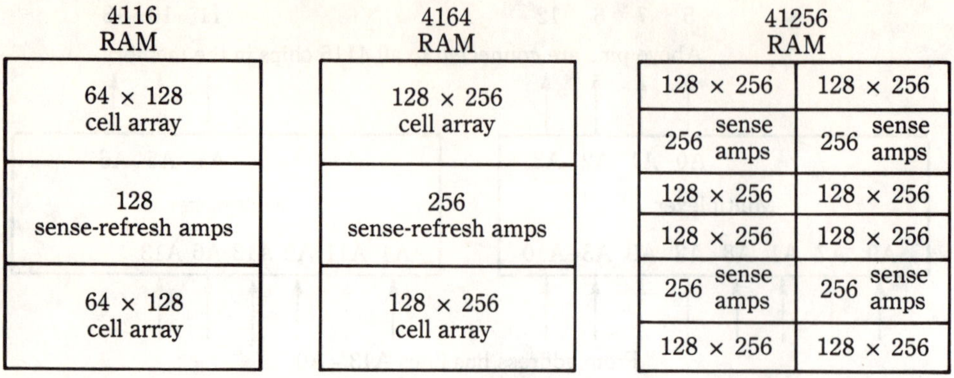

| 4116 RAM | 4164 RAM | 41256 RAM |

4116 RAM
64 × 128 cell array
128 sense-refresh amps
64 × 128 cell array

4164 RAM
128 × 256 cell array
256 sense-refresh amps
128 × 256 cell array

41256 RAM

128 × 256	128 × 256
256 sense amps	256 sense amps
128 × 256	128 × 256
128 × 256	128 × 256
256 sense amps	256 sense amps
128 × 256	128 × 256

3-17 The RAM cell arrays in the dynamic chips use amplifiers for refreshing. Notice that the 41256 is like four 4164 chips.

columns with a matrix of 512 rows and 512 columns. The 41256 is similar to the 4164 and the 4116 in the way they use the RAS input pin 4, the CAS input pin 15, and the WE input pin 3. The main differences are the number of address lines. The 4116 uses A6 through A0 to input 14 multiplexer address bits, seven at a time. The 4164 uses A7 through A0 to input 16 multiplexed address bits, eight at a time. The 41256 needs A8 through A0 to input 18 multiplexed address bits, nine at a time. The 41256 uses pin 1, which was not connected in the 4164, as address bit A8 (Fig. 3-18). These RAMs all use the same package, but the 1M RAMs use a different package.

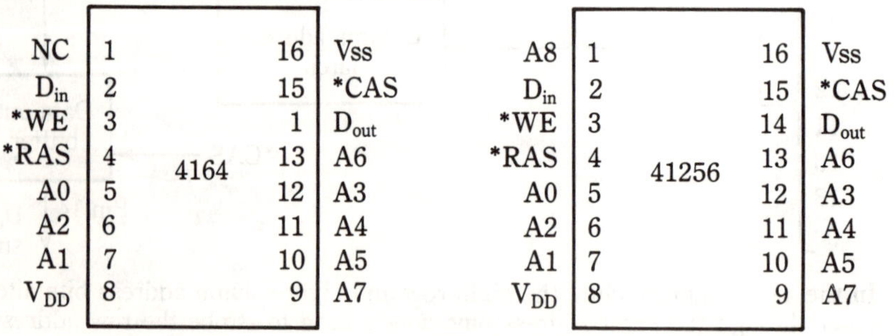

4164

NC	1	16	Vss
D_{in}	2	15	*CAS
*WE	3	1	D_{out}
*RAS	4	13	A6
A0	5	12	A3
A2	6	11	A4
A1	7	10	A5
V_{DD}	8	9	A7

41256

A8	1	16	Vss
D_{in}	2	15	*CAS
*WE	3	14	D_{out}
*RAS	4	13	A6
A0	5	12	A3
A2	6	11	A4
A1	7	10	A5
V_{DD}	8	9	A7

3-18 4164 and 41256 pinout. The only pin difference is the extra address bit on the 41256.

1M RAMs The 1M RAM uses a matrix of 1024 × 1024 (Table 3-2). A set of eight can provide one million bytes of dynamic memory. In order to address this set of chips, 20 address bits are needed. The 1M chips use 10 pins (A9 through A0) for multiplexing the 20 address bits. One type of package that is used is a 26-pin *surface-mount device (SMD)*, which has three pins on each side of the pin arrangement that are removed in the center. This provides space for additional components or circuit paths. In the larger chips, the bit matrixes are divided into several sections. The sense amplifiers aid in the refreshing operation, which must be performed every few milliseconds.

Table 3-2. Memory chip differences

Chip number	4116	4164	41256	411024
Total bits	16K	65K	256K	1024K
Bit array	128×128	256×256	512×512	1024×1024

Testing memory chips

Memory chips use MOS circuits for the memory cells. These chips are sensitive to static electricity. A grounded wrist strap and other precautions can be used to avoid damage as a result of static electricity. Memory chips should be handled carefully.

Figure 3-19 shows the top view of a 4164 chip with the typical voltages or logic states present at each pin. This can be used as a test-point chart. A logic probe or VOM can be used to check at each pin. A bad reading will usually indicate a problem with the chip if the signal is an output. If a bad reading is found at an input, it is more likely that the trouble is caused by the circuit that provides the input (unless the signal is being shorted by the memory chip).

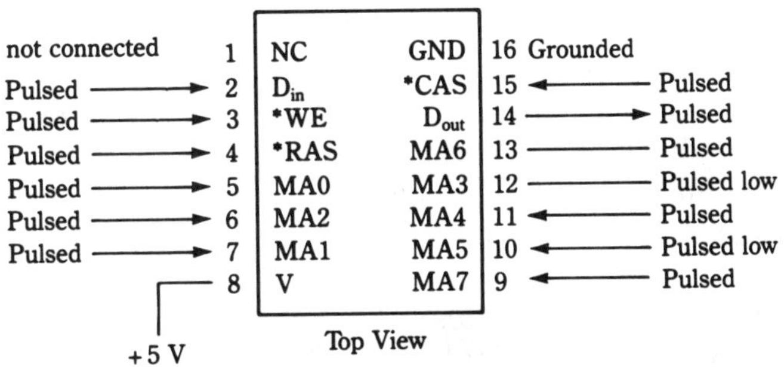

3-19 The pin diagram of the 4164 RAM chip with typical voltage states, which can be used for troubleshooting.

Eight chips are usually in a set to provide a byte, but a ninth chip might be used as a controller of the set or as a parity-checking bit. *Parity checking* involves counting the bit states and determining if the total is odd or even. This total is then compared with a stored total to determine if a bit was lost during an operation.

When a RAM or ROM fails, usually a short or open is somewhere in one of the internal circuits. This causes a problem in storing data when a program is being run and you must locate the bad chip and change it.

In some cases, a short might produce some smoke from the chip and the chip will appear to be charred or visually damaged. Most of the time, the bad chip looks the same as the other chips. Usually, only one chip at a time is defective, although multiple-chip failures can happen if a chain reaction is caused by, for example, a power-supply problem.

A defective memory chip will usually cause a problem in running part of a program. A shorted cell location could cause faulty data or addressing to occur. The results could be minor, like a slight error in calculations or the program might not run at all.

Diagnostic programs Many diagnostic programs are available for testing memory because this failure is common. Most computers use an automatic memory diagnostic that is run whenever the computer is booted up. This type of test program will often identify a bad memory chip and display some sort of memory location number for the bad chip on the screen.

The following diagnostic scheme is typical. The microprocessor will write to all of the RAM locations, then it will read all of the locations to check that the data was properly loaded. If the read check is okay, the memory location passes the test. If the read check indicates a bad bit location, the chip should be replaced.

RAM chip testers RAM chip testers are designed to check $256K \times 1$ and $64K \times 1$ RAM chips. They use test algorithms similar to those used in advanced diagnostic software. One design uses an 8088 processor to run a program that includes routines to test the chip's peripheral circuitry, and a routine that writes, reads, and refreshes every memory cell several times. The chip to be tested is placed in a Zero-Insertion Force (ZIF) socket. The test results are displayed and indicate the type of chip and its condition. Also, current limiters protect the chip and prevent any damage if the chip is placed in backwards. Options include a 1M adapter, speed verification, and automatic loop-testing.

The 1M adapter lets you test 1M, $256K \times 4$, and $64K \times 4$ Drams, in addition to $256K \times 1$ and $64K \times 1$ chips. The speed verifier test measures the memory chip's actual access time. Access time is a maximum parameter; a chip rated at a certain speed can be expected to meet or exceed that speed. Actual access times will show a considerable variance, and the speed verifier test can be used for sorting chips according to their true speeds. When a bank of memory chips fails, the speed test can be used to find a slow chip that might be causing the failure.

The auto-loop testing option is useful for detecting intermittent temperature and time-related problems in memory chips. It automatically retests the chip, using different data patterns, until the chip is removed. Detected errors are stored on the display.

The clock

The computer clock acts as the timekeeper for all processing. It runs at an assigned frequency and all operations are done in step with the clock. The clock consists of a crystal-controlled oscillator. A crystal oscillator produces a continuous sine-wave output. This sine wave is converted to a square wave for the digital circuits that need to use it. The square wave pulses provide the quickly rising and falling edges that are needed to trigger events. The faster the clock frequency, the faster the data will be processed. The processing frequency is derived from the clock frequency.

In the IBM PC, the clock components are part of the clock generator chip (U11-8284) (Fig. 3-20). This chip divides the crystal frequency to provide the frequencies needed.

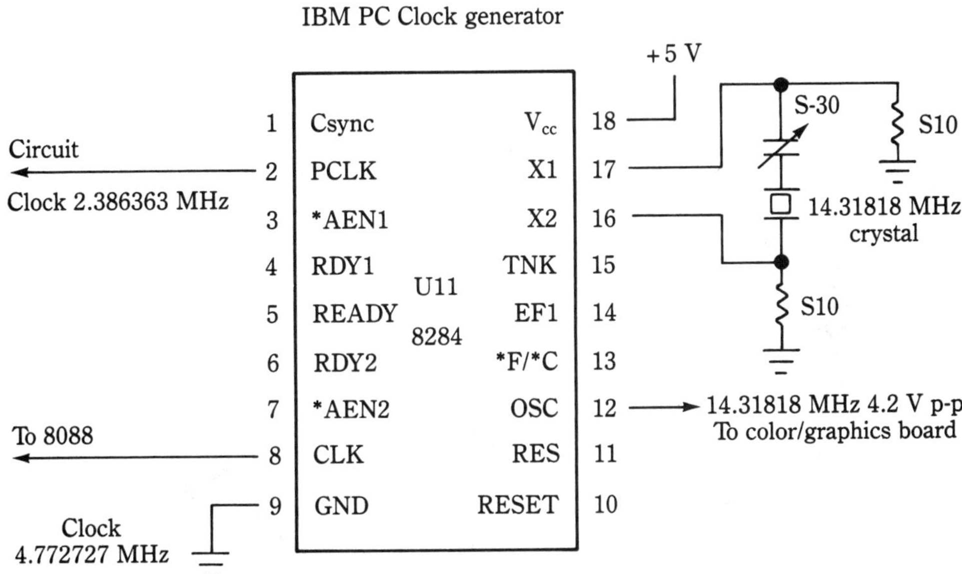

3-20 Clock generation.

The 8284 clock generator in the IBM PC has the crystal connected across pins 16 and 17. The crystal used in the PC is cut to run at 14.31818 MHz. When power is applied to the crystal, the effect of the voltage across the crystal causes it to oscillate at this frequency, which is called the *master frequency*. The clock generator circuitry divides this master frequency by 3.

This produces the system operating frequency of 4.772727 MHz. Computers that run at a faster rate use a higher frequency crystal.

The 4.772727 MHz is sent to the processor, which is an 8088 in the IBM PC. It is also available on the expansion connectors. The 8284 also divides the master frequency by 6 to provide a frequency of 2.386363 MHz. This signal is sent to a 74LS175, which divides this frequency by 2. This 1.1931817-MHz frequency is used to drive the 8253 programmable-interrupt timer chip.

The keyboard

The IBM PC family and its clones use a separate encoded keyboard, which is connected to the system unit. The encoded keyboard for the IBM personal computer has five connections on the output plug (Fig. 3-21). Two of these provide the power (+5 V and ground). The other three provide the interface between the keyboard and the system board.

In the IBM keyboard, a key depression causes the encoded circuits to generate the ASCII code for the key. The keyboard feeds its ASCII output

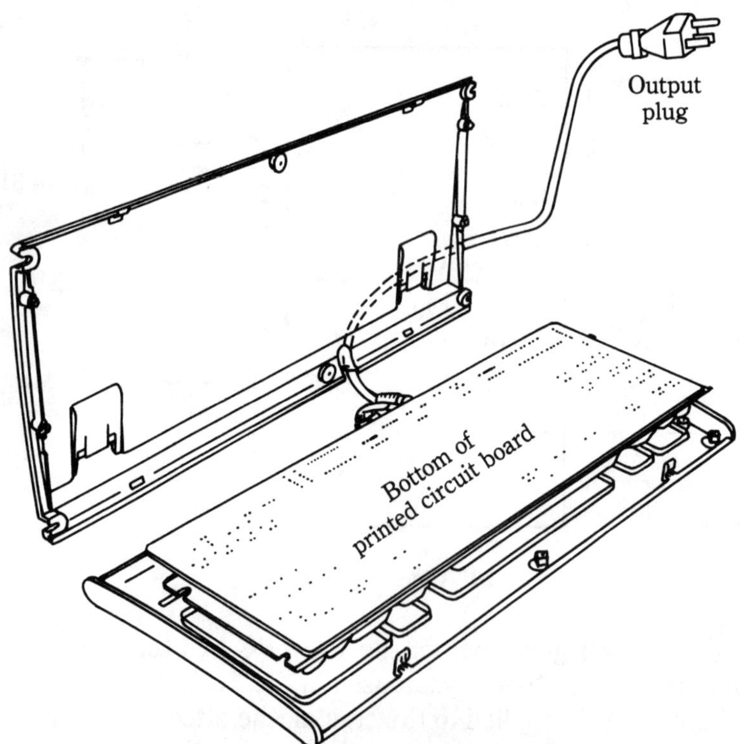

3-21 A keyboard with the bottom removed.

to the system unit. The keyboard uses a keyboard processor, an 8048 microprocessor chip. The 8048 chip is an 8-bit processor and contains 2K of ROM. The ROM is preloaded with a character code that is known as a *scan code*.

The processor uses a row-scanning technique to monitor the keyboard matrix. Each key makes a connection at one of the row-column intersections when depressed. The 8048 processor scans the rows for keystrokes by sending a high-level logic signal to each of the columns, one at a time. It scans the matrix once every 5 ms. The 8048 will receive a high-level logic signal from each row if a key in that row has not been pressed. The signals are stored in the scanning buffer resister in the 8048.

If a key is pressed, then the intersection connection is made and a low is received. The 8048 matches the column that is being scanned with the row that changed state. This sets the intersection point. The 8048 then looks up the character for this key in its character ROM. The coded bit pattern for the character is then sent out through the keyboard cable to the system board.

Inside the keyboard is a PC board with the row-column matrix and some electronic components—including the IC chips and supporting discrete parts (Fig. 3-22). The main circuit chip is the 8048 processor, which has internal clock circuits. The clock crystal generates the timing for the processor, which is also sent to the system board. The clock output syncs the keyboard timing with the system board.

The matrix is divided into rows and columns. The rows are held in the high state by $+5$ V through a pull-up resistor. The columns use inverter amplifiers to couple the outputs to the 8048 buffer register. The rows are constantly scanned by the 8048's internal circuits. If a key is not pressed, the column outputs are all high. The set of bits leaves the 8048 and is input to the main board in a serial form.

The data output line and the clock output line are sent to a NOT gate before going to the main board. The gate inverts the output and also amplifies it so that it can drive the system board circuits.

A busy line goes from the system board to the keyboard. It also uses an inverter. The busy signal tells the 8048 when it can send data; the system board might be busy and not be able to accept data at that time.

Debouncing

The mechanical contact (Fig. 3-23) that occurs when you strike a key is not perfect. As you press the key and the key closes the metallic connection, a condition of oscillation occurs for a few milliseconds until the connection is finalized. During this time, the keyswitch voltage is unstable and bounces

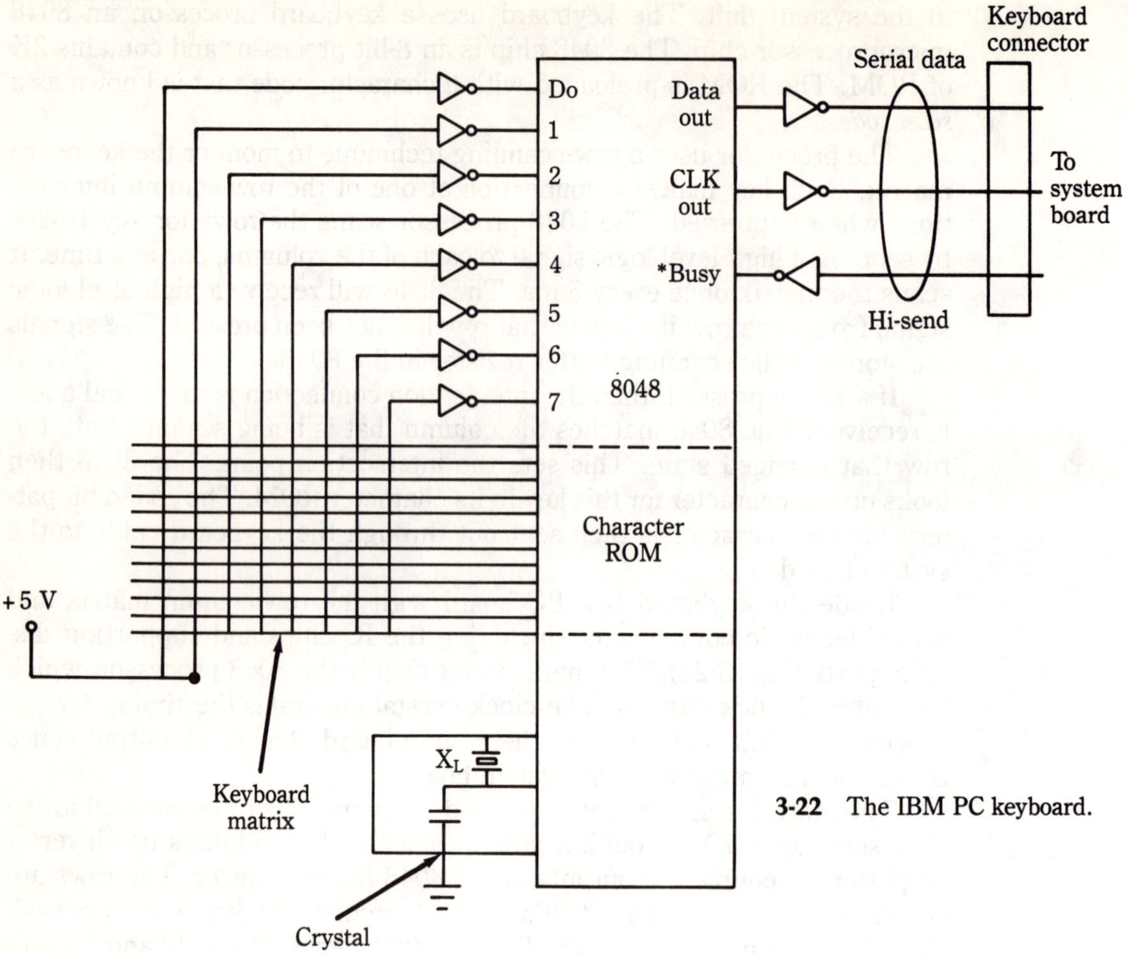

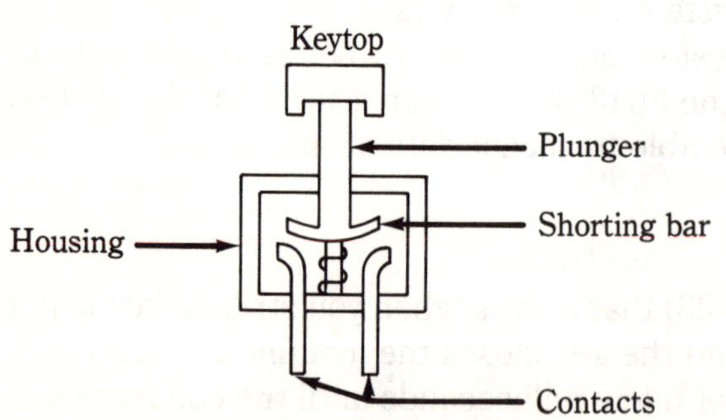

3-22　The IBM PC keyboard.

3-23　Typical keyswitch construction.

between the two switching voltages. The same type of oscillations occurs when you release the key.

In nonencoded keyboards, a resistor and capacitor are connected as a filter to reduce the oscillations and the bouncing effect. In the encoded keyboards (the IBM PCs and its clones), a delay of a few milliseconds is used before the keystroke is encoded. The delay is accomplished with a programmed loop that inserts the delay. This inhibiting of the key action during the switch bouncing is called *debouncing*. The 8048 microprocessor debounces by generating an interrupt during the time that the keyboard voltage is bouncing.

Keyboard and system-board operation

The encoded keyboard signals are sent to the system board (Fig. 3-24). The keyboard output is a serial data signal that is sent to the system board. A busy signal is used to control when the keyboard can send keyboard bits to the system board. The keyboard bits are sent in a serial format with the least-significant bit sent first and the most-significant bit of the data byte sent last.

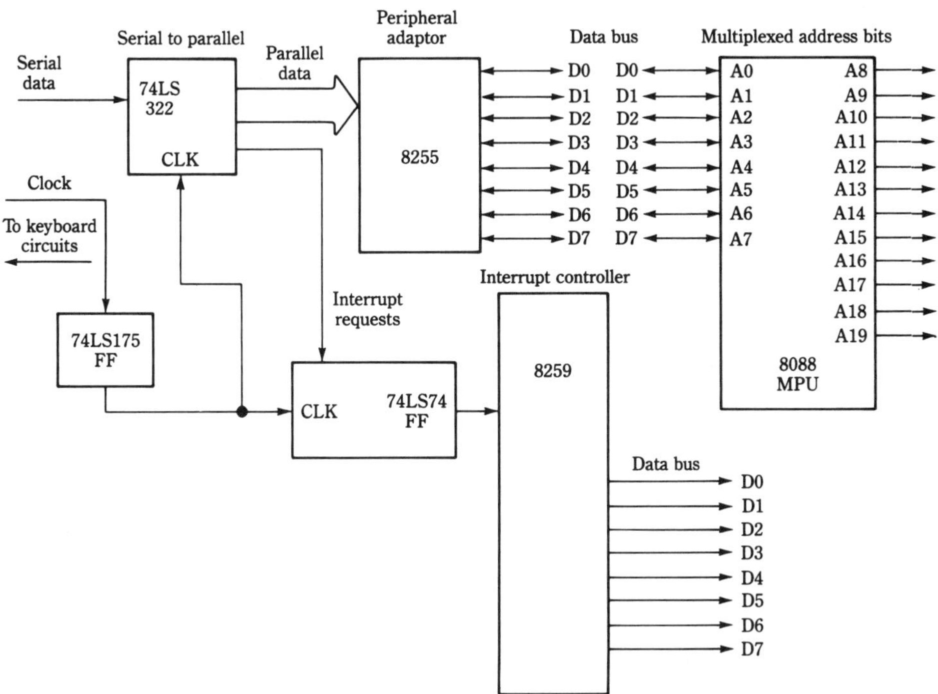

3-24   System board/keyboard processing.

The serial data is sent to a serial-to-parallel 74LS322 register, which changes the serial format to parallel. The 74LS322 is also connected to a dual-D flip-flop, the 74LS74. The latched clock signal from the keyboard is sent from the 74LS175 to the serial/parallel register and from the 74LS74 to sync these chips with the keyboard.

The 74LS74 flip-flop is used to generate an interrupt request to the 8259 programmable-interrupt controller. This chip generates an output signal that interrupts the main processor (the 8088). The 74LS322 shift register sends its parallel bits to one of the ports of the 8255 I/O chip. The parallel bits are then sent to the system data bus. These bits, which hold the keyboard characters, are then read by the 8088 processor and stored in the video RAM section of memory. They can then be used by the video display system and be sent to the monitor or to the printer for hard-copy output.

Audio outputs

Several types of audio outputs are available in personal computers. The sounds are usually created in software. The IBM PCs and most clones have their own speaker and audio circuits (Fig. 3-25). The audio circuit that responds to the program usually uses four chips. The speaker is typically driven by a 75477 relay driver chip. This chip amplifies the incoming bit signals so that the signals can be applied to the speaker cone. By controlling the frequency of the movement, you can produce a range of sounds. BASIC can be used to produce sounds up to about 1,000 Hz, and machine language can be used to produce sounds up to 3,000 Hz.

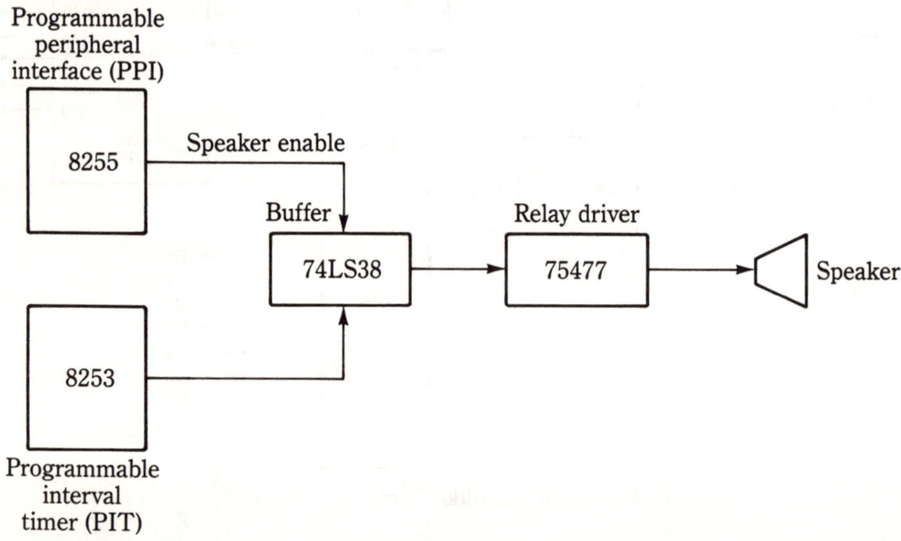

3-25   An audio driver circuit.

An 8255 Programmable Peripheral Interface (PPI) chip provides one of its output port pins (pin 1) for switching the audio on and off. A high-level signal turns the speaker system on and a low turns it off. This acts under software control and is called the *speaker enable*. This signal is connected to a 74LS38 NAND buffer.

Another signal from an 8253 Programmable Interval Timer (PIT) is also sent to the NAND buffer. This signal is a software-control sounder. If the two signals are both true, the buffer will provide an output to the relay driver. The speaker then responds to the buffer output. The audio frequencies generated will be a result of the signals from the PPI and the output of the PIT.

4
Diagnostic hardware and software

Two general types of computer-aided diagnostic tests can be used to detect and isolate problems that might occur in the system:

1. An internal diagnostic test that runs upon power-up, reset, or self-test.
2. A diskette diagnostic test that runs a series of test programs that reside on a diskette (Fig. 4-1).

The internal diagnostic test runs automatically upon power-up and checks the internal logic of the system. It is usually known as the *power-on self-test (POST)*. If this test runs successfully, a system message appears on the monitor (Fig. 4-2) and the system is ready for a command.

Error messages

If an error message appears (as discussed in the following examples), one of the computer's operational modes is not working. For example, if a disk drive fails, you would get a message number. In most cases, you must find the cause of the error before you can continue. The error message should direct you to the problem.

Self-test errors

In the IBM PC, if you turn off the computer, wait 10 seconds and turn power back on, the system self-test will run. If no problems occur, the speaker will beep and the computer will try to boot the disk drive. If no disk is in the floppy drive and no hard drive is connected to the PC, the

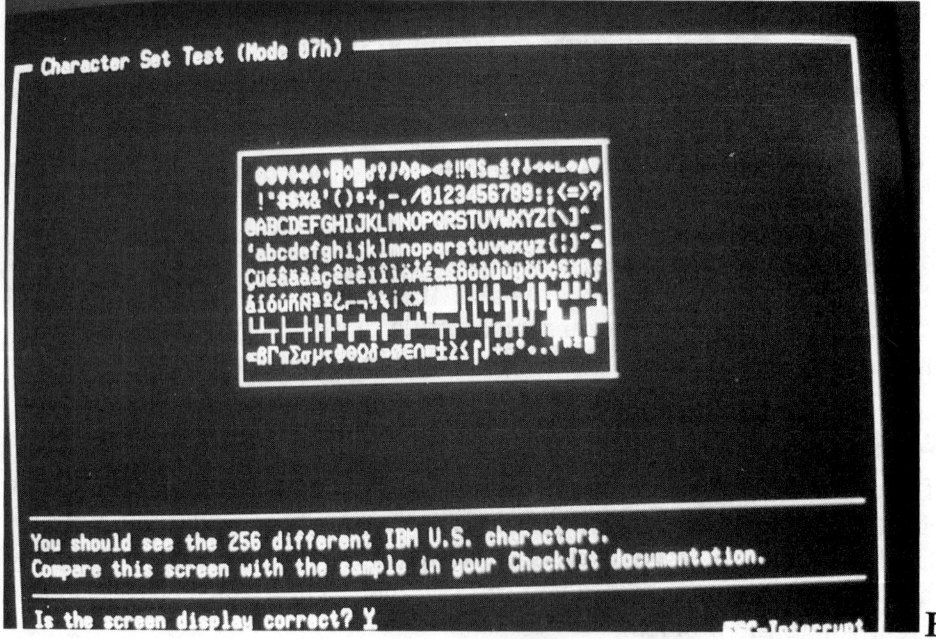

4-1 (A) Typical diagnostic test programs that reside on a diskette. (B) A screen for checking the character set.

operating system will shift into ROM BASIC. A failure during the self-test will generate an error-code message and the machine might beep.

An error code will appear if the switch settings do not match the

```
SILENT PARTNER CORPORATION
WELCOME TO THE BIOS AT.

Current date is Sun 12-30-1990
Enter new date (mm-dd-yy):
Current time is 6:02:10.44
Enter new time:

Microsoft(R) MS-DOS(R) Version 3.20
          (C)Copyright Microsoft Corp 1981-1986


C>
```

4-2 A typical message after the self-test.

installed components. The switch settings for the original IBM PC are:

Switch Block 1	Function
1, 7, and 8	5¼ Disk-drive setting 1 on, 7 on, 8 on = no drives 1 off, 7 on, 8 on = 1 drive 1 off, 7 off, 8 on = 2 drives
2	Coprocessor 2 on = no coprocessor installed 2 off = coprocessor installed
3 and 4	Memory setting 3 off, 4 off = 64K memory or more 3 on, 4 off = 48K memory 3 off, 4 on = 32K memory 3 on, 4 on = 16K memory
5 and 6	Monitor type 5 on, 6 on = no monitor 5 off, 6 off = monochrome monitor/ printer adapter or more than one monitor 5 off, 6 on = 40 × 25 color monitor 5 on, 6 off = 80 × 25 color monitor
Switch Block 2	
1 through 8	Memory size (used with SW1 3, 4) 1, 2, 3, 4, 5 on, 6, 7, 8 off = 64K or less

> 1, 3, 4, 5 on, 2, 6, 7, 8 off = 128K memory
> 1, 2, 4, 5 on, 3, 6, 7, 8 off = 192K memory
> 1, 4, 5 on, 2, 3, 6, 7, 8 off = 256K memory

If the system self-test finds a RAM failure, a four-character error code followed by the number 201 will appear in the top left corner of the screen. The 201 indicates a RAM problem and the four-character code indicates the bank and the row of the memory chips in which the error occurred. The first two characters show the memory bank in which the failure occurred and the last two characters show the bit position of the RAM failure in that particular bank of memory. This is shown for the IBM PC 5150:

System Board Bank	Failed Chip	RAM Error
00 - Bank 0	00 - Parity	201
04 - Bank 1	01 - D0 chip	201
08 - Bank 2	02 - D1 chip	201
0C - Bank 3	04 - D2 chip	201
	08 - D3 chip	201
	10 - D4 chip	201
	20 - D5 chip	201
	40 - D6 chip	201
	80 - D7 chip	201

This translates the error codes to the malfunctioning bank and bit position. For example, a failure in the bit 2 position of bank 2, a code 0804 201 should appear in the upper left corner of the screen. If the third and fourth characters in the error code do not match the codes, swap the entire bank of RAM chips and try again. Another technique is to power down and swap each chip in the bad bank one at a time with the same bit-position chip in an adjacent bank. Then, power up and retest. When the error code shifts to the adjacent bank, the last chip swapped was bad. On the 64K/256K boards, a four-character code is also displayed when a ROM failure occurs. The self-test routine resides on ROM U33. This ROM does not get tested by the self-test program. The other ROMs are tested and the error codes for the IBM PC5150 follow. These ROMs are used to store the internal BASIC program in these machines.

Error Code Displayed	Problem
F600 ROM	Cassette BASIC ROM U29
F800 ROM	Cassette BASIC ROM U30
FA00 ROM	Cassette BASIC ROM U31
FC00 ROM	Cassette BASIC ROM U32

Power-on checklist

If your computer does not work when you try to start it up, go through the following checklist. Almost 90% of the failures that occur are likely to be solved by going through this checklist:

1. Check that the main power cord is fully plugged in—one end to the JS286 chassis, the other end to a grounded (3-prong) wall outlet.

2. Check that the monitor's power cord is connected either to the computer chassis power outlet or a wall outlet and the display cable to the connector of the display adapter.

3. Check that the monitor is turned on.

4. Turn up the monitor's brightness control knob.

5. Check that the five-pin keyboard cable is plugged in securely to the system unit. The plug must be in the correct orientation. The bump on the plug should be on top and the plug should fit completely into the socket.

6. When booting from the floppy disk drive, check that a DOS diskette is in the floppy drive and that the drive door is closed or that the lever is correctly positioned.

7. When booting from the hard-disk drive, make sure no diskettes are in drive A.

Error codes   If you see an error code on the screen, look it up on your error code list and follow the accompanying instructions. If the instructions fail to clear up the problem and the error pertains to a peripheral product in the system, such as a monochrome display adapter, check the manual that accompanies that product and try to isolate and correct the problem. You should always write down the error code that you receive. In the event that the unit requires additional troubleshooting, this information will be valuable. The following error codes are typical for most clones:

101   System board error. Board requires repair.

201   Memory error. One of the RAM chips might be bad or missing or incorrectly installed. You need to locate the bad or incorrectly installed chip and replace it.

301   Keyboard error. This is one of the most common error codes. Usually, the five-pin keyboard cable has pulled out from the system unit. The plug must be in the correct orientation, the bump on the plug must be on top, or the cable will not fit completely into its socket.

401   Color or monochrome adapter error. Check that the monitor is securely plugged in both to an electrical source and to the connector of the display adapter. Check the adapter manual, and verify that any jumpers and/or switches on the adapter are set correctly. If you still get this error code, the monitor needs repair.

501   Color adapter error. Use the same procedure as for 401.

601/ 602   Floppy drive or controller error. The cables between the floppy drive and its controller might have disconnected or are connected backwards. Check that the cables between the floppy and hard-disk controller, and the floppy drive, are properly connected.

701   Math coprocessor error. Check that the math coprocessor is completely pushed into its socket. The math chip might be defective, or if it was installed backwards, it has probably been damaged.

901   Printer adapter error. Check that the printer cable is correctly attached to the adapter. If you have two or more printer adapters in the system, such as one port on a display adapter and one on a multifunction card, check that they are not configured for the same LPT.

1101/ 1201   Asynchronous communications adapter (serial port) failure. I/O adapter cards, multifunction cards, and some display adapters might include serial ports. Identify the serial ports in the system and check the cabling attached to each. Check for COMN port conflicts using the manual or documentation for each serial port adapter. You will need to determine the factory default COM port setting and whether that COM port setting can be reconfigured or (if it isn't needed) disabled. The proper procedure for reconfiguring/disabling that COM port should be indicated in the documentation. You must reconfigure or disable conflicting serial ports. You can check each port by disconnecting each one at a time and rebooting. If you do not get the error code when one of the serial-port adapters is disconnected, that adapter is the problem.

1301   Game port adapter error. Check the cabling and if you have more than one game control device, such as a game paddle and a joystick, test each one in turn to isolate the problem.

1401   Graphics printer error. Check the cabling of the printer to the system unit and to electrical power (see chapter 7 for printer troubleshooting).

1501   SDLC (Synchronous Data Link Control) error. Check the attachment of the modem to the system. Reboot the system without the modem installed. If the error does not repeat, the problem is in the modem.

1701 Fixed disk error. This error code will occur, and it can be ignored, the first time you boot up with a new hard disk. This will occur if the disk is formatted. If the error still exists after the disk has been formatted, repeat the format procedure. It can last up to 40 minutes for a 20M drive, so do not interrupt the procedure before it is complete (see chapter 5 on disks for more information).

Power-on self tests When the power to your computer is first turned on, it automatically runs the internal Power-On Self-Test (POST) program, which is built into the BIOS. The *BIOS* is the *Basic Input Output System* software that is programmed in ROM chips on the computer's system board. The POST program tests the critical system components, one at a time. As each component is tested, the POST program generates a test number code that is sent to an output port (usually number 80). If all of the tests confirm proper operation, the system boots normally.

If a problem is detected during these tests, the POST program stops and the system boot is aborted. Depending on when this happens, an error code might appear on the screen or the screen might just go blank. Diagnostic cards allow the missing codes to be captured.

POST diagnostic cards The POST-IT ISA card can be placed in an expansion slot of an Industry Standard Architecture (ISA) bus computer to monitor the code numbers being sent by the POST to output port 80. The code numbers appear on a seven-segment digital LED display during the test.

If a problem is detected by the POST program, the number shown on the POST-IT ISA display indicates which component test failed. The BIOS manufacturer's POST codes can then be used to identify the problem. In order to troubleshoot, repair, or maintain PCs, a number of tools are available to aid these tasks. The diagnostic card verifies that the correct power is being supplied to the expansion bus with a series of green and red LEDs. Information about critical internal bus lines and clocks can be checked with the clock test function.

The POST-IT ISA card fits in a short XT slot and runs in an IBM PC, XT, AT or a compatible computer that uses an 8-bit bus and Industry Standard Architecture (ISA). A dual hexadecimal LED digital display shows the POST codes. Four LEDs are used to monitor $+5$ V, -5 V, $+12$ V, and -12 V. A single LED and jumper block is used to monitor signals from the Address Latch Enable, Input/Output Read, and clock systems. KickStart 1 is another card designed for engineers, technicians, and advanced PC users who want to identify the cause of motherboard and other system failures.

Because many computer failures can blank the screen, software diagnostics can be difficult. With a POST card installed in a slot, when the power comes on, the CPU executes the POST program built into BIOS in the ROM chips on the main circuit board. The LEDs on the card show whether power is applied to the board. Prior to running each step in the POST program, BIOS sends test number codes to output port 80, which lights the LEDs on the card. If the computer hangs up, stops, or runs in a loop during the test, it is because an error has been detected.

The last test number sent to port 80 signals the problem that caused the system to fail. You might be able to find the number in the BIOS manufacturer's POST code list in the manual and know which circuit to repair.

KickStart 2 is a multifunction diagnostics card designed for service technicians, it performs both low-level and advanced diagnostics for the motherboard, memory, and peripherals. This card relays low-level POST failure codes using a digital display. Advanced diagnostics are performed by a set of tests in a 512K paged EPROM. It also measures the power-supply voltage.

System tests include CPU, math chip, real memory, extended memory, interrupt control, DMA control, clock, timer, and CMOS RAM. Peripheral tests include serial port, parallel port, floppy-disk drive, hard-disk drive, keyboard, and video (MONO, CGA, EGA, and VGA). Tests can also be run from a remote terminal.

Errors can be logged to either a remote terminal (via onboard serial and parallel I/O), or printer. The board includes an 8K CMOS battery-backed up RAM for storing configurations and password information, a real-time clock, an Ethernet BNC terminator, a serial cable assembly, and loopback plugs (9-pin serial, 25-pin serial, 25-pin parallel) for communication port testing and special ROMs to replace BIOS ROMs, which do not send POST code errors.

PC Probe is an example of a disk that offers advanced diagnostics and provides system information, utilities, and benchmark testing. It is suitable for the advanced end user and service technician. It uses pull-down menus that can be keyboard or mouse driven, and on-screen help. It can also be run remotely with programs like CoSession.

Typically, these tests can run in single pass, multiple pass, or batch mode for isolating intermittent errors. Results can be logged to a disk file, display, serial port, or printer. Tested components include the system board, RAM, video board and display, keyboard and mouse, parallel and serial ports, floppy controller and drive, and hard drive (Figs. 4-3, 4-4, 4-5, 4-6, and 4-7).

Also, a number of built-in utilities are available for fixing common operating problems. You can reformat your hard drive, revitalize hard-disk

4-3 A system configuration display.

```
                         Loading

            Investigating system configuration

       Local - Check for remote operation
  (Standard) - Identify BIOS manufacturer
    Complete - Determine system components
    Complete - Look for RAM (base, extended, expanded)
 Not present - Look for math co-processor
 Not present - Look for mouse


          System configuration checks complete.

                 Press any key to continue
```

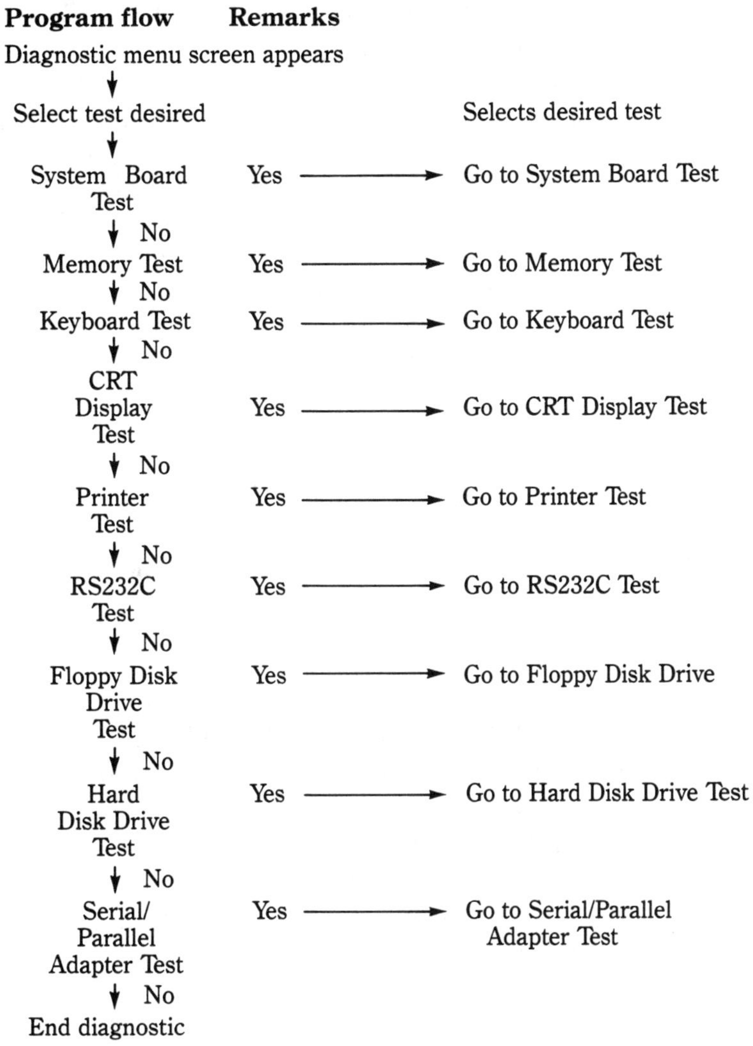

4-4 A typical diagnostic program.

1. All tests	7. RS232C
2. System board	8. Floppy disk drive
3. Memory	9. Hard disk drive
4. Keyboard	10. Serial/parallel adapter
5. CRT display	11. End diagnostics
6. Printer	Select option number__

4-5   A typical diagnostic menu.

data, list and edit bad track tables, display and edit CMOS RAM, and locate a bad RAM chip. Serial and parallel port loopback plugs are included in some utilities for communications port testing. A speed test is also built in to test the CPU, FPU (math coprocessor), and video speeds. It can display CPU, FPU, BIOS, Video, RAM, EMS, IRQ, DMA, I/O, CMOS RAM and Cache information.

IBM Advanced Diagnostics Diagnostic programs, such as IBM Advanced Diagnostics, are useful for troubleshooting the IBM AT and the compatibles. However, because the IBM AT keyboard and most compatible keyboards are not identical in their electronics, this program might sometimes generate a keyboard error when none exists. If you use IBM Advanced Diagnostics, be prepared for this problem.

Extended self-test Many compatibles come with an extended self-test program which runs a more extensive internal diagnostic than that which is run upon power-up or reset. The extended self-tests are usually menu driven.

You can run the extended self-test when you suspect a problem in the disk drive, a diskette, or any option added to the system board. To run the extended self-test, bypass DOS in some compatibles by loading the diagnostic disk, and turning on the computer. See Figs. 4-8 to 4-10.

The diagnostic test will typically run the following types of programs:

1. Floppy or hard disk tests. These tests check each hard- or floppy-disk drive.

2. Extended tests. These tests include the drive tests above, a memory test, and a video, printer and communications test.

3. Individual test selection. This allows you to run the tests one at a time. It might allow you to run tests that check the communications port and the printer. The selection can help isolate a problem to a specific device (Fig. 4-11).

4. Install new diagnostic tests. This selection allows you to add new diagnostic tests to the diskette.

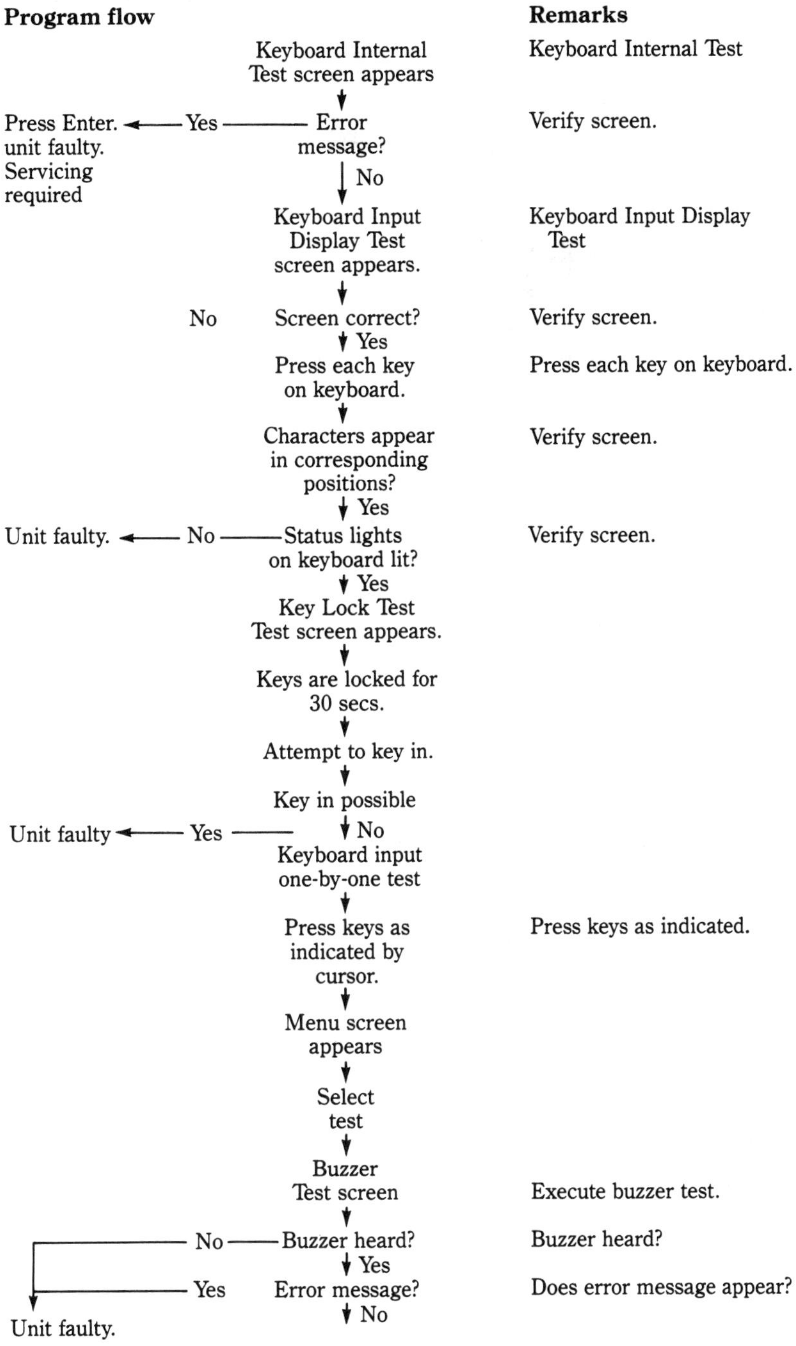

Program flow   **Remarks**

Keyboard Internal   Keyboard Internal Test
Test screen appears
↓

Press Enter. ◄── Yes ────── Error   Verify screen.
unit faulty.   message?
Servicing
required   ↓ No

Keyboard Input   Keyboard Input Display
Display Test   Test
screen appears.
↓

No   Screen correct?   Verify screen.
↓ Yes

Press each key   Press each key on keyboard.
on keyboard.
↓

Characters appear   Verify screen.
in corresponding
positions?
↓ Yes

Unit faulty. ◄── No ──── Status lights   Verify screen.
on keyboard lit?
↓ Yes

Key Lock Test
Test screen appears.
↓

Keys are locked for
30 secs.
↓

Attempt to key in.
↓

Key in possible
Unit faulty ◄── Yes ────── ↓ No

Keyboard input
one-by-one test
↓

Press keys as   Press keys as indicated.
indicated by
cursor.
↓

Menu screen
appears
↓

Select
test
↓

Buzzer
Test screen   Execute buzzer test.
↓

── No ──── Buzzer heard?   Buzzer heard?
↓ Yes

── Yes   Error message?   Does error message appear?
↓ No

Unit faulty.

4-6 Typical keyboard tests.

A. Normal end

```
TESTING – KEYBOARD INTERNAL
END KEYBOARD TEST
PRESS "ENTER" . . .
```

B. Error message

```
TESTING – KEYBOARD INTERNAL
XX:XX:XX LOOP COUNT = XX
3XX XXXXXX
END KEYBOARD TEST
PRESS "ENTER" . . .
```

C. Typematic Test
menu

```
PRESS EACH KEY, HOLD FOR TYPEMATIC TEST
IF OK PRESS "Y THEN ENTER"
IF NOT OK PRESS "N THEN ENTER"
```

4-7   Typical displays (keyboard tests). (A) A normal end. (B) An error message. (C) A Typematic test menu.

Typical diagnostic operation flow	**Action**
Start	
↓	
Load diagnostic floppy disk	
↓	
Diagnostic Utility Menu appears	Activate Diagnostic Utility Menu
↓	
Input desired item and Enter	Select desired item
↓	
Floppy Disk Utility	Go to Floppy Disk Utility
↓	
LOG Utility	Go to Log Utility
↓	
Setup Utility	Go to Setup Utility
↓	
Hard Disk Utility	Go to Hard Disk Utility
↓	
End Diagnostic Menu	

4-8   A main diagnostic program.

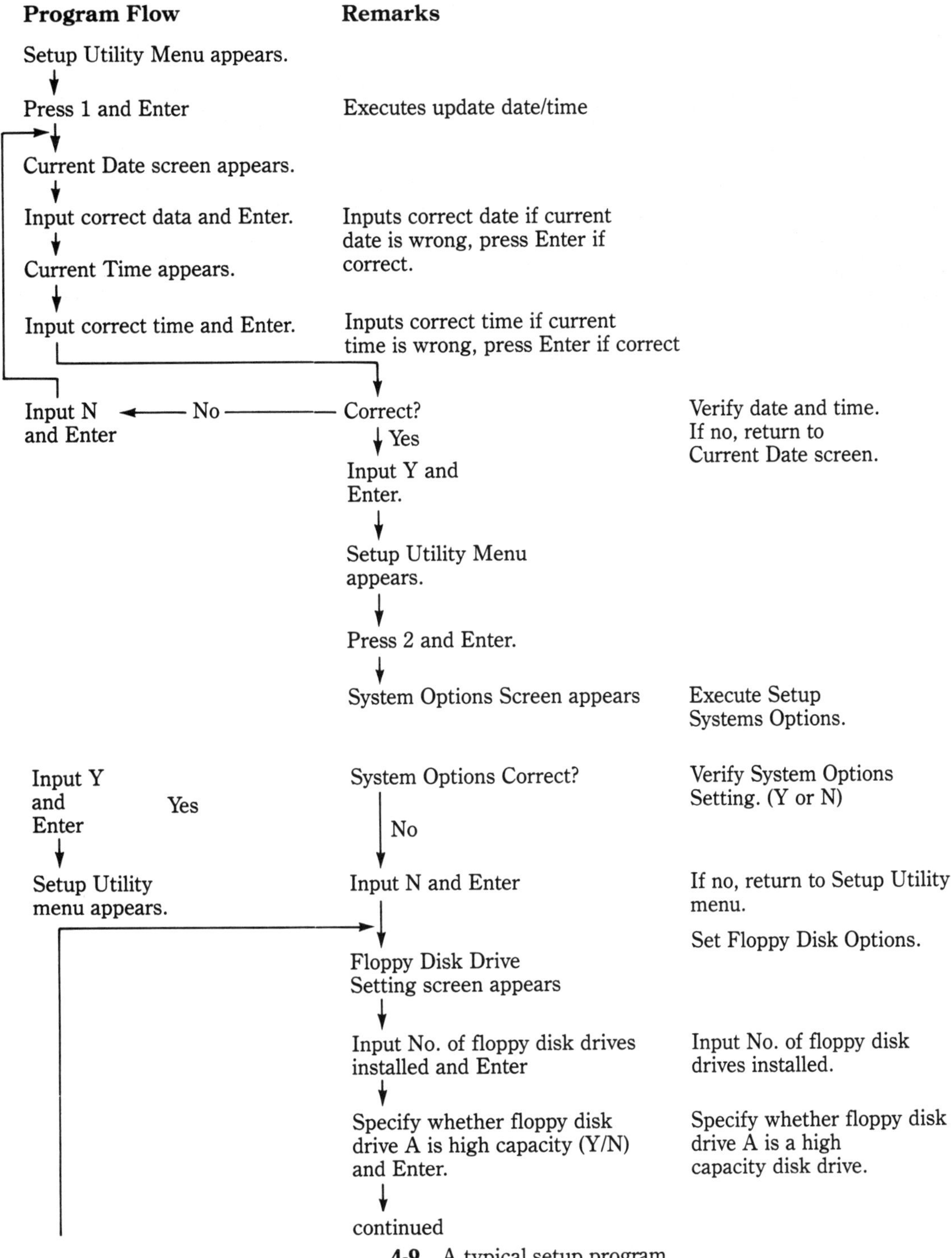

4-9 A typical setup program.

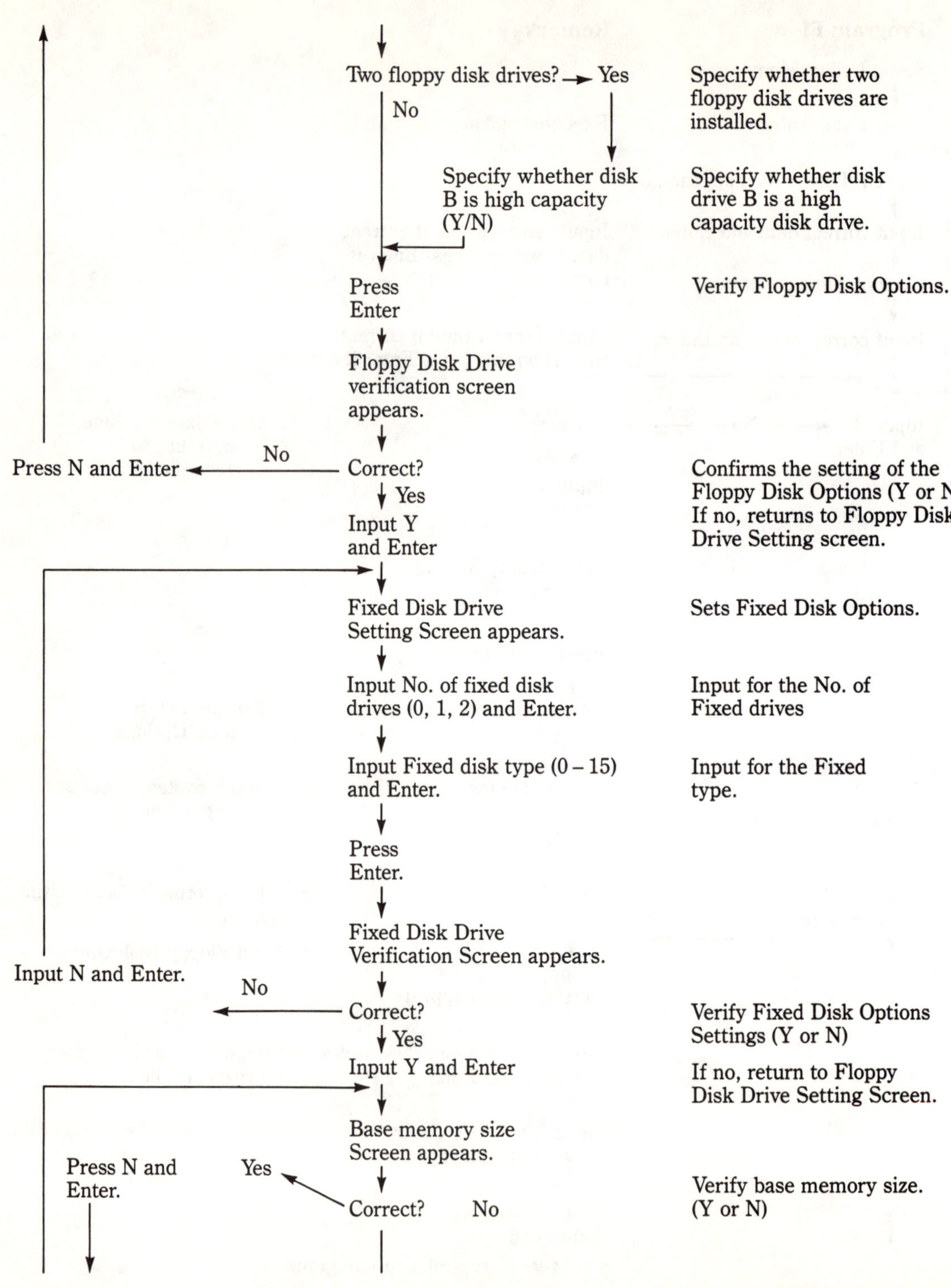

4-9 Continued

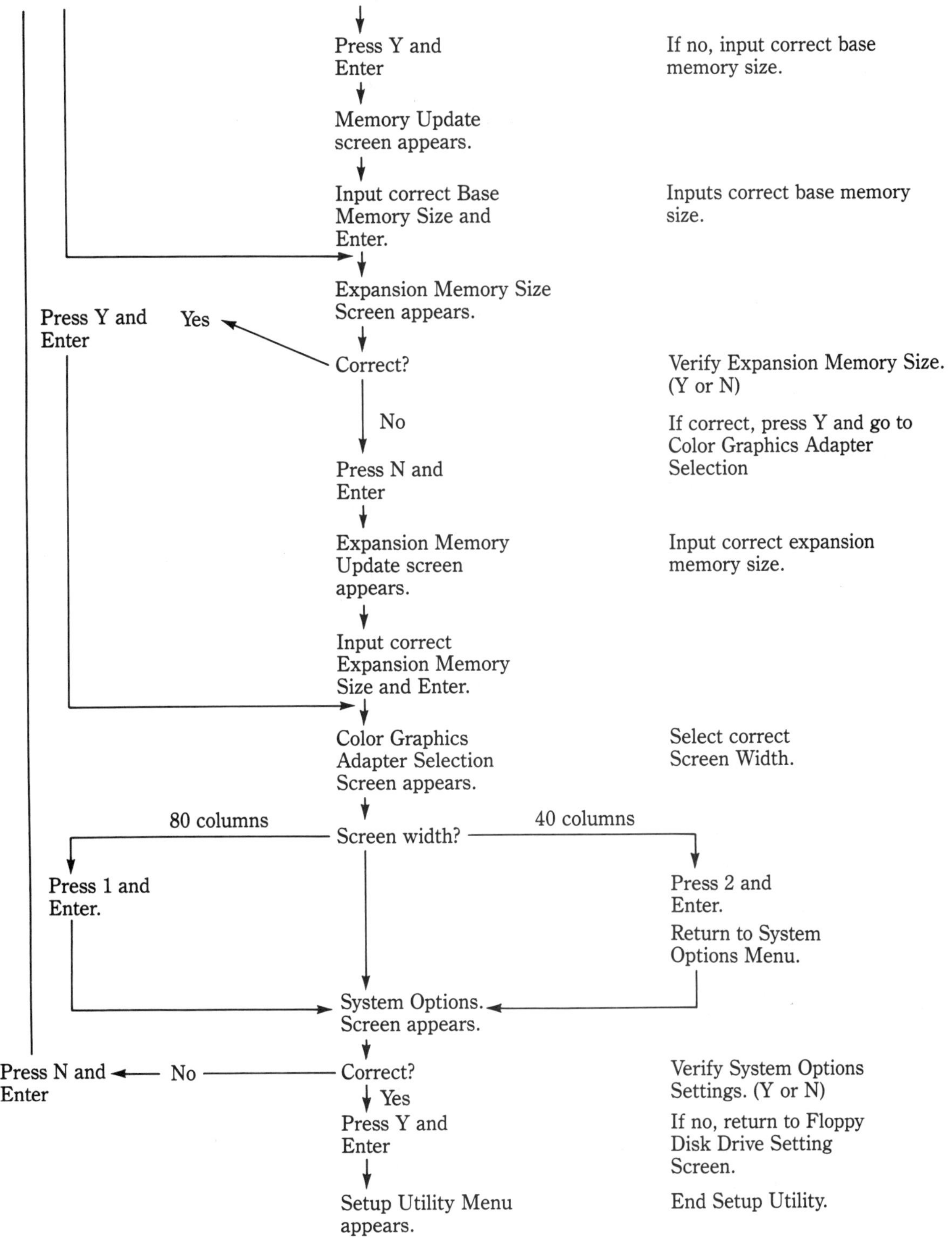
Press Y and
Enter

If no, input correct base
memory size.

Memory Update
screen appears.

Input correct Base
Memory Size and
Enter.

Inputs correct base memory
size.

Expansion Memory Size
Screen appears.

Press Y and
Enter

Yes

Correct?

Verify Expansion Memory Size.
(Y or N)

No

If correct, press Y and go to
Color Graphics Adapter
Selection

Press N and
Enter

Expansion Memory
Update screen
appears.

Input correct expansion
memory size.

Input correct
Expansion Memory
Size and Enter.

Color Graphics
Adapter Selection
Screen appears.

Select correct
Screen Width.

80 columns

Screen width?

40 columns

Press 1 and
Enter.

Press 2 and
Enter.

Return to System
Options Menu.

System Options.
Screen appears.

Press N and
Enter

No

Correct?

Verify System Options
Settings. (Y or N)

Yes

Press Y and
Enter

If no, return to Floppy
Disk Drive Setting
Screen.

Setup Utility Menu
appears.

End Setup Utility.

```
SETUP UTILITY
1  UPDATE CURRENT DATE/TIME
2  SETUP SYSTEM OPTIONS
3  END SETUP UTILITY
   SELECT OPTION NUMBER __
```

A. Main Menu

```
CURRENT DATE IS: XX-XX-XXXX
ENTER NEW DATE:
CURRENT TIME IS: XX-XX-XXXX
ENTER NEW TIME:
```

B. Option 1

```
CURRENT DATE IS: XX-XX-XXXX
CURRENT TIME IS: XX-XX-XXXX
IS THIS CORRECT (Y/N)?
```

```
ENTER NUMBER OF FLOPPY DISK DRIVES (1 or 2) INSTALLED ? 1
IS FLOPPY DISK A
A HIGH CAPACITY DRIVE (Y/N) ? Y
```

C. Floppy Disk Drives

```
FLOPPY DISK DRIVE A—HIGH CAPACITY
FLOPPY DISK DRIVE B—NOT INSTALLED
IS THIS CORRECT (Y/N)?
```

D. Floppy Disk Drive
   Configuration

```
ENTER NUMBER OF FIXED DISK DRIVES (0, 1, OR 2)
ENTER FIXED DISK TYPE (1 – 15) FOR DRIVE C
PRESS ENTER TO CONTINUE . . .
```

E. Fixed Disks

```
FIXED DISK DRIVE C—TYPE 2
FIXED DISK DRIVE D—NOT INSTALLED
IS THIS CORRECT (Y/N)?
```

F. Fixed Disk Configuration

```
BASE MEMORY SIZE IS 640KB
IS THIS CORRECT (Y/N)?
```

G. Base Memory

```
BASE MEMORY SIZE IS 640KB
IS THIS CORRECT (Y/N) ?N
ENTER CORRECT BASE MEMORY SIZE (256, 512, or 640).
```

H. Base Memory
   Configuration

```
EXPANSION MEMORY SIZE IS 0KB
IS THIS CORRECT (Y/N)?
```

I. Expansion Memory

```
EXPANSION MEMORY SIZE IS 0KB
IS THIS CORRECT (Y/N) ?N
ENTER CORRECT EXPANSION MEMORY SIZE
```

J. Expansion Memory
   Configuration

```
FLOPPY DISK DRIVE A—HIGH CAPACITY
FLOPPY DISK DRIVE B—NOT INSTALLED
FIXED DISK DRIVE C—TYPE 2
FIXED DISK DRIVE D—NOT INSTALLED
BASE MEMORY SIZE—640KB
EXPANSION MEMORY SIZE—0KB
PRIMARY DISPLAY IS COLOR GRAPHICS ADAPTER (80 COLUMNS)
ARE THESE OPTIONS CORRECT (Y/N)?
```

K. System Options
   Configuration Menu

4-10   Setup utility menus. (A) A main menu. (B) Option 1. (C) The floppy-disk drives.
(D) A floppy-disk drive configuration. (E) Fixed disks. (F) A fixed disk configuration. (G) The base memory. (H) The base memory configuration. (I) The expansion
memory. (J) The expansion memory configuration. (K) The system options configuration menu.

Individual Test Selection

  1. RAM Test
  2. RAM Arbitration Test
  3. Video Controller Test
  4. Floppy Diagnostic Test
  5. COMM Port Test (no loopback plug)
  6. COMM Port Test (loopback plug)
  7. Printer Port Test (loopback plug)
  8. Printer Confidence Test
  9. Synchronous COMM Test
10. System Test
11. Video Alignment Pattern
12. Private RAM Test
13. Keyboard Test
Type Selection Number and <ETR>

4-11 The individual test selection menu.

Extended tests

The extended test checks each disk drive, tests the memory, and checks the communications and printer connectors. The message PASS is displayed on the monitor as each test is completed without error (Fig. 4-12). After successful completion of the extended test, the message TEST PASSED or something similar will appear on the monitor.

Proceeding from an error If an error is detected during a diagnostic test, a message like the following might appear after the error message:

```
ERROR
PERCENT FAILURE XXX%
```

After the test is performed 10 times, the percent failure is updated. You might be asked to: Type P to exit the loop, and proceed with the next test.

Individual test selection If you have a printer installed on your computer, you can select the printer tests from the menu. You would type the number of the test needed, and follow the instructions that appear on the monitor for that test.

Memory testing

Memory testing involves testing the base memory, including memory that is currently being used by DOS or any other program. If errors occur, a failure indication will appear and the errors can be listed in an activity report. Any extended memory can also be tested. Like the base memory test, any errors found will result in a failed status on this part of the test and the specific memory locations can be listed in an activity report.

Next, the expanded memory is tested. Like the other tests, if any errors are found, the specific memory locations will be listed in an activity report.

Test Being Executed   Pass/Fail
                      Indicator

Other
messages

Floppy Test	Pass	Comm Port Test	Pass
RAM Test	Pass	RAM Arbitration	Pass
RAM Test	Pass	System Test	Pass
Video Test	Pass	Keyboard Self-Test	

Number of drives to be tested? Select 2 or 4
Remove diagnostic disk and insert formatted disks
Warning contents of diskettes are destroyed???
Number of test – 1
Test 1 – Internal Register Test
Test 2 – Head Load Test
Test 3 – Loopback Test
Test 4 – Restore Test
Test 5 – Step Test
Test 6 – Motor Test
Test 7 – Seek Test
Test 8 – Forced Write Errors Test
Test 9 – Write Sectors Test
Test 10 – Forced Read Errors Test

Error
messages
and status

Error: Drive A, failure
Status: testing

4-12   Typical test messages.

A test for high address lines can find problems caused by incorrectly sized chips, bent or broken pins, and other addressing problems where one byte can affect another. It is similar to a bad address test, but generally it works on blocks of memory that are larger than 64K. A high address-line problem can occur when 256K chips are inserted in a 1M bank or when a chip pin is broken off.

Most memory tests are designed to be nonintrusive. The memory tested during the test will be restored to its original state and the system should run normally afterwards. At the end of the memory test, you should have a list of any bad memory locations and bad bits, if any.

Correcting the problem   Most of the time, memory errors are caused by a bad RAM chip. Other times, the problem can be caused by a poorly inserted RAM chip or even a defective memory board.

The first thing to do when a memory problem is reported is to try replacing the chip where the error occurred. Some test programs will locate the bad RAM chips for you on the display to show which RAM chips should be replaced.

Once the defective chip has been located, carefully remove the bad chip from the board. Check to see if any pins have been broken or are folded under. If this is the case, carefully straighten or correct the damaged pin. Sometimes, it is possible to solder a new section on a broken pin. Try to reinsert the chip and make sure that all pins are fully inserted in the socket. Then, you should run the memory test again to be sure the problem has been corrected.

If the bad chip is part of a SIMM, make sure the module is fully inserted on the board. If this does not cure the problem, the entire module must be replaced because the individual chips are soldered into the module.

Sometimes memory problems are caused by other factors. If you have replaced the reported memory chips and the same error appears, the problem might be caused by problems on the memory board. For example, a cut or bridged address line on the memory board could cause a memory error. If memory errors occur repeatedly at different locations, the errors might be caused by a power supply problem.

Test patterns

The following test patterns are commonly used for testing memory bits. Each pass of the memory test can check the bit being tested several times. Each time, a pattern is written to memory, then the inverse of the pattern can also be written. The common patterns used are:

Pattern used	Description
Pseudo-random	This test copies a random pattern into each byte. This is the most common test. It is always run when only a basic test is selected.
Walking bit left	Each memory location is filled with the following initial bit pattern: 00000001 On each successive pass through memory, the 1 is moved one position to the left until all the bits are tested.
Walking bit right	Each memory location is filled with the following initial bit pattern: 10000000 On each successive pass through memory, the 1 is moved one position to the right until all the bits are tested.

Inverted walking bit left	Each memory location is filled with the following initial bit pattern 11111110 On each successive pass through memory, the 0 is moved one position to the left until all the bits are tested.
Inverted walking bit right	Each memory location is filled with the following initial bit pattern: 01111111 On each successive pass through memory, the 0 is moved one position to the right until all bits are tested.
Checkerboard	This is a test of each memory location with the following bit pattern: 01010101
Inverted checkerboard	This is a test of each memory location with the following bit pattern: 01011010
Bit stuck	A test of each memory location is set to all 0s then set at all 1s.
Lo/Hi Address	This test will find memory addressing problems caused by improperly installed chips, those with broken pins, wrong size chips in a bank, such as a 64K chip in a 256K bank and bad solder traces on a board.

System board test

The *system board test* is a test of the primary components of the computer, such as the processor (CPU), coprocessor (NPU), DMA (direct memory access) controller, and interrupt controller. The tests usually have a number of different stages.

CPU testing *CPU testing* has four stages or steps to check the key functions of the processor. First, there must be a test of the general, math, and logic instructions of the CPU. A failure on one of these tests indicates a major failure in the PC's main processor, which should then be replaced. These tests will check for the following conditions: branching, overflow, two's complement and BCD math, shifts and rotates. These functions are necessary for the reliable operation of your PC. A repeated failure indicates a bad processor. Chip replacements can usually be purchased from a well-equipped electronics parts outlet.

Interrupt problems *Interrupt testing* will identify CPUs that allow interrupts to occur at the wrong times. This is a problem in some older 8088 and 8086 chips. If your machine has one of these faulty processors, it could lock up at random times. If this problem shows up on your machine, you need to replace the processor.

Protected mode problems If your PC has an 80286, you might need to test your processor's ability to function in protected mode. When you are using DOS, your CPU is operating an 8086 emulation mode. This mode is called *the Real Mode*. When your PC is accessing DOS extended memory or running OS/2 or Xenix, your CPU is running under its native mode, called *the Protected Mode*.

A failure of this test only indicates a problem under this mode of operation, and your PC might operate without problems under normal DOS operation. A failure means that your PC will not function correctly if you add extended memory or when you run in an operating system, such as OS/2 or Xenix. The tests sends the 80286 processor into the protected mode and then back into the real mode. In the protected mode, the processor can access memory above the 1M address range.

NPU testing The *NPU test* will check if the math coprocessor (NPU) is functioning properly. It might be improperly installed or defective. One test will force the NPU to perform a set of floating-point calculations. Then, a comparison is made between the actual results and the expected results. If they do not match, an error is reported. Another test actually verifies that the NPU's floating-point comparison operations are working properly. A test of the trigonometric functions might also be available on the math coprocessor. The NPU could be asked to complete several tangents, for example. All of these tests will be done with floating-point numbers.

DMA controller testing The *DMA controller test* checks the communication between the CPU and the DMA controller. The DMA controller is responsible for transferring data between the CPU and memory. A failure indicates that either the DMA controller or the CPU is defective. AT computers use a second DMA controller that should also be tested.

The DMA test must check each channel and register of the DMA controller. It also must check that the DMA refresh is operating normally. Problems with the DMA refresh cycle can sometimes cause what appear to be memory errors.

Interrupt controller testing The *interrupt-controller test* checks that the PC's interrupt controller is operating properly. This controller is responsible for the interrupting that occurs to the CPU when certain events are commanded to happen (such as when a character is about to be received over the serial port). Normally, when an interrupt occurs, the CPU momentarily stops what it was doing, runs a program, such as a device driver to handle the cause of the interrupt, and returns to where it was. If this test fails, the problem could be either that the interrupt controller or that the CPU is bad. If you are using an AT machine, the second interrupt controller must also be tested.

This test will set interrupt priority level and interrupt vectors for the 8259 interrupt controller. It will generate an interrupt for each level. It will temporarily reassign any predefined interrupt vector and replace them when the test is completed.

As the system board test is completed, the screen might look similar to the following:

Pass	CPU general test
Pass	CPU protected mode
Skip	NPU arithmetic test
Skip	NPU trigonometric test
Skip	NPU comparison test
Pass	DMA controller test
Pass	Interrupt controller test

Sometimes if a component has a problem, it can cause the computer to lock up. Usually, typical test times are given for each test; make sure you wait at least as long as the times listed for each test step. Then, if the PC still does not respond, copy down the last lines displayed and reboot. The last display will usually indicate the area where the problem lies.

Clock tests   *Clock tests* compare the real-time clock time to DOS time. This test checks both times to make sure they are almost the same. Differences of as much as 15 seconds are usually considered close enough. Most systems will show a difference of from 1 to 5 seconds. A test can also be made to compare the real-time clock date to DOS date. This will compare the two clocks to make sure that the dates are the same. If the real-time clock time or date is incorrect, you must set the time or date.

Most AT clocks have an alarm feature that can also be tested. The test will set the alarm to go off in a few seconds. If it does not do this on time, the test fails. This can indicate a problem with the CMOS clock hardware. Some AT systems do not support the alarm and will lock up when this feature is used. This can be a potential problem. If you have this type of problem and wish to correct it, you can usually replace the BIOS chip with a later version.

A comparison of the elapsed time can also be made. This test will compare the amount of time elapsed on each clock to see if they are keeping time at the same rate. Any difference here usually means that the real-time clock needs batteries or that a component is malfunctioning.

5

Disks and disk drives

The 5¹/₄-inch floppy disk (Fig. 5-1) has been standard for the IBM personal computer family. The 3¹/₂-inch floppy is used in the PS-2 and has some advantages. The smaller one is more compact, has a more rugged container, and saves some space.

The floppy disk looks like a small phonograph record. But, although a record uses grooves that a needle travels in while producing mechanical vibrations that are converted into audio frequencies, computer disks are more like magnetic tape. A layer of iron oxide is coated on the smooth surface of the disk. The coating can be magnetized in small spots on the coating. The spots are microscopic and each one acts like a very small permanent magnet.

When a spot is magnetized, it can be used to indicate a true (on state) by setting the magnetic poles in one orientation. The spots that are magnetized in another orientation or direction are used to indicate a false (zero state).

Each line of spots is called a *track*. A floppy disk might have 40 concentric tracks, which are numbered, 0 through 39. The outside track is numbered 0 and the inside is numbered 39. The tracks are not a continuous spiral, like a phonograph record, but each track is an isolated closed circle.

Sectors are used to divide up the disk into pie-slice sections. Ten sectors could be on each track and each sector has a unique address. With 40 tracks of 10 sectors each, the 400 sector addresses would be numbered 0 through 399.

When the disk is placed in the drive, the mechanism starts rotating the disk to its designed speed (usually 300 or 360 revolutions per minute). The

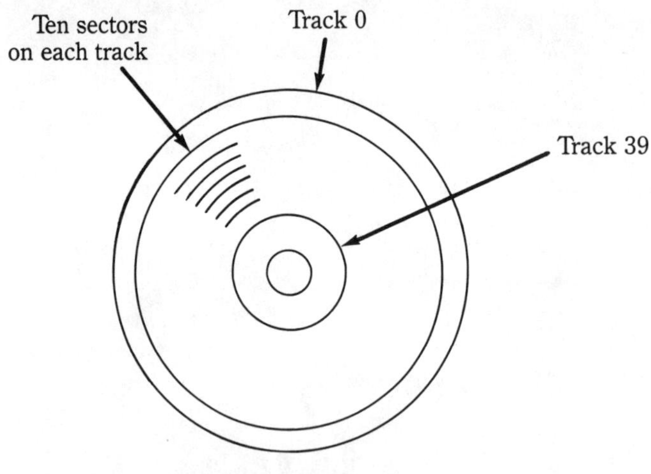

5-1   A floppy disk.

hard-disk drive speed is usually 10 times this speed. At a speed of 300 rpm, the floppy disk rotates at a spacing of about 30 microinches from the read/ write magnetic head.

The disk head is on an indexed shaft, which moves it from the outer track of the disk to the inner track of the disk. The indexing system allows the head to be positioned over any of the 40 tracks. Because the disk rotates at 300 rpm, the 10 sectors on each track pass under the head five times a second and the head positioning takes about one second to locate a sector.

The mechanical system, called the *drive* (Figs. 5-2, 5-3, 5-4, and 5-5), spins the disks and moves the index arm that holds the magnetic recording head. The drive resembles a small record player in some ways, but it is much faster. However, the mechanical parts can wear out and break down like a record player.

The drive provides the mechanical functions and the electronics required to control the rotation of the disk and access data. The diskette is made of a flexible milar material. It is coated with magnetic oxide and rotates in a plastic jacket (5¹/₄ inch) or case (3¹/₂ inch). A long opening is cut in the jacket or case to provide access to the read/write head. The plastic case used to hold the 3¹/₂-inch disk has a spring loaded metal that also protects the media.

The same head is used for read/write and erase (Figs. 5-6, 5-7, and 5-8). The head is moved to the proper track by a positioning motor, usually a stepping motor. The jacket has an index hole, which is punched in the disk and marks the beginning of the first sector. The hole is detected by a photosensing circuit (Fig. 5-9).

A

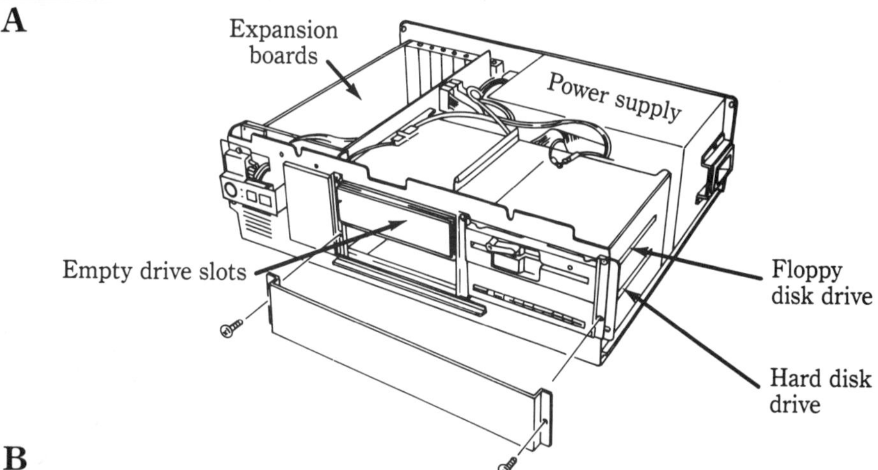

B

5-2 The disk drive locations. (A) An XT clone showing the floppy-disk drive over the hard-disk drive. Controller board is next to power supply. Note controller cables. (B) AT clone with floppy-disk drive over hard drive. Two additional drive slots are available.

The drive must perform the following functions:

1. Move the head to the track.
2. Use the head to perform either a read or write.
3. Generate or interpret control signals or status information, including index hole detection.
4. Drive the spindle motor at a constant speed.

A

B

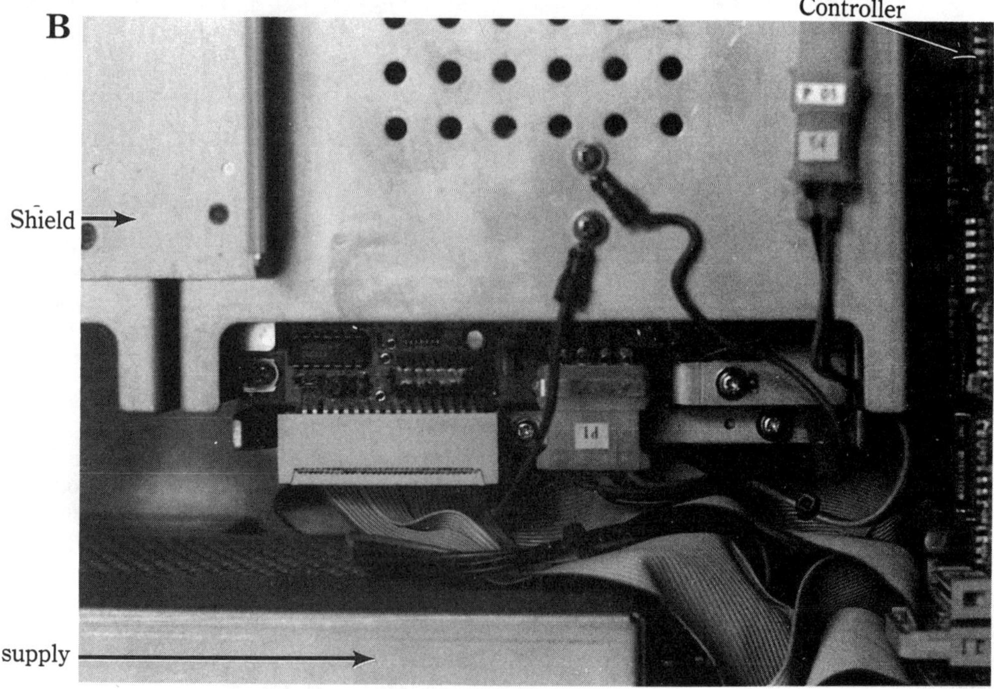

5-3 The disk drive connectors. (A) The rear view of floppy drive over hard drive. The floppy drive motors can be seen as well as the drive power connectors. Notice that the sealed hard drive has an additional connector. (B) A closeup of the connectors with floppy drive installed in an AT. P1 is the power connector. The controller board is shown at the extreme right. The controller connector is shown in lower right corner.

5-4 A top view of the floppy disk drive. Notice the drive spindle in the center with a photosensor for sectoring next to it. The other photosensor for write protection tab is in lower left corner.

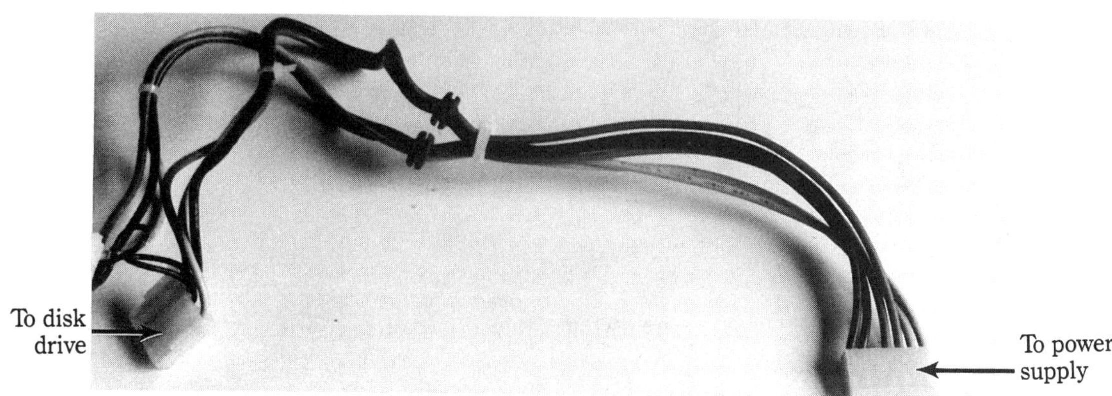

5-5 A drive power cable.

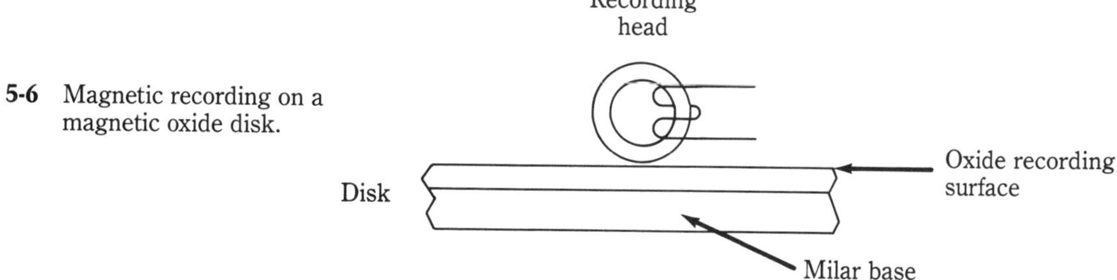

5-6 Magnetic recording on a magnetic oxide disk.

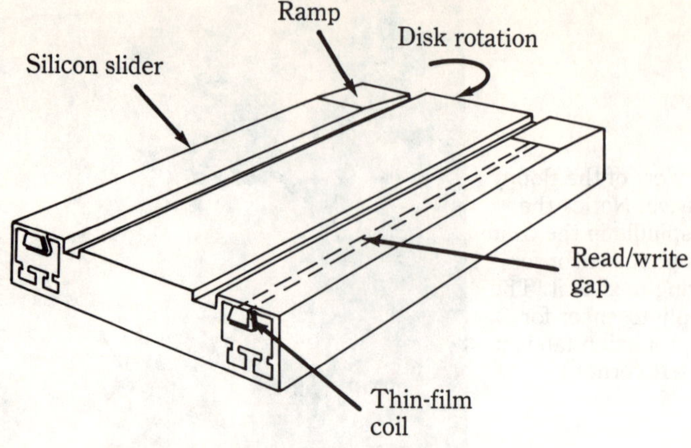

5-7   A thin-film head.

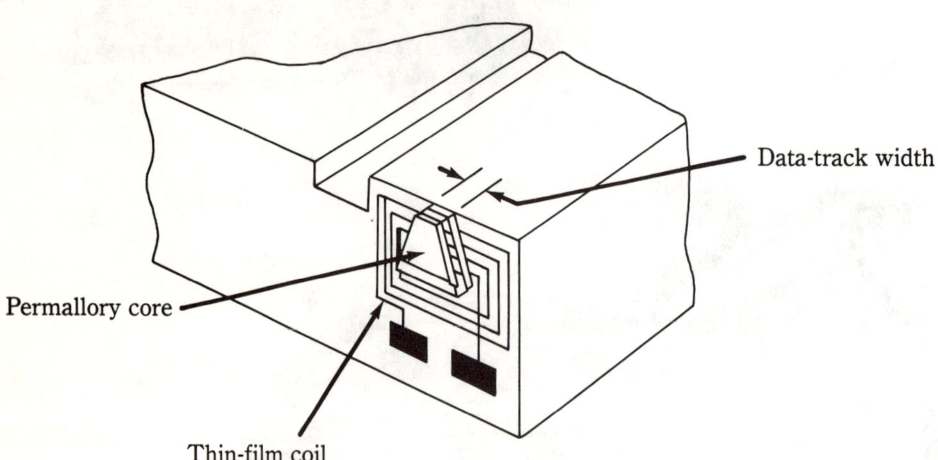

5-8   Spiral conductors are used in a thin-film head.

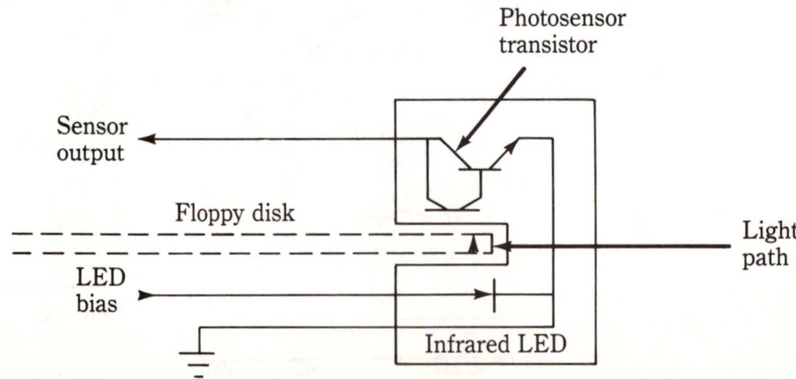

5-9   A photosensing circuit that is used for indexing.

Read and write operations

A read or write operation requires the drive to access the specified track and sector, and to then transfer a block of data. Three operations must be performed: head positioning, read-write control, and data transfer. The head is usually stepped with an incremental stepping motor and requires 3 to 10 ms per step. A head settling delay of 8 to 15 ms is also used to allow for vibrations to die out. The position is verified by reading the track number on the disk and comparing it to a track register.

Signals of the disk drive

The signals required by a floppy disk drive include the following six signals, which are used to communicate with the disk drive:

1. **Motor control**   This signal will turn the motor on or off. When turning the motor on, one second is usually allowed after activation and two seconds after deactivation. This is done to extend the life of the drive.

2. **Direction select**   This signal will select the direction in which the read/write head will be moved. The actual motion is accomplished by pulsing the step line.

3. **Step control**   This signal moves the head by one track position toward the center or away from it. The movement usually occurs on the trailing edge of the pulse.

4. **Write gate**   The write is enabled when this line is active. A read is specified when this line is inactive.

5. **Track 0**   This signal indicates that the head has reached the outermost track (track 0). The head will move no further even if additional step commands are issued.

6. **Index/sector**   A signal is issued whenever a hole is sensed in the disk. Two types of holes can be used, an index hole and a sector hole. The index hole marks the beginning of the first sector on the disk.

Soft sectoring

A hard-sectored disk has a number of holes marking the beginning of every sector. Soft sectoring is used in most PCs, including IBM. In a soft-sectored disk, one pulse is issued per revolution at the beginning of a track. This is usually done every 200 ms. In a soft-sectored disk, sectors must be identified by a header. Less data can be stored than with hard sectoring, but reliability and flexibility are improved.

The INDEX line provides a pulse that marks the beginning of sector 0, where the hole in the disk is detected by a photosensitive circuit. The READY line is true when the diskette has been correctly inserted and is up to speed. A special tab can be covered on the disk cover. An optical sensor in the drive will detect the covered notch, which protects a diskette from accidental writing.

Data recording

Information is recorded on the tracks of the disk in binary format. Usually, an NRZ technique is used. *NRZ* means *NonReturn to Zero* and each bit position is magnetized in one direction (1), or the other (0). There is no intermediate state (or true zero), so this is called NRZ. *FM encoding* (Frequency Modulation) is used as the basic modulation technique. Each data bit appears exactly half way between two successive clock pulses. Other recording methods are used to increase the bit density. The basic idea is to eliminate as many unnecessary clock or data bits as possible. Double-density diskettes use *modified frequency modulation (MFM)* or modified MFM to increase the recording density. These techniques use a clockbit only if a zero is found in two consecutive frames.

Data on the disk is structured in bytes (groups of 8 bits). Each block of information is given a special marker. When the diskette is first used, it is initialized or formatted with these markers. A serial-to-parallel conversion must be performed to assemble 8 bits into a byte. This operation is usually done by the disk controller.

Density

Two methods, *increased density* and *dual heads*, are used to increase the amount of information that can be stored on a floppy disk. Double-density doubles the number of bits per track by using a packed recording technique, such as *modified MFM* (*M2FM*). It requires tight tolerances for reliable operation and is less speed-tolerant than regular FM encoding. Dual heads are used for reading and writing both sides of the floppy. The dual heads increase the mechanical complexity of the drive.

Both clock and data information are encoded into the same signal. Clock pulses are issued for every bit. A 0 is indicated by no further pulse during the bit cell time. A 1 is indicated by a data pulse that occurs in the middle of the bit cell interval.

Disk formatting

Soft sectoring, as discussed, relates to the division of the disk or track into sectors by software. This is opposite to hard sectoring, where the beginning of each sector is detected from a hole in the disk. In soft sectoring, each track is marked by a physical index pulse, corresponding to the detection of the index hole on the disk. This is done during the formatting operation.

Every data record is marked by a unique identifier and successive records are separated by gaps. Gaps are used to protect the following or the preceding record. Because of speed variations in the disk-drive motor, whenever a record has all or some of its contents rewritten, the end of the record might extend beyond the previous record end.

Error detection

A checksum technique is usually used to detect any data that is written on the disk. *Cyclic-redundancy-checking (CRC)* is one method used. Special CRC bytes are used at the end of a group of data bytes. The data bits are divided by a special equation, usually a polynomial. The remainder from this division becomes the CRC bytes. When reading data from the diskette, the CRC bytes are checked for errors. The floppy-disk controller performs the CRC generation and checking.

Disk controllers

Many manufacturers make disk drives that can be used with the IBM PC family. Some drives are external to the system unit and have their own enclosure. In the IBM PC, a disk-controller card is used to plug into one of the expansion slots. The disk-controller card has a ribbon data cable that connects to the disk drive. A typical controller card can support four disk drives.

The data that moves between the disk and the processor is usually controlled by an 8237 Direct Memory Access controller (Fig. 5-10) on the main board. It controls the data-transfer operations and is used to move data from the disk to computer memory, from the computer memory to disk and from one disk drive to another disk drive.

When a disk drive needs to send data, it sends a signal to one of the DREQ (data request) lines of the DMA controller. The chip first turns on one of its DACK (data acknowledge) lines. Then, the chip sends a signal to the other I/O devices that puts them into a three-state condition. Next, the starting addresses and the number of bytes to be transferred are sent to the DMA controller. The data is sent from the disk through the disk-controller card onto the data bus and into RAM. After the transfer is complete, control of the data bus is returned to the processor.

The floppy-disk interface must be able to convert data from serial-to-parallel format and from parallel-to-serial format. The interface must be able to match the data bus in the computer with the disk drive. The data from the bus is converted from parallel to serial and conditioned into the

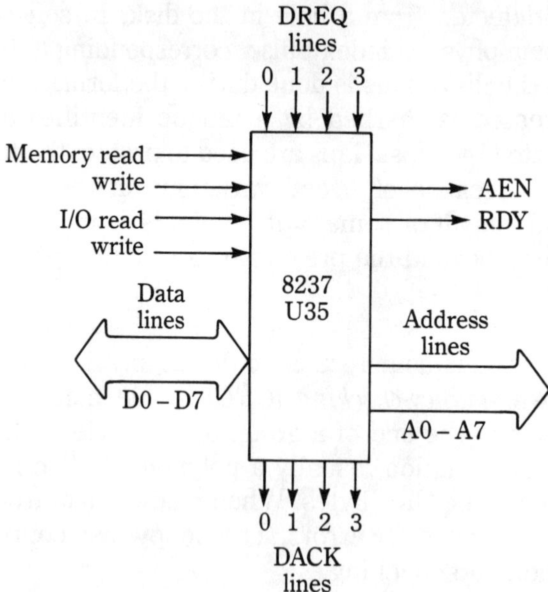

5-10 An 8237 direct memory-access controller.

bit-pattern format that is needed by the disk-drive circuits. When data is going the other way, from the floppy disk to the computer, the bits must also be conditioned. Sync bits are used to surround the actual data so that variations in speed of the rotating disk do not cause errors. When the data transfer is complete, the controller turns the operation of the computer back to the processor.

Maintaining disk drives

It is normal for some oxide to build up on floppy disks. The oxides form from dust and other contaminates in the atmosphere. Because the disk runs so close to the read/write head, some of these oxides will be transferred to the head. If enough oxide is collected on the head, the drive will make read or write errors. If this problem is allowed to continue, the disks or the head could be damaged.

Clean the heads with medical alcohol and a cotton swab that is wrapped in a lint-free material. Use the alcohol sparingly and do not wet any of the components around the head. A disadvantage with this manual cleaning procedure is that you must remove the system unit cover and usually the head cover from the disk drive. Each drive manufacturer has its own way to cover or protect the head assembly. It is a good idea to make some notes before you attempt to take it apart. Once you do access the head, then you can clean the oxides off. When the head appears to be clean, let the area dry before you reassemble the head cover and the system unit.

A quicker method is to purchase a head cleaning disk. A special cleaning solvent on this disk is designed to clean the head. The cleaning disk is inserted into the disk drive and allowed to rotate. The turning motion of the drive rubs the solvent material against the head and the oxides are rubbed off.

Floppy-disk testing

Floppy-disk drives can be tested with a diagnostic disk. Insert the diagnostic disk and select the floppy tests from the main menu. A message, such as the following, will appear on the monitor:

```
Floppy Tests—Drives A and B
Number of Drives to be Tested? select 1 or 2
```

You might be asked to remove the diagnostic disk and insert a formatted scratch disk. Then, a selection menu (Fig. 5-11) will appear. Select the floppy-disk tests that you desire from this menu, and your selection will take you to the next menu.

Title	Floppy tests – drives A and B
	Drive to be tested? select drive Remove diagnostic disk and insert formatted disk Warning: contents of diskettes are destroyed!!! Number of tests – 11
Runtime messages	Test 1 – Internal Register Test Test 2 – Head Load Test Test 3 – Loopback Test Test 4 – Restore Test Test 5 – Step Test Test 6 – Motor Test
This area can scroll as new messages are added.	Test 7 – Seek Test Test 8 – Forced Write Errors Test Test 9 – Write Sectors Test Test 10 – Forced Read Errors Test Test 11 – Read Sectors Test Rewriting Sectors Used in Test 9 End of Tests. Insert Diagnostic Disk Controller Board – Head Load Timing Failure
Error messages and status	Enter P to proceed or L to loop on error

5-11 A floppy disk test menu.

When you remove the diagnostic diskette and insert blank or scratch diskettes into drives A and B, a message, such as the following, will appear on the monitor:

WARNING CONTENTS OF DISKETTES ARE DESTROYED!!!

The tests can usually be run automatically, first testing drive A and then testing drive B, if desired.

Floppy-disk random read and write tests

The read test will check the entire floppy disk to make sure that it can be successfully read. The tracks are chosen randomly and this simulates normal operating conditions during the test. The write test will write data to the disk and verify that it can be read back again. Like the read test, the tracks are chosen randomly.

Types of errors   Three basic types of errors can occur during a read/write operation. These errors are often caused by a problem with the disk media.

1. **Write errors**   This type of error will occur when data on the disk is not written correctly. One technique used to verify whether data has been correctly written is to use a write-check. Normally, the user will be asked to write the data again repeatedly. If this fails repeatedly, the sector or the track might be damaged and the disk might not be usable. A reformatting can be tried as a further check.

2. **Read errors**   There are two types of read errors. **Soft errors** mean that the error is not permanent and can usually be corrected by rereading or by moving the head. Typically, the head is moved one step in its previous direction, then moved back. Usually, this will correct the read errors, but if this fails, it is a hard error and the information is unrecoverable. This type of error can occur during the read test or during the write test, while reading the data to be compared.

3. **Seek errors**   This occurs when the head does not reach the correct track. When this type of error is detected, the track counter of the disk drive must be reset. The head is moved back to the first track and a new seek order is issued. This error will occur when the drive's stepper motor is not working properly or when the movement of the read/write head on the drive is obstructed. The following errors can occur when a problem is with the drive. Some of these problems can be caused by a bad cable or an improperly installed drive.

4. **Comparison errors**   This error will occur during the write test if the data read from a disk is not the same as what was written.

This is a major problem because it shows that the drive is not properly detecting errors.

5. **Disk changed**   This error will appear if the disk is changed during the test. It will also appear if any of the hardware used for the disk change function is malfunctioning on the drive. This includes the sensors that monitor the opening of the drive door. This error usually aborts the test.

6. **Drive not ready**   This error indicates that the drive motor is not working or that the drive door is open or that its sensors are malfunctioning during the test.

7. **Write protected**   This error indicates that a write-protect tab is on the disk being tested. It can also appear if the write-protect mechanism is malfunctioning on a drive. This error usually aborts the test.

Disk problems   You should rerun the test with several different disks to rule out the possibility of bad media. Another probable cause for errors is dirty read/write heads. You can try cleaning the heads and rerun the test. If the head cleaning or new media does not correct the problem, the disk drive might have a defective component or need alignment.

Most tests will check the entire disk by using random jumps from track to track. This helps to test head alignment, the stepping motor, and timing of the drive. More extensive floppy-disk tests use a special spiral diskette for timing functions.

Disk-drive problems   When a disk drive fails to boot a system disk, one of several problems can exist, the disk might be bad, the drive electronics or cable might have failed, the drive mechanics might be out of tolerance, the disk-drive controller in the expansion slot might be at fault, or the system board itself might have a failure.

Check to see if you have the configuration switches set correctly. For example, in the IBM PC, if SW1 positions 1, 7, and 8 are on, this indicates to the system that you do not have any floppy drives attached.

The boot-up diagnostics usually provide some clues. If you get a short beep, the Cassette BASIC display, and no disk boot with the IBM PC, the problem is probably the diskette or in the drive itself. An error display of 601, 606, 607, 608, 611, 612, 613, or 621 through 626 indicates a malfunction in the disk system (disk media, drive, cable, or controller).

When a disk-related malfunction occurs during operation, you must verify that the problem is not in the disk being used. Reboot with a good copy of the system disk. If the disk seems good, try to reboot with the same disk that you were using when the problem occurred. If a failure occurs, the disk is bad or needs formatting.

Will not boot from drive A   If you cannot boot and run from drive A, power down, unplug the drive data cable from drive A and try connecting it to drive B. Also, you can swap the jumper at 1E on the IBM controller card between drives A and B. Power up again and reboot using drive B. If drive B boots normally, drive A has a malfunction. If not, power down and check the cable for continuity. Clean and examine the cable and the adapter card edge connectors. Check for +5 V on pin 4, and +12 V on pin 1 of the power-supply cable. If the power at the plug is normal, check the disk-drive controller card.

Both drive lights on   If both drive run lights turn on when reading or writing a disk, check the cables to see if the drive A cable is connected to drive B. An active low signal on either the Motor on, Motor enable (A), Drive select (A), or Drive select (B) lines can cause the LED (CR27 on IBM drives) to turn on. Other possible causes could be failure of the U16 output NAND 7438 or U17 output D flip-flop 74LS273 on the IBM controller card. Most cards use similar circuits, although the U numbers will differ.

Cannot read data   If you cannot read data from either floppy drive, the U6 FDC UPD765 or U7 driver MC3487 in the IBM controller might have failed.

Seek error problems   If you get a Seek Error message, a track is unreadable or head misalignment has occurred. Try to read another disk. If this does not work, it could be the U4 2-input AND gate 74LS08, U6 floppy-disk controller D765AC (UPD765), or U18 tristate octal inverter buffer 74LS240 on the IBM controller.

Cannot write-protect data   If you have a problem protecting data on a write-protected disk, it could be a failure in the U6 FDC UPD765, U10 multiplexer 74LS153, U11 D flip-flop 74LS175, or U18 tristate octal inverter buffer 74LS240 in the IBM controller.

Floppy-drive diagnostic tests   A number of products are available for diagnosing floppy drives. They can identify most major causes of floppy-drive failure without drive removal. Many of these offer online help and are menu driven.

Typical floppy-disk drive diagnostic tests include: head alignment, head read span, head step linearity, hysteresis, track zero alignment, drive speed, overwrite/read, noise interference, and write protect. Some products use a separate analog alignment disk and a digital diagnostic disk. Products are available that allow you to diagnose and align 360K, 720K, 1.2M, and 1.44M MS-DOS-compatible drives.

Most alignment products use a special spiral track disk and a test and alignment can be done in about 10 minutes. An accuracy to several tenths of a mil is possible on tests, such as radial head alignment. These spiral-alignment disks have a limited life and can only be used several hundred times. In this way, they are similar to lubricated cleaning disks, which also can be used for only about 200 uses.

Adjusting disk speed Most floppy drives rotate at 300 rpm. When the drive speed changes as a result of mechanical wear, the read/write head might not be able to function properly. If the speed is not correct, the head might read a wrong address or write to a wrong sector on the disk. If this occurs, you can adjust the drive speed and make as it as close as possible to the designated value.

A small resistive control on floppy disk drives can be adjusted with a screwdriver. A method of measuring the drive rpm is needed so that the adjustment can be made at the proper speed.

Drive speed can be measured via two methods. On the bottom of the many drives is a marked pulley with timing marks (Fig. 5-12). The outer marks are designed to be used with a 60-Hz light. To use these timing

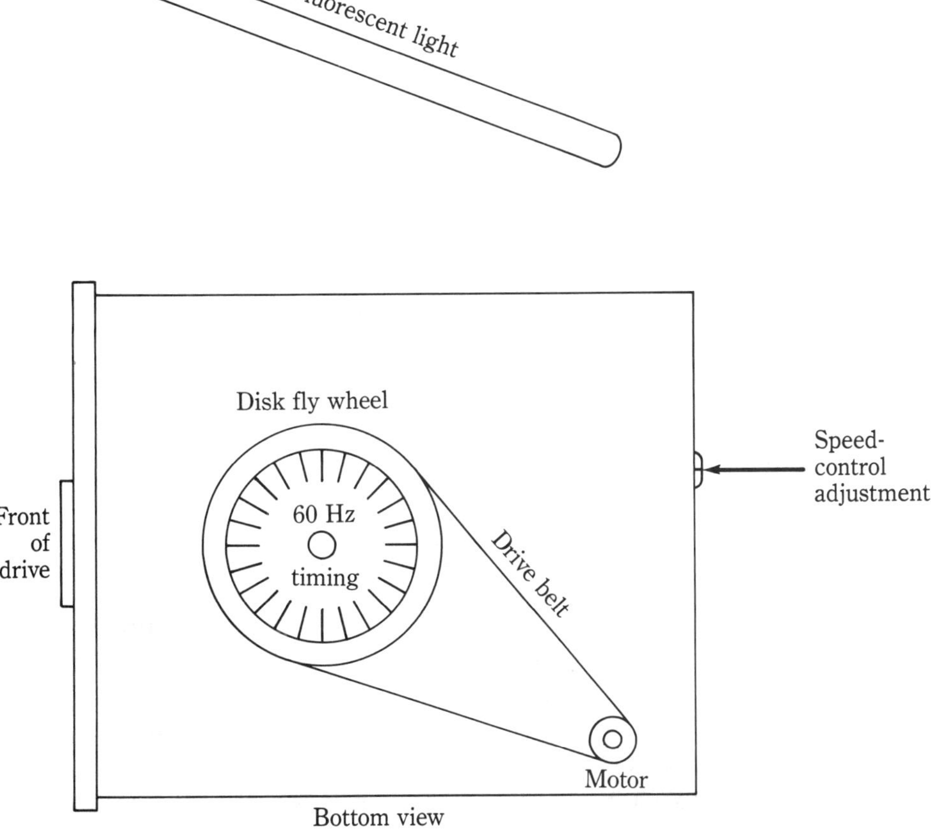

5-12 A disk-drive speed adjustment.

marks, shine a 60-Hz light on them. The timing marks should appear to be stationary when the disk is running at the desired speed. If the timing marks appear to be rotating during the test, the resistive control needs to be adjusted. The marks could be rotating in either direction. Adjust the speed control until the marks appear stationary.

Another technique is to use a disk-drive speed program disk. Run the speed test program and the display shows the current speed setting (Fig. 5-13). You can then adjust the speed control until the display shows the speed at 300 rpm.

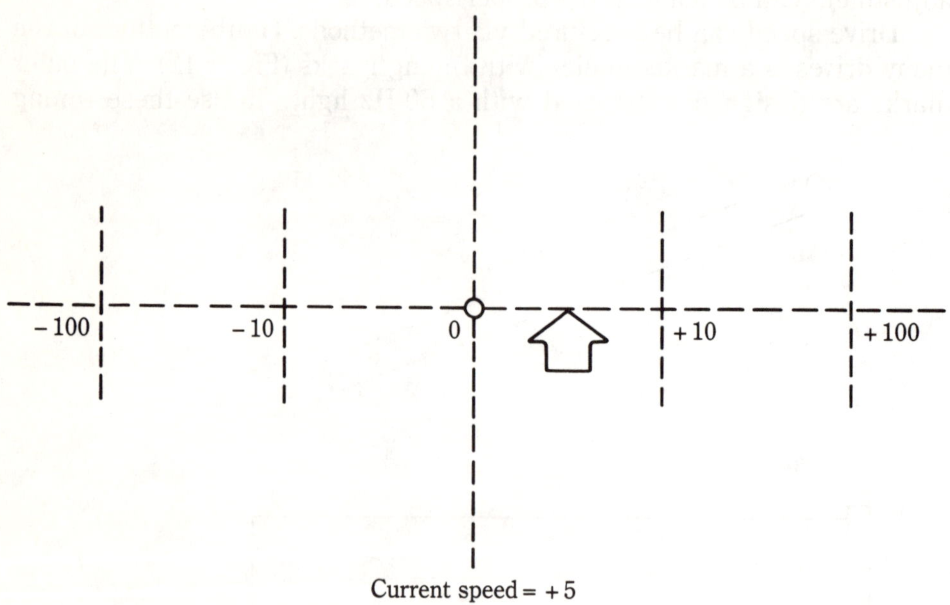

5-13   A typical disk-drive test program display (disk-drive speed test).

Hard disks

Hard disk drives, as discussed earlier, are very similar in concept to floppy-disk systems. The main differences are the media (aluminum disks that are coated with magnetic particles) and the drive speed (about 10 times that of a floppy). Because the speed is much higher and the media is rigid, the heads are much closer for read and write operations. Even though the drive assembly is sealed to prevent dust from getting between the heads and the disk (Fig. 5-14), problems can occur from oxide build-up on the heads, which will eventually cause a *head crash* (when the head touches the disk and destroys data).

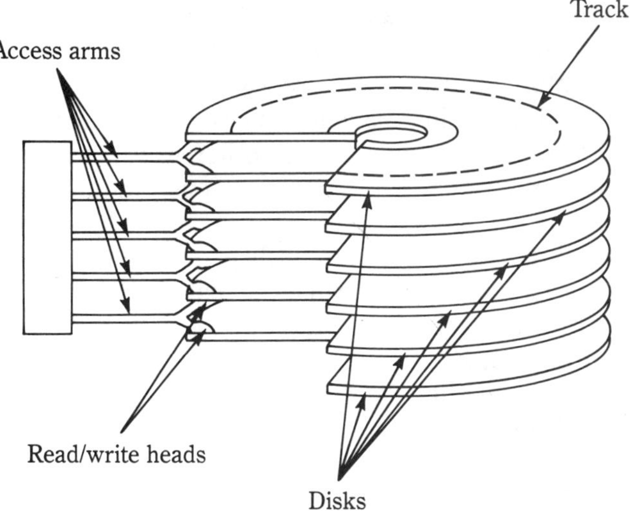

5-14   The sealed components of the hard disk drive.

Hard-disk utilities

Software known as *disk utilities* can be used to recover after a hard disk crashes. Utilities can also help after you have deleted files and want to bring them back. The reason a utility can do this is because when DOS gets a command to delete a file, it does not actually erase the data from the disk. Instead, it changes the first letter of its name in the directory to a special symbol. Then, when the file is called for by its original name, the operating system will not recognize it.

Unerase and undelete   A utility program with an unerase or undelete function will prompt you for the deleted file name. It will then find it on the disk and rename it so that it can be accessed. The *file access table (FAT)* stored by DOS shows the way the files are arranged on the disk. When a disk is accidentally reformatted, the FAT is erased. Some utilities make a copy of the FAT (and other crucial information, such as bindery and trustee rights for a NetWare-formatted disk) and store it at the back of the disk. This copy is not erased during reformatting and you can replace the original FAT from the copy.

Defragmenting   Another important service that most disk utilities provide is the ability to *defragment* your disk. When DOS writes data to disk, it might not put parts of the same file in adjacent sectors. It usually starts from the outside of the disk and moves inward. When it erases a file, it fills up the spaces that erasure creates by moving in a section of a new file. This process fragments the files, and it takes the disk heads longer to read a file because they must take extra passes over the disk surface, while they are reading the different fragments of the file.

A defragmenting utility facility reorganizes the disk surface so that parts of the same file are in adjacent sectors, which saves time when that file is read. Defragmenting also aids in other ways. Accidentally deleted files are easier to recover if they have previously been stored on disk in clusters.

Instead of using a defragmenting utility to straighten out the disk, you can back up your disk on tape, reformat the disk, and restore the data to the disk. When DOS sends the files to the tape, it collects the bytes for each file from their different locations on disk and sends the file whole. When this data is copied back onto the disk, it comes off the tape in whole files. This way, it gets back on the disk with all the bytes belonging to individual files in adjacent sectors.

If you use disk utilities, you should make a complete backup of the disk before you even put the utility software diskette in. It is good insurance— even if the software vendor guarantees that the program will not damage your data and not all of them do. The power could fail while the utility is performing the defragmentation and you could permanently lose your data.

Norton Utilities   The Advanced version 4.0 of the *Norton Utilities* can be used for file recovery and to provide system information. But, like all DOS-based disk utilities, Norton will not work on a NetWare server disk. It can be used with DOS-based network operating systems, including 3Com's 3+.

Norton Utilities runs from a command post program called the *Norton Integrator*, which also provides online help for each utility. The advanced version uses a program called *Speed Disk*, which arranges the logical structure of the disk. It can be used to optimize the seek time and improve the disk performance.

The Format Recover utility is used to unformat an accidentally reformatted hard disk. A special maintenance mode can be used for badly damaged disks. It bypasses the DOS logical organization to work at the cluster or sector level. Other included editors are: the File Allocation Table Editor, the Partition Table Editor, and the Directory Editor. Also, an Absolute Sector mode can be used for absolute physical sector access and verification.

Golden Bow Utilities   *Golden Bow Utilities* are another set of DOS-based disk utilities. *Vopt* is a disk-organizer package that defragments files, does benchmark timing, and allows you to do system maintenance, such as flagging bad clusters. It can be run in under one minute and uses a best-fit algorithm.

Vcache is a disk caching program that can be used to cache up to 15M hard-disk data in RAM. It is a write-through cache and all written data is recorded immediately onto the hard disk, unlike a RAM disk. Changes will not be lost if a power failure occurs.

Vfeature Deluxe provides hard disk partitioning for bootable DOS partitions up to a gigabyte. It supports nonstandard drives, can span two drives into a partition and includes formatting and security options.

Vtools is a set of tools to display and sort directories and files, delete files or directories, modify them in ASCII or hex format, walk the directory tree, find and display all copies of a file, and compare/update similar files in different directories or disks.

Mace Utilities *Mace Utilities* has three programs for DOS-based disks: *Recovery*, *Hot Rod*, and *dbFix*. Recovery is an unformat utility that you can use if you accidentally reformat your disk. It saves a copy of the index tables at the back end of the disk. If the DOS index tables get deleted during an accidental format, recovery uses this copy to restore the tables.

Even if Mace Utilities are not installed before an accidental format, the program can still be used to restore those files not in the root directory that are relatively continuous on the disk. If the data is subdirectories, you can get back the names of the subdirectories from the names of the files in them. DOS's CD command is used to move to the subdirectories where you can find the files. An Undelete facility allows you to restore deleted files and subdirectories.

HotRod is a utility for speeding up disk operations by defragmenting your files, providing RAM cache and sorting directories. dbFix is designed for users of dBase, FoxBase, and Clipper. Files that are lost, unreadable, corrupted, or overwritten can be located, repaired, and recovered.

Disk crashes

Disk utilities can restore a disk when you have accidentally deleted a file or crosslinked files in the same clusters. However, they cannot rebuild a destroyed master boot record or get data back after a hardware problem. If this happens and you do not have a backup of the data, or if the backup system fails along with the drive, data from a crashed disk can often be recovered using an outside service. These firms generally perform data recovery, along with rebuilding disks in a clean room facility.

Some sources for disk-drive repair include:

AA Computech, Inc.
28210 Avenue Crocker #306
Valencia, CA 91355
(805) 257-6801

ACI Depot Repair Inc.
550 E. Thornton Parkway, Suite 100
Denver, CO 80229
1-(800) 231-0743

Bell Atlantic Computer Technology Services
4700 Calle Bolero
Camarillo, CA 93012
(805) 987-8628

BL Memories
17070 Royal View Road
Hacienda Heights, CA 91745
(818) 913-1851

Depot USA
4545 Industrial Suite #6E
Simi Valley, CA 93063
(805) 520-9411

Ficomp Fidelity Computers
3114 W. Alpine Avenue
Santa Ana, CA 92704
(714) 546-1608

JB Technologies, Inc.
5105 Maureen Lane
Moorpark, CA 93021
(805) 529-0908

NRG Data Corporation
1502 Arbuckle Court
Santa Clara, CA 95054
(408) 727-1008

Peripheral Repair Corp.
9233 Eton Avenue
Chatsworth, CA 91311
1-(800) 627-DISK

Peripherals Unlimited
240 Mayfield Drive, Suite 103
Smyrna, TN 37167
(615) 459-3639

Reset
49 Strathearn Place
Simi Valley, CA 93065
(805) 584-4900

Sprague Magnetics, Inc.
15720 Stagg Street
Van Nuys, CA 91406
1-(800) 553-8712

Tech ZAM
7745 Alabama Avenue, Unit #8
Canoga Park, CA 91304
(818) 887-3046

Common hardware problems include controller-card failure, where the card may write data improperly to the drive. Other hardware problems can be solved by replacing the circuit board in the drive. If the stepper motor has burnt out, it must be repaired or replaced before the data can be retrieved.

If the heads have truly crashed and touched the surface of the platter, iron oxide particles will be removed from the platter, which physically destroys data. If a crashed drive is quickly put out of service, it is still possible that some or most of the data can be retrieved.

Drive mounting screws   Four mounting brackets on the side of your disk drive allow you to secure the disk drive to the drive housing. If the screws you use are too long, the threaded end of the screw can go through the bracket and touch the disk-drive housing. When this happens, it is possible for the disk-drive housing to become distorted and not work at all. When the screws are backed out, the disk drive will work. The screw size for mounting the disk drive to the housing is usually a $6/32\text{-}\times\text{-}1/8$ Phillips pan-head machine screw; the $1/8$-inch length being critical.

Stiction problems   *Stiction* is the bonding together of the read/write heads and the media (disks) of a hard-disk drive. It occurs primarily with plated (thin film) media, but it has also been observed on oxide media.

The most common cause of stiction is from the read/write heads becoming contaminated with the lubricant used on the media. The lubricant is a *fluorocarbon*. Fluorocarbons are similar in chemical structure, but not exactly the same as Teflon™. This type of fluorocarbon is used because of its lubricity and ability to bond securely to whatever it's applied to. Because the spin motor rotates at 3,600 rpm, the fluorocarbon needs to bond to the media or it will be lost.

If a new disk is measured at various points of the surface, the lubricant will measure between 70 and 110 Angstroms, about two molecules thick. The thickness of the lubricant after three years of use is more consistent over the surface of the disk, than a brand new disk.

Even though the lubricants are selected for their ability to bond securely to a high speed, rotating device, some of the material still spins off. After a period of time, this material evens out the disk coverage. This excess lubricant flies off of the disk and some lands on the read/write heads.

Contamination and bonding   Although contamination can occur on all parts of the head assembly, the contamination located on the *air bearing surface (ABS)* causes the stiction. Bonding of the head to the disk can begin the first time that the ABS gets contaminated. When the contamination is minor, the torque action of the disk drive spin motor (the motor which rotates the media), during power up, is stronger than the bonding of the heads to the disk. As the contamination increases, the bonding strength can become equal to the spin motor torque. At some point, the bond will exceed the motor torque, which prevents spin up.

In addition to the amount of contaminant, the strength of the bond increases as the amount of time in which the head is in direct contact with the disk. Thus, stiction might not occur when the drive is turned off for a short time, but it will occur when the drive is off for a longer period of time.

Head cleaning fluids   In order to break the adhesive bond that the fluorocarbon adds to the heads, you must break down the chemical structure of the fluorocarbon. Alcohol and freon, which are generally used for head cleaning, do not break down the chemical structures of fluorocarbons. Some chemicals will break down the fluorocarbon structure, but they can also damage the other parts of the head assembly, such as the epoxy adhesive on the head, copper wires, wire coatings, plastic wire covers, and stainless-steel suspensions.

Some special chemical mixtures can be used to remove the fluorocarbon contamination from the read/write heads. These mixtures, if applied correctly, will clean the heads and not damage any of the other head components.

The use of nonlubricated disks will eliminate stiction, but will eventually cause a failure by the heads wearing down the surface of the disk. This type of failure is worse than those caused by stiction, and the failures will occur much quicker.

Some disk-drive repair companies are replacing the plated media in the drive with oxide disks. Oxide media does not provide the long-term data integrity and reliability in drives that were originally designed for plated media.

Oxide media   *Oxide media* begins with a blank, high-precision aluminum disk. The plain disk is then plated with aluminum alloy 5086. The purpose of this alloy is to give the next layer of material, which is a resin mixture, better adhesion to the raw disk. After this alloy is applied, the resin mixture (an organic polymer with oxide particles mixed in) is applied using a method called *sputtering*. With the disk spinning at 2,400 rpm, starting at the inside of the disk, the thick resin mixture (which is almost like a slush or slurry) is sprayed onto the disk at a thickness of about 30 microinches. The spray moves outward until the entire disk is covered. Then, the disk is baked to cure and harden the resin mixture.

After baking, the disk is burnished to remove the high spots and surface irregularities. A lubricant is then applied and the disk can be burnished again. The actual magnetic recording of data occurs with the orientation of the oxide particles in the resin mixture. The movement of these particles creates the north-south magnetic poles.

A problem with oxide media is that you cannot store large amounts of data on the disk because of the nature of the oxide particles in the resin mixture. These particles cannot be produced in a consistent size or shape. So, large, medium, and small particles are mixed together. The larger particles require greater amounts of magnetic force for polarization. The smaller particles require less magnetic force.

Also, when the oxide particles are mixed into the resin slurry, they do not always mix evenly. In one part of the slurry, there might be a high concentration of particles, but another part might have almost no oxide particles. Even under the best of conditions, the oxide is not distributed evenly.

The resin mixture is essentially a plastic type of paint that is sprayed on the disk. Over a period of time, sections of the resin might become harder or softer spots, depending upon temperature changes and read/ write activity. As the texture of the resin changes, the integrity of the disk deteriorates and data can be lost.

Thin-film disks   Like an oxide disk, a plated, *thin-film disk* is built up in layers, starting with a high-precision aluminum disk. The first two layers are nickel and chromium, which provide greater adhesion and a flatter, smoother surface for the next material. This material, cobalt phosphorus, allows the actual magnetic recording of the data to occur. This layer has a thickness of 2 to 3 microinches, compared to an oxide's 20 to 40 microinches.

On top of the chromium phosphorus, some disks use a layer of chromium for corrosion resistance and a layer of carbon graphite with diamond particles. The carbon graphite acts as a lubricant and the diamond particles help keep the heads clean. A lubricant is always the last layer because it provides the heads with a smoother lift and landing during power up and power down. As the drive is powered up, the heads float at 5 to 25 microinches above the surface of disk. The variation depends on the design of the drive.

Write frequency and drive density

If a low frequency is used for writing data, it will penetrate deeper into the media than a higher frequency. A lower frequency is used for oxide disks, so it can penetrate through the resin mixture of 40 microinches and manipulate the oxide particles.

A lower frequency produces a wider and taller data bit. This requires wider data tracks, which reduces the number of tracks that can be physically placed on the disk. As the write frequency is increased, the data bit becomes smaller. At some point, you won't be able to read the smaller data bit on an oxide disk because of the limitations of oxide in: particle size, distribution, and resin thickness. The width and height of the data bit can be adjusted slightly by changing the write current, but this is a minor adjustment that is primarily used for precompensation.

Thin-film disks use a cobalt phosphorus thickness of only 2 to 3 microinches, which allows a higher frequency to be used for writing data. The higher frequency produces a narrower data bit and allows more bits on a single track. Because the data track does not have to be as wide, more tracks are available. The standard MFM and RLL disk drives use frequencies of 5.0 MHz and 7.5 MHz, respectively. These frequencies are close to ideal for oxide disks, but, some newer drives write data with frequencies of 10 to 15 MHz. Some newer controller cards are able to write data at frequencies as high as 100 MHz. They will have be used with disk-drive technology that allows higher frequencies.

Stepper motor operation

Many drives use a stepper motor for moving the heads from track to track. See Figs. 5-15 to 5-17. The stepper motor circuit is an open loop, which means that no signal indicates that the stepper motor has reached the track to which it was sent. Instead, a calculation is made by the processor to determine the amount of time that the stepper motor needs to position the read/write heads above the proper track. When this time is reached, the processor will send out a SEEK COMPLETE signal, pin 8 on the 34-pin cable from your drive out to the controller card. This will issue a WRITE DATA command to the disk drive or to begin reading the data that is already on the disk.

The calculation for the SEEK COMPLETE signal depends mainly on the distance that the heads must travel. This distance is combined with the amount of torque that the stepper motor needs to accomplish, along with

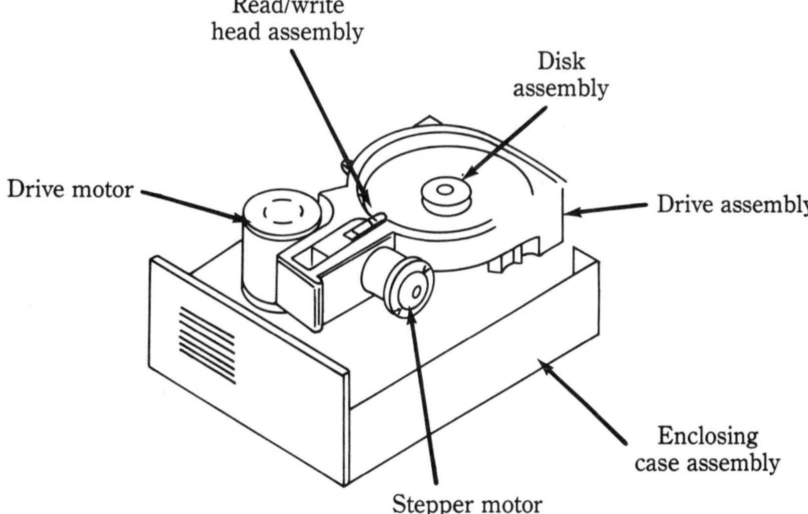

5-15 A typical hard-disk drive.

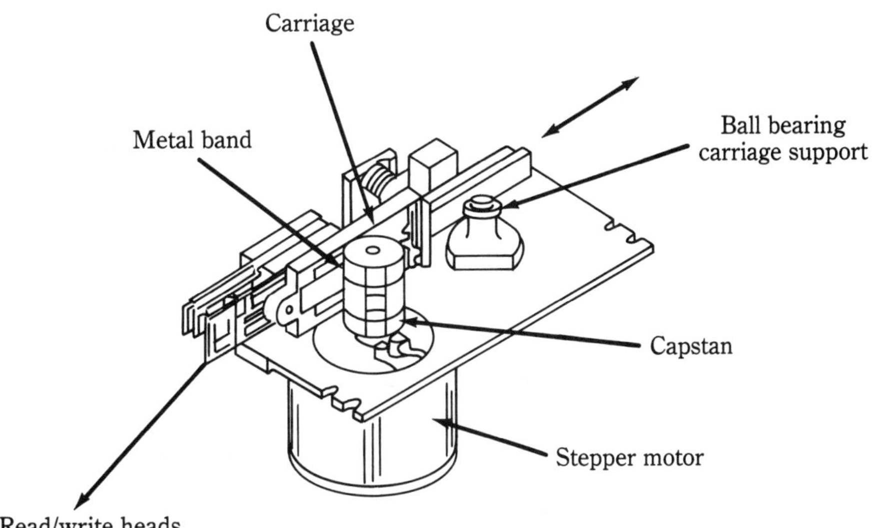

5-16 Hard-drive components.

the amount of head settling time. *Head settling time* is a back-and-forth action that occurs with the read/write heads as the energy is dissipated before coming to a complete stop.

In the open-loop circuit, the SEEK COMPLETE signal is sent as soon as the calculated time is reached—even though the head movement has not stabilized. High or low voltages will increase this head-positioning error, which tends to be a common problem.

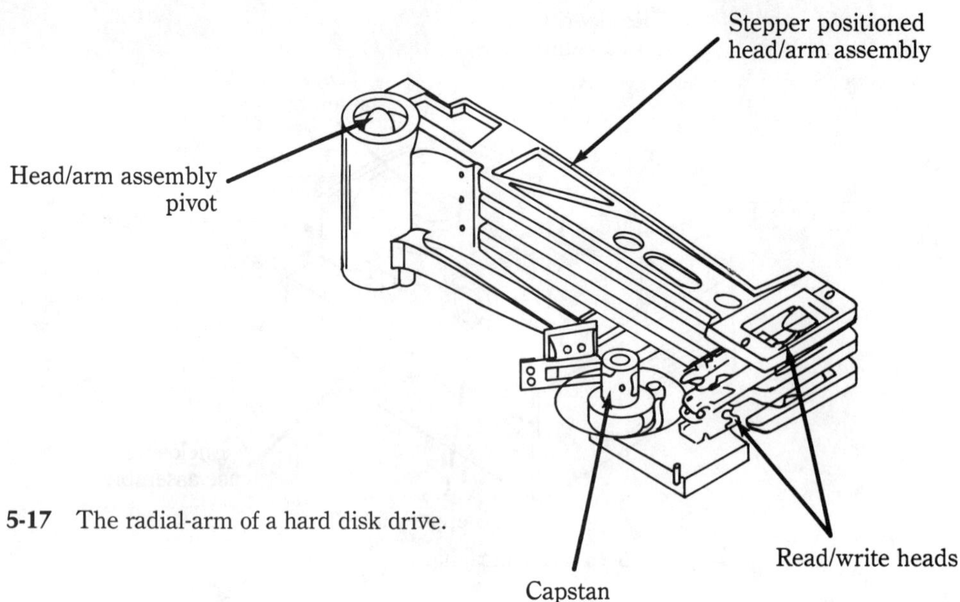

5-17 The radial-arm of a hard disk drive.

Disk-drive voltage comparator problems

Disk drives use a voltage comparator built into the circuit board on the drive. This drive helps to maintain the integrity of the data on the disk, in case the voltage levels going into the disk drive fall below predefined levels. If the voltage drops below 9.60 V for the 12-V line or 4.25-V for the 5-V line, then the comparator circuit will shut down the disk drive.

As soon as both voltage levels (5 V and 12 V) are at, or above the minimum range, the voltage-compare circuit sends out a VOLTAGE-SAFE signal and the processor will reset all of the circuits on the disk drive and the drive will begin its power-up sequence. If the voltage drop is long enough, the comparator will shut down the drive, otherwise, the low voltage will not be detected, but it can still cause problems with your system.

Power supplies and data loss

Power supplies can be defective and still supply power to the system to present the illusion that they are working properly. A properly working power supply must be able to control the output voltage within 5% of the expected voltage levels, which includes leveling out power-on spikes. This 5% tolerance is on the power supply itself. So, the 12-V output range becomes 11.40 to 12.60 V and the 5-V output range becomes 4.75 to 5.25 V.

Leaky inductors and diodes in the power supply can cause problems in two ways: *spiking* and *rippling*. Rippling can cause an output to fluctuate outside of the acceptable range of the disk-drive voltage comparator. The voltage comparator in the disk drive allows the 12-V line on a disk drive to drop to 9.6 V. If the power supply drops that low, the system will shut down and you could easily diagnose a defective power supply. However, if the power supply produces a ripple or momentary change in voltage, the change in voltage might not be long enough to cause a complete disk-drive shutdown. Instead, the individual functions of the drive won't work properly. The stepper motor might not be able to step completely to the desired track. This problem would cause a write or a read failure.

The constant changing of the voltage might cause the spin motor to speed up or slow down. The speed difference might not be large, but to properly read the data bit, the drive motor spin rate must be stable at 3,600 rpm, with a 1% or 36 rpm tolerance. Some newer drives must maintain the spin speed to a tolerance of $1/10\%$ or 3.6 rpm.

The typical disk-drive read/write circuitry uses 5 V at the head centertap for a read, and a write function is accomplished by applying 12 V to the centertap. If the drive is writing data to a sector, the voltage drop might not be enough to shut down the drive, but some data might be lost during the low-voltage excursion.

The operation of a disk drive is accomplished by the precise timing of motors spinning, the heads stepping, read or circuit activating, and other timed events. If a circuit chip is malfunctioning and providing inconsistent voltage outputs, a problem can develop. If the main source of power for the drive (the power supply) is failing, expect problems in the disk drive, the system memory, and even the refreshing of characters on the monitor.

Hard-disk tests　A number of diagnostic programs are available to test hard disks. Typical of these is *CheckIt*, which is a general PC diagnostic with hard-disk tests and *Spinrite*, which is a set of hard-disk utilities. As errors are found during the tests, they are displayed on the screen, usually with a short explanation of the problem.

Controller-card tests　*Controller-card tests* are usually done at the beginning of the hard-disk tests. The operation of the hard-disk controller must be checked because a malfunctioning controller card can cause errors and corrupt data; it will make a good fixed disk act badly or even damage it. If the controller does not pass, the test should be aborted to avoid the possibility of losing data or damaging the hard drive.

Read tests　*Read tests* are used to verify each track to make sure that the data on the hard disk can be read. During the test, the cylinder and head currently being tested will be displayed. Several different types of read tests are used. Each is designed to find a different type of problem.

Linear read test　In the *linear read test*, each cylinder is checked from cylinder 0 to the last cylinder on the disk. This test makes sure that all of the data can be read under the most basic conditions.

Butterfly read test   In the *butterfly read test*, each cylinder is read: first the outer cylinders, then the inner cylinders. This tends to be a worst-case test for the hard-disk seeking operation.

Random read test   This test is useful for finding problems that are related to head movement. The previous tests represent a more orderly progressive movement for the heads. The random read test is more realistic of the actual head movement.

Error messages   A single error can be reported by several of the previous tests. The following types of errors are typical. The first types of errors on this list are the least critical and the errors become more critical as you move down the list.

Marked by low level format

This message is not considered a problem. It indicates that the error has already been identified by the system. The message tells you that there is a bad spot on the hard disk. When you run a low-level format on the disk, you should consider this track to be bad.

Marked by DOS

This message shows that DOS already knows that this track is bad and the bad spot will not be used by DOS.

Soft error

This message indicates that a minor error occurred. The drive might have some trouble reading the data. But it was either able to reconstruct the data using *using correction codes (ECC)* or by rereading the track. This also indicates a potential problem with a track that is starting to fail.

Not in a partition

This message indicates that the bad track is outside the limits of any partition, for any operating system, on the hard disk. This can occur if you have not assigned all tracks of your hard disk to partitions. Although it might not be a problem now, it could become one when you use FDISK to change the partitions of the hard disk.

Non-DOS partition

This message indicates that the error occurred in a partition on the hard disk assigned to Xenix or another operating system. You will need to use utilities for that operating system to determine the status of the bad track.

DOS free space

This error was caused by a defect on the disk area that is not allocated to DOS. This can cause data to be lost. If you get this error, always back up your data and format the drive. The DOS Format command can be used to identify the bad track and mark it as unusable.

DOS file

This error occurs when one of your files on the named volume is written on a bad part of the disk. If this occurs, back up your data and reformat the drive. The DOS Format command can identify this bad track and mark it as unusable.

DOS boot record
DOS file allocation
  table
DOS root directory

These three types of errors can occur when one of the required sections of the DOS partition is bad. If this occurs, the entire volume may be unusable. Depending on the number of defects and where they are located, you might be able to map out these sectors using the DOS FDISK utility. If this cannot be done, you might have to get the disk repaired at a disk-drive repair facility or it might have to be replaced. This is especially true if the defects are on the first volume of the disk.

Partition table

This error indicates a major problem. The master boot record (logical sector 0) on the hard disk is bad. If this error occurs, you might need to replace your disk because you normally cannot reformat.

Extensive damage

This error indicates a serious problem with the hard disk. As the test program was attempting to report the status of a bad sector, it found more bad sectors on critical areas of the disk. You can try reformatting and if this does not work, the drive must usually be sent to a repair facility or be replaced.

When a hard drive has many failures, the test will usually be aborted. This is done to avoid damaging the drive any further. If the drive is failing badly, you should copy all of your important data. Normally, the program will read through the partition table until it finds a partition that contains the bad track. Then, if the partition contains DOS data, it will look through the *file allocation table (FAT)* for information on how the space is used. Errors are reported at the track level while DOS stores files at the sector level so that the FAT is used for each sector on the track.

Backup

Although hard disks are a reliable form of data storage, they do fail and valuable information can also be erased by an operator error. Because the volume of information contained on a hard disk is large, the failure of a hard disk that is not backed up can be a major loss. A hard disk can be backed up in several possible ways. One method is to copy files onto floppy disks using the DOS backup and retrieve commands. However, floppy-disk backup is time-consuming and tedious, so many users fail to do it often enough. When the hard disk fails, they find themselves without backups of critical files. Also, the quantity of floppy disks needed to back up a high-capacity hard disk can quickly become unmanageable. At first, floppy-disk backups appear to be inexpensive, because it requires no special hardware or training. However, the cost of the time spent backing up with floppies grows quickly.

The other popular method of hard-disk backup involves using a tape drive. The two basic types of tape drives are: floppy tape and streaming tape. The floppy-tape type of backup runs directly from the floppy-disk controller, so it does not take up an extra expansion slot. Streaming tape has the advantages of being very fast, standardized, and reliable. Streaming-tape drives can be activated automatically at a specified time of day, which frees the operator from backup operations. Because streaming tape is easy to use, people tend to perform backups more regularly.

The industry standard, *QIC (quarter-inch cartridge)*, units allow tapes to be interchanged among drives, which is required for archival storage. The disadvantage of streaming tape is cost, which can exceed the cost of the hard-disk drive, but this must be weighed against the cost of regenerating lost data after a disk failure.

Another backup method that is sometimes considered is a second hard disk that is used for backup. This is an unreliable choice because the reason that causes the main hard first disk to fail, such as an unexpected physical shock to the system chassis, will damage the backup disk at the same time.

The use of an external tape drive requires the installation of a controller card that will use the drive. Internal tape drives are available in half-height packages. These can be installed under the floppy drive in the right drive bank of an AT PC. The plastic or metal bezel that covers the opening is removed.

The controller card should be installed in a suitable slot that is close to the drive, because a ribbon cable will be connected from the card to the tape drive. You will also need to connect power cables to power the tape drive.

Floppy disk-drive alignment tester/exercisers

Floppy disk-drive alignment tester/exercisers are designed to realign floppy-disk drives on site. They provide all of the standard alignment testing and exercising functions. All ranges required for amplitude, radial, index, track 0, head load, and sector can be incorporated. One design digitizes the analog signal from an alignment diskette and does not require an oscilloscope. It is portable and designed not to lose calibration during travel.

Problems with radial, index, sector, amplitude, skew, track 0, and head load are identified by LEDs. The disk drive is adjusted until the proper lights are shown. The range of adjustments includes:

1. **Radial** An eight-LED sequence provides the adjustment indication. It shows 60%, 70%, 80%, 90%, and 100% indications.

2. **Index** A four-LED sequence provides the adjustment indication. The standard setting is 1.2 to 2.2 ms. An LED indicates the positive presence of index.

3. **Sector** A five-LED sequence provides the adjustment indication. LEDs are used to indicate which section, sector, or index to burst position is present and will indicate the reaction, as adjusted.

4. **Amplitude** A seven-LED sequence shows the positive indication on a prerecorded track of the alignment diskette.

5. **Head load sequence** A GO, NO/GO LED indicates the presence of signal in initiated head load and provides a positive indication during the first 10 ms of operation. This adjustment is most often used in dual-sided drives for the loading head. The 10 ms time is factory adjusted and can change according to the manufacturer's specifications.

6. **Head load bounce**   A single LED indicator shows bounces on a load sequence of the secondary head. A typical sequence can show bounce indications of less than 75 s in duration.

7. **Track 0**   Two LED indicators show the presence of Track 0 status.

The selectable options include:

Amplitude input   Amplified and nonamplified radial test points.
Index   Rising and falling edge indexes.
Sync   Internal and standard sync operations.
Head select   Switches for dual head drives.
Load/Radial   Provide head load sequence and bounce circuits.
Speed   300- and 360-rpm settings.

The exerciser switches include:

1. Drive select: 1, 2, 3, 4
2. Head load
3. Head select: 0/1
4. Track addressing up to 255
5. Seek track
6. Enable
7. Continuous write
8. 1f/2f pattern
9. Variable step rate
10. Off/On/Test

LED indicators are provided for the following functions:

1. Track address
2. Track 0 I/O
3. Write protect
4. Write continuous
5. Reset/on/off

Disk drives can be tested from the following manufacturers:

Canon	Panasonic
CDC	Perci
Control Data	Philips
Data General	Qume
Digital	Sharp
Epson	Shugart
Franklin	Siemens
Hewlett Packard	Sony
Hitachi	Sykes Data

IBM
Memorex
Micro Peripheral
Micropolis
Mitsubishi
NEC

Tandom
Teac
TEC
Winchester
YE Data

Hard-disk drive testers

Hard-disk drive testers can be used for field testing and repair of hard-disk drives. One design uses a small keyboard for single key commands and a 64-character LCD display. It can be used to test stepper motors, index assemblies, circuit boards, spindle motors, track-O sensors, and wiring harnesses. This equipment allows tests onsite and a 20M drive takes about 10 minutes. It provides track- and head-error counts, maximum step rate, rpm, index speed, and other reports. It can be preprogrammed to perform a series of tests while unattended. Errors flash on the LCD display and an audible tone signals test completion.

6
Video systems

Displays and adapters

A *video display adapter* is a card that takes up one of the expansion slots and controls the monitor (Fig. 6-1). The display adapter and the monitor must be compatible. A monochrome monitor cannot be used with a display adapter that is designed only for color monitors. Some display adapters will run two or more monitors. Others offer features (such as 132-column extended display, dual displays, and the ability to run color graphics software on a monochrome monitor).

The display adapter installs in one of the expansion slots (Fig. 6-2). Most are designed for eight-bit slots, but some 16-bit display adapter cards are available. Many display adapters are not designed to run reliably at the higher MHz speeds, so this can be a problem if you run at high MHz speeds.

Some computers have a slide switch on the system board. It determines whether the system boots up in color or monochrome mode, and you must refer to the manual for the correct switch setting. Often a display adapter will have several different display modes, which are set jumpers or dip switches (Fig. 6-3). It is important to use the correct switch settings for the system board, because you can damage some monitors by attaching them to a display adapter configured for the wrong mode.

Monochrome monitors

A monochrome monitor runs at a horizontal frequency of 18.432 kilohertz (kHz) and a vertical frequency of 50 hertz (Hz). It is usually available in

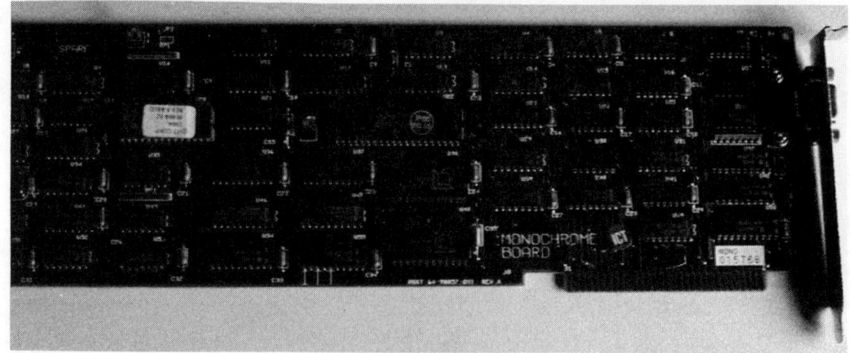

6-1 An early monochrome full-slot display adapter.

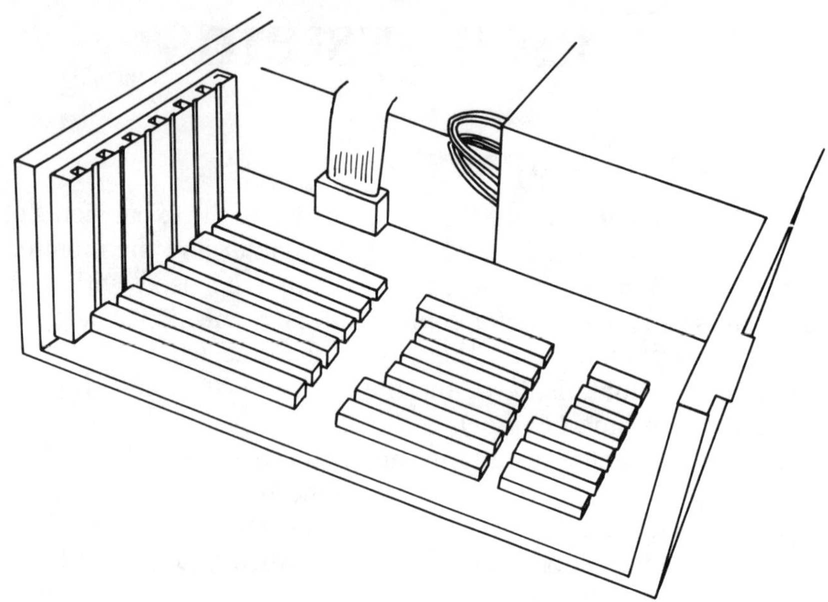

6-2 The expansion slots in a typical AT computer. The display adapter will take up one of these slots.

amber or green. A monochrome monitor will display a 9-$\times$-16 pixel text character with 25 rows of 80 characters.

Pixel is short for picture element. Pixels are the individual points of light that make up the patterns on the screen. The resolution of a display is defined by the numbers of pixels across and up and down the screen. A standard monochrome video adapter displays 720-$\times$-348 pixel graphics and can emulate *color/graphics (CGA), enhanced graphics (EGA),* or *visual graphics (VGA)* displays. These color emulation boards display the colors as varying tones of amber or green.

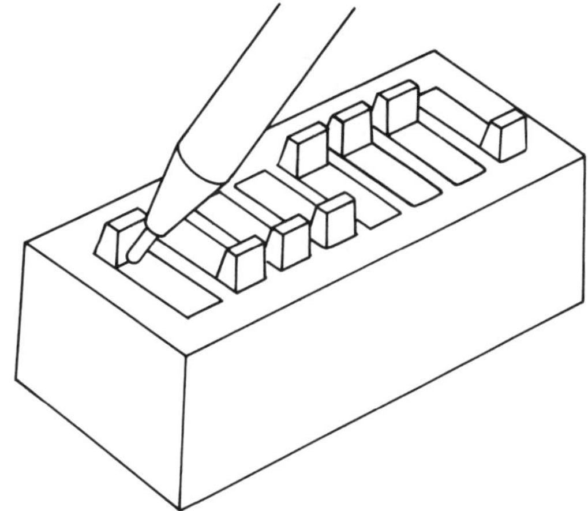

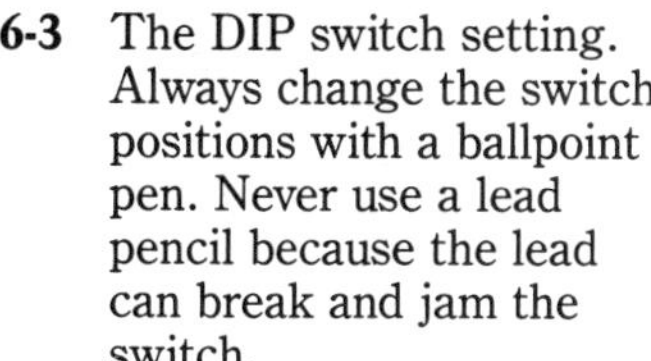

6-3 The DIP switch setting. Always change the switch positions with a ballpoint pen. Never use a lead pencil because the lead can break and jam the switch.

Often adjustable external vertical and horizontal sync controls are also included. It might be necessary to adjust the sync frequencies to change the monitor's resolution for different video modes. This adjustment would allow all modes to operate properly on the monitor. In some cases, a temperature change can cause the monitor to alter its sync characteristics. This change might cause a monitor to roll vertically.

The case can be exposed to direct sunlight, which would warm up the monitor and change its vertical sync frequency. A small adjustment of the vertical sync control can correct this problem. The original IBM monochrome display did not have external sync controls and even minor adjustments of the sync frequency required the case to be removed.

The more expensive monochrome monitors use *phase-lock loop (PLL)* circuitry to track drifting of the input sync signal. Many color emulation boards will not work properly, unless the monochrome monitor is equipped with PLL.

In order to display clean, clear text that is free of interference from external sources, some monitors filter the input signal to remove noise. Color emulation boards alter the signal characteristics to produce grey shades. The filter circuit can interpret this alteration as noise and convert it back to a clean monochrome signal. This can reduce the scaling and allow just a few shades. Monitors that use only a shielded cable for filtering will not have this problem.

RGB monitors

An *RGB monitor* (often called a *CGA monitor*) has an input frequency of 15.75 kHz horizontal and 60 Hz vertical (Table 6-1). Separate red, green, blue, and intensity inputs (RGBI format) allow a total of 16 colors to be displayed. The characters are 8 pixels high by 8 pixels deep on an 80-×-25

Table 6-1.   Color display systems

Display Name	Resolution	Bandwidth	Input	Horizontal sweep	Vertical sweep
		Typical characteristics			
CGA Color Graphics Adapter	320 × 200 4 of 16 colors	35 MHz	Digital	15.75 Hz	60 Hz
EGA Enhanced Graphics Adapter	640 × 350 16 of 64 colors	35 MHz	Digital	21.8 Hz	60 Hz
VGA Video Graphics Array	320 × 200 256 of 256,000 colors	35 MHz	Analog	31.5 kHz	60 Hz
NEC Multisync	1024 × 768 and lower	65 MHz	Analog Digital	Variable 15.75 to 35.5 kHz	60 Hz

character display. Graphics can be displayed to a maximum of 640 × 200 pixels.

Multivideo adapters, which allow an RGB monitor to also display monochrome and EGA graphics, are available. Because the maximum vertical resolution of an RGB monitor is 200 pixels, these adapters use an interlacing technique to produce the 350 lines required for EGA or monochrome graphics.

Interlacing involves creating a virtual screen in memory and forming the display with two alternating 200-line segments. The result is a screen with 400 lines. Interlacing does not change the vertical frequency, but it does change the screen refresh rate to 30 Hz and it can produce flicker. When interlacing is used, the RGB monitor should have a high-persistence phosphor to reduce the flicker.

External sync controls are usually needed if EGA or monochrome emulation boards are to be used with an RGB monitor. Changes to invertical sync characteristics can distort screen images and make the text characters difficult to read.

Dual-frequency monitors

A *dual-frequency monitor* is a display that can operate at either monochrome or color sync frequencies. These monitors usually have a monochrome screen and produce shades when operating as a color display. This type of monitor is seen in many computers and is also available as a standalone unit. These monitors can switch from monochrome sync frequencies

(18.432 kHz horizontal, 50 Hz vertical) to color sync frequencies (15.75 kHz horizontal, 60 Hz vertical) by analyzing the input sync frequency. Some monitors check the pin configuration (usually pins 3, 4, and 5) to determine if a color adapter is connected.

When using a dual-frequency monitor with a multivideo board, it is best to operate the monitor as a monochrome display. This allows the highest resolution and eliminates the need for interlacing. However, an adapter with the capability to display video on a color monitor will have circuit connections for pins 3, 4, and 5. In order to use monochrome operation, a special cable is needed between the monitor and the video board to disconnect these pins.

EGA monitors

An *EGA monitor* displays an 8-$\times$-14 pixel character on an 80×25 display. It can be driven by a CGA adapter (15.75 kHz) or by an EGA adapter (21.8 kHz) to deliver graphic resolutions from 320×200 pixels to 640×350 pixels. The vertical sync frequency is constant at 60 Hz. A total of 16 colors, from a choice of 64, can be displayed at any one time. Colors are generated through primary and secondary red, green, and blue inputs (RGB format). Special programs allow an EGA monitor to support downloadable character fonts.

Most EGA adapters also emulate monochrome text and graphics on the EGA display. Some EGA monitors do not support the 15.75-kHz horizontal scan frequency, which limits the monitor to EGA resolution (640×350). These monitors can be recognized by the absence of the 15.75-kHz frequency from the monitor specifications. Some video adapters double scan CGA graphics to produce better graphics. Most EGA monitors can handle these frequency changes, but some monitors will lose vertical sync.

25-kHz 400-line monitors

The *25-kHz monitor* was designed to produce better CGA graphics by double scanning each of the 200 lines used on a CGA graphic screen. Some adapters are only CGA compatible, while others can emulate EGA and provide their own 640-$\times$-400 and 752-$\times$-410 pixel graphics modes on the 25-kHz monitor. These monitors do not have an established standard. Many manufacturers use their own specifications for video frequencies and color format. Horizontal frequencies can vary from 23 to 27 kHz. Some 25-kHz monitors use a combined horizontal and vertical (composite) sync signal, instead of the separate horizontal and vertical signals used in the standard RGB monitor. An important consideration for matching a 25-kHz monitor to a video adapter is the sync polarity.

A CGA monitor uses a positive sync for the horizontal frequency and a negative sync for the vertical frequency. An EGA monitor uses a negative sync for horizontal and vertical frequencies in high-resolution modes and switches to a positive horizontal/negative vertical sync in CGA resolutions. A 25-kHz monitor might use one of the above formats or it might use its own.

VGA monitors

VGA monitors are the latest in the IBM PC graphics standards. They operate at a horizontal frequency of 31.5 kHz and a vertical frequency of 70 Hz. These monitors provide 640-×-480 pixel resolution. The VGA monitor uses an analog RGB input scheme to achieve the 262,144 different colors available in VGA modes. By switching the vertical and horizontal sync polarity, the VGA adapter signals the monitor to change its vertical-sizing characteristics for lower vertical resolution modes.

Multisync and multimode monitors

Multisync monitors adapt themselves to the sync characteristics as the video board. They can operate with most video boards including special purpose and workstation video adapters. Multimode monitors are different from multisync monitors in that they can only match input sync characteristics within one of several frequency ranges. Most of the multisync and multimode monitors support both digital (monochrome, CGA, and EGA) and analog (VGA and graphics workstations).

Some multisync monitors will not sync on frequencies below 21 kHz. They cannot be used with CGA adapters, but they can be used with video boards that double scan CGA. With the use of multimode monitors, some multivideo-board emulation modes might be within an unsupported frequency range. This can occur with EGA and VGA boards. Some high-resolution modes might not be supported when using these adapters on multimode monitors. Connecting a multisync or multimode monitor to a VGA adapter requires a special cable to mate the video board's connector with the monitor's analog input connector.

A VGA adapter can cause a multisync monitor to experience changes in the vertical-display size when the video mode changes. This is because the monitor might not sense the sizing signals, which are sent by the VGA adapter.

Special monitors

High-resolution graphics are also available for other CAD applications. These monitors are usually designed to accommodate the monitor manufacturer's proprietary video system. If another videosystem is used, then it is important to match the monitors sync characteristics with those of the video adapter. The following characteristics must match:

1. Vertical/horizontal sync frequency
2. Analog/digital signal
3. Sync polarity
4. Color format
5. Composite/separate sync

Dual display

This is the ability to run two monitors with different displays on each one, at the same time. This feature is supported by some software packages (such as Lotus 1-2-3 and Symphony). With a dual-display card running one of these packages you can graph on an enhanced monitor and simultaneous text on a monochrome monitor. You could type changes on the mono-chrome monitor, and the graph on the enhanced monitor would modify itself to show the changes. *Dual-monitor support* means that the system supports two different types of monitors, and *dual displays* refers to the dual simultaneous independent display on two separate monitors.

The following definitions are important to computer video systems. A *bit map* is a computer representation used to define the color and intensity of each pixel on a raster screen that is required to create an image. A pixel is the smallest unit that is available for display on a raster screen. It represents a single graphics point and is also called a *picture element*. A *raster display* refers to the common type of video display, which operates like a television set, where images are created by illuminating individual pixels using a line-by-line scan of the screen by the electron beam. *Resolution* is the number of pixels that are displayed on a monitor per horizontal line, by the number of horizontal lines displayed on the vertical axis. For example, *640×350* indicates 640 pixels wide by 350 vertical lines of pixels.

Display-adapter compatibility

Many graphics display adapters are compatible with several types of moni-tors. The graphics capabilities that are available with a particular adapter, including resolution and the number of colors, vary depending on what type of monitor is used and which display adapter you wish to simulate. The capabilities of a particular monitor can be affected when other graph-ics display adapters are installed in your system.

The following list shows several compatible IBM monitors and display adapters:

1. The 5151 monochrome display (MD) is designed to be used with the monochrome display adapter (MDA).

2. The 5153 Color Display (CD) is designed to be used with the color/ graphics adapter (CGA).

3. The 5154 Enhanced Color Display (ECD) is designed to be used with the enhanced graphics adapter (EGA).

Tables 6-2A and 6-2B shows the typical compatible modes that are possible. Descriptions follow for each type of IBM monitor. Information is also included about the type of graphics adapter most often used with that monitor.

Table 6-2A.   Typical graphics modes

Adapter	No. of colors	Resolution (h × v)	Monitor
EGA	16/64*	640 × 350	ECD
EGA	16	640 × 200	CD,ECD
EGA	16	320 × 200	CD,ECD
EGA	4/64	640 × 350	ECD
EGA	2	640 × 350	MD
CGA	4	320 × 200	CD/ECD
CGA	2	320 × 200	CD/ECD
CGA	2	640 × 200	CD/ECD

*Refers to 16 displayable colors from a 64-color palette and usually requires 256K of graphics memory on the adapter.

Table 6-2B.   Typical text modes

Adapter type	Number of colors	Character size (pixels)	Characters per screen	Monitor needed (2)
EGA	16/64*	8 × 14	80 × 25	ECD
EGA	16/64*	8 × 8	80 × 43	ECD
CGA/EGA	16	8 × 8	80 × 25	CD/ECD
CGA/EGA	16	8 × 8	40 × 25	CD/ECD
CGA/EGA	2	8 × 8	80 × 25	CD/ECD
CGA/EGA	2	8 × 8	40 × 25	CD/ECD
MDA/EGA	2	9 × 8	80 × 43	MD
MDA/EGA	2	9 × 14	80 × 25	MD

IBM 5151 monochrome display monitor   The IBM 5151 monochrome display was designed to be used with the IBM MDA. This monitor has a screen refresh rate of 50 Mz (noninterlaced), and a maximum bandwidth of 16.257 MHz. The MD monitor is transistor-transistor logic (TTL) compatible and has a horizontal scan frequency of 18.432 kHz.

IBM 5153 color display monitor   The IBM 5153 color display was designed to work with the IBM CGA card. This monitor can display 16 different colors, by combining digital outputs of red, green, blue, and intensity values. Monitors of this type are sometimes called *digital RGB monitors* because they combine the colors red, green, and blue to create color variations. This monitor has a high-contrast black screen. Many IBM-compatible digital RGB monitors are available; some of the older monitors provide only 8 colors instead of 16.

The maximum bandwidth for this type of monitor is 14.318 MHz and the screen refresh rate is 60 Hz (noninterlaced). The monitor is TTL-compatible and uses a horizontal scan frequency of 15.750 kHz.

IBM 5154 enhanced color display monitor   The IBM 5154 Enhanced Color Display was designed to be used with the Enhanced Graphics Adapter (EGA). This type of monitor can usually support software that is written for either the EGA or the CGA. The ECD monitor has a screen-refresh rate of 60 Hz and the horizontal-scan rate can be either 15.75 kHz or 21.850 kHz. This type of monitor can be considered an RGBI monitor because each color can be intensified.

Software/hardware compatibility

If an adapter is compatible with an IBM standard, such as EGA, it will also be supported by the Virtual Device Interface (VDI) specification described by IBM and Graphics Software Systems (GSS). Software that is written with the VDI interface will run on most adapters with an EGA driver. Most, but not all, CGA software that runs on IBM's EGA will also run on other EGA adapters.

Using multiple-display adapters   Depending on your software applications, you can use your display adapter with another coexisting display adapter. Most color adapters can only be used with another display adapter if one adapter is operating in a color mode, and the other is in a monochrome mode. For example, if a color adapter coexists with a CGA, then one color adapter must be configured in monochrome mode.

When two display adapter cards coexist, you must specify which adapter is primary and which is secondary. This is accomplished through switch settings. The adapter designated as primary will be the adapter in use when you boot up your system. The secondary card will not be used unless it is activated through a DOS MODE command.

For example, to switch over to a monochrome display adapter that is designated as secondary, you would enter the following command at the DOS prompt:

```
C> MODE MONO <Enter>
```

Display problems

During system power-up, one of the BIOS routines initializes and starts the 6845 CRT controller and tests the video read/write storage. The program causes the 8088 CPU to check the setting of video switch SW1 by reading port A of the 8255 PPI. This port is connected to the two configuration switches, SW1 and SW2. The CPU logically ANDs the port data with the hex value 30H, which thus checks the settings of switch SW1-5 and SW1-6. If they are not off, the program jumps to a subroutine that tests to see which type of video card is installed. If SW1-5, 6 are off, the program goes into an I/O memory parity test and then into setting the video mode. If a parity error occurs, a message is displayed. If a problem occurs setting the video mode, another error message is displayed.

The program also conducts a test of the video storage memory. If a failure occurs, the speaker is beeped. By reading the CRT controller status port and logically ANDing the reading with binary 1000, a test is made to see if the video/horizontal line changes state. If it does not go low during this timed test, a timer clocks out and an error message is displayed and the speaker is caused to beep. Several times during this power-up testing, the INT 10H video I/O procedure is called.

No video   You must localize the failure to the display unit or to the system board. You can do this by connecting a good test monitor with a good cable to the PC and recheck. If the problem is corrected, try the original display unit with the good cable. If this works, replace the cable. If it does not work, the problem is in the display unit.

If no video is available using the test monitor and cable, and no cursor appears, check the configuration switches on the system board, (SW1-5 and SW1-6 in the 5150 PC). These switches are used to configure the system for the particular type of monitor adapter that you are using.

Inspect and wipe clean the pins of the edge connector on the adapter card. On some older adapter cards, the bracket on the adapter must be grounded to the chassis for proper operation.

If it still has a problem, check the +5-V power on the adapter board. If the voltage is incorrect, it could be a power supply problem. If the system seems to work fine without the color card installed, but shuts down when it's mounted in the expansion slot, check ICs U26, U42, U60, U66, or U67 (these and the following IC numbers apply to the IBM CGA card). If the horizontal or vertical sync has a problem, the U21, U63, U67, or U101 IC could be faulty. If the cursor is not blinking or is missing, check U12. Color fading or the wrong color can be caused by U20, U22, U43, U44, U45, U65, or U67. Video RAM problems require checking ICs U50 through U60. Error code 501 will appear when the color/graphics adapter card has a problem.

Monochrome display problems When problems occur on systems that have a monochrome display/printer adapter installed, run the following preliminary checks. Connect the system to a good monitor with a known good cable to eliminate the display unit and cable as the problem cause. A 401 error code will appear if there is a problem.

With no video, check for +5 V on the adapter board. If this voltage is not present on the monochrome video board, troubleshoot from the +5-V power input to the point where a loss of power is.

With no cursor on the screen, check the system board configuration switches (SW1 and SW2 in the IBM PC 5150). Both should be turned off; check that these have not shorted. Also, clean the pins and reinstall the adapter card. If the cursor is not blinking properly or is missing, check U55 in the IBM PC (DM74LS174N).

Video interfaces

In the IBM personal computers, the video outputs are on plug-in expansion cards, as has been mentioned previously. The outputs are designed to be displayed on specific types of monochrome or color monitors with various resolutions.

Regardless of the type of monitor used, the output of the video circuits must contain all the elements needed to create an image on the display screen. These circuits must be able to encode a number of different display forms. They must be able to show the alphanumeric characters that are on the keyboard as well as graphics.

The monitor screen

A monochrome screen has a display face with a single color phosphor, usually green, amber, or white (Fig. 6-4A). At the other end of the cathode-ray tube is the electron gun. It sends a beam of electrons to the face of the tube that lights up the phosphor and causes it to glow. The beam lights up only a small dot on the screen at any one time.

The color tube (Fig. 6-4B) contains small patterns of color phosphor dots (red, green, and blue) on the face of the screen. Three electron beams are sent from the electron gun (Fig. 6-4C). One beam controls the red dots, another the green dots, and the other controls blue dots. The three colors are additive and produce the colors that are needed for a color image. In higher resolution monitors, the color dot patterns are made as closer to each other and produce a more natural color display.

The beams scan the face of the tube, on a line-by-line basis from the top down. As the scanning occurs, each dot is switched either on or off (Fig. 6-5). This scanning is done by the video circuits that control or focus the beam. Most tubes use electromagnetic focusing. As the beam travels

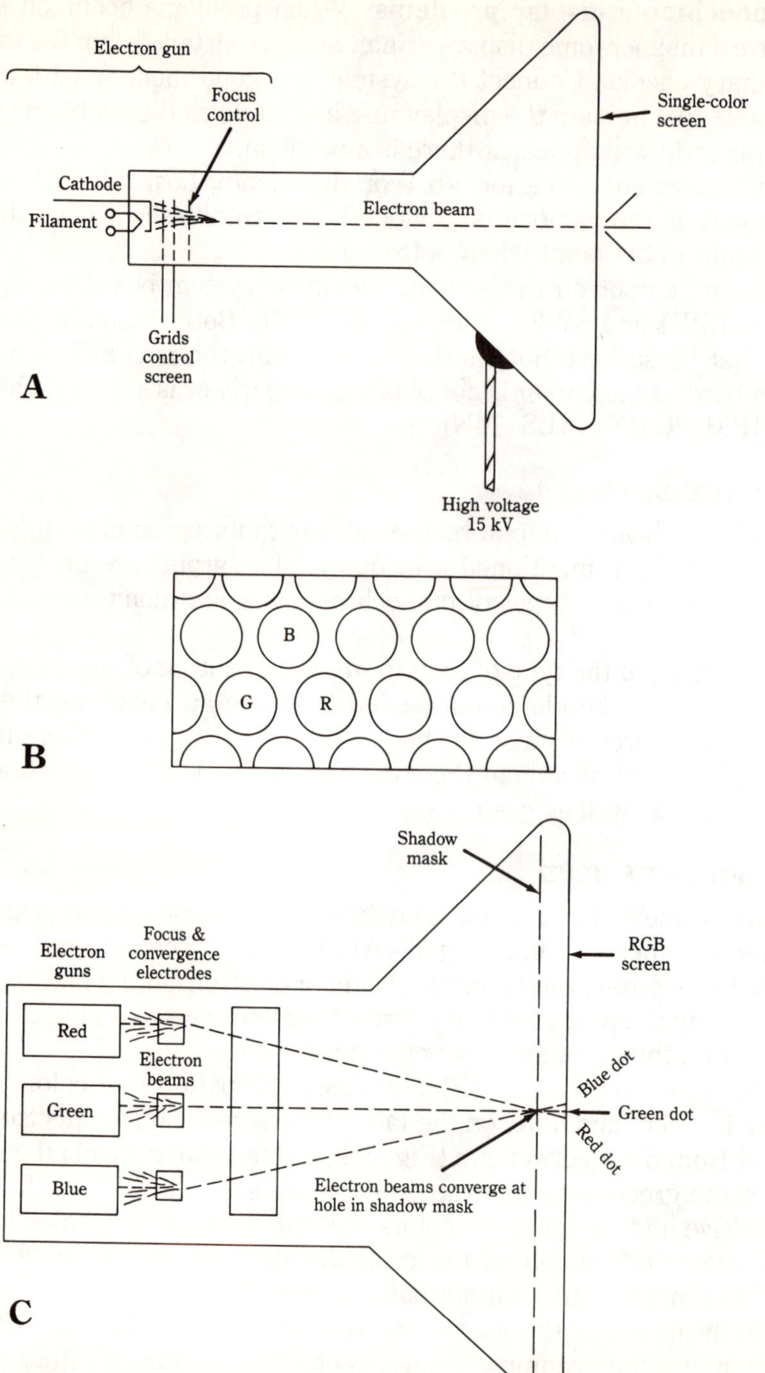

6-4 (A) A monochrome cathode-ray tube. (B) A color tube screen with alternating red, blue, and green dots over the face of the screen. (C) Color tube operation.

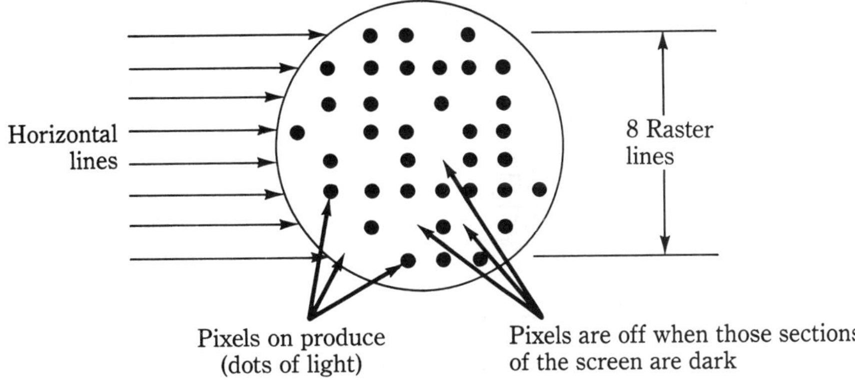

6-5 A closeup view of raster lines and pixels.

from the gun to the phosphor, it must go through the focusing coils. One coil is used for horizontal focusing and the other for vertical focusing.

The horizontal coil moves or sweeps the beam from side to side at a rate of more than 15,000 times every second (Fig. 6-6). The vertical coil moves the beam up and down about 60 times a second. This scanning operation writes 264 lines of light on the screen 60 times a second (Fig. 6-7).

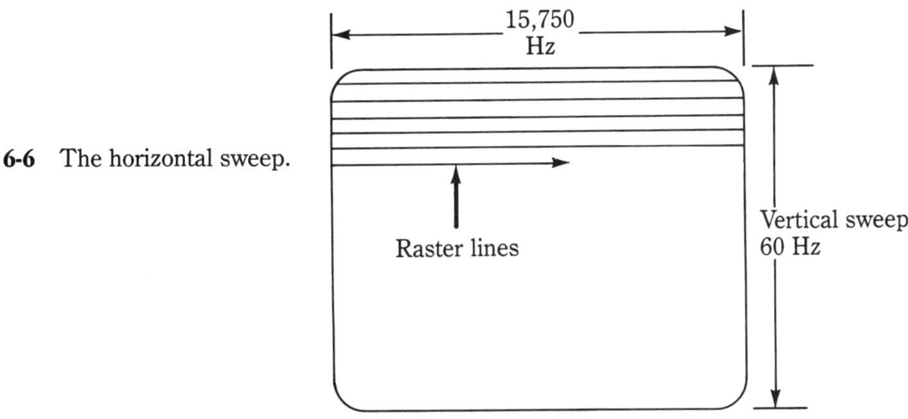

6-6 The horizontal sweep.

The scanning occurs using the timing of the monitor's sweep circuits. A higher scanning frequency produces more scanning lines. The scanning must be in sync with the computer's clock. The computer sends horizontal and vertical sync signals to the sweep circuits to lock the horizontal and vertical oscillators in step with the computer's operating frequencies (Fig. 6-8).

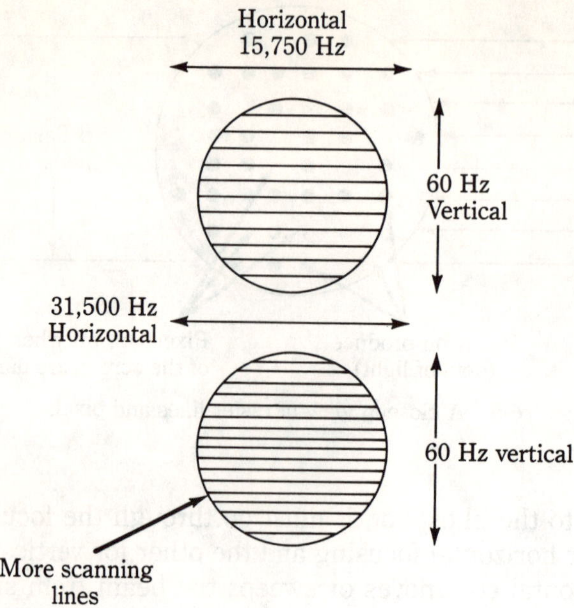

6-7 A high-scanning frequency produces more scanning lines and improves the resolution.

The monochrome I/O card

The IBM PC uses a separate adapter card (Fig. 6-9) that plugs into one of
the I/O sockets and provides a port on the rear of the system unit for a
monochrome display. The modular approach is convenient for troubleshooting. On the card is a video output chip, usually a 6845 CRT controller

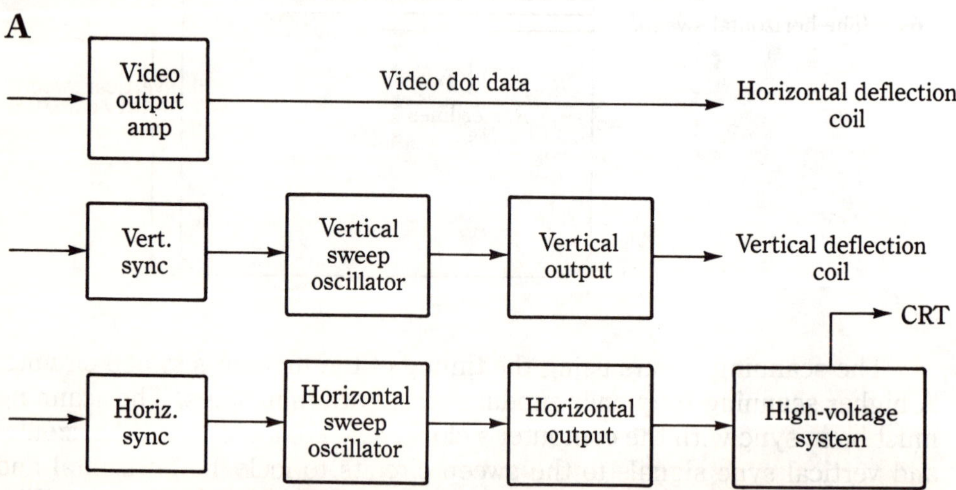

6-8 (A) A video system block diagram. (B) Signal characteristics. (C) Timing chart
fH = 15.70 kHz. (D) Timing chart fH = 21.85 kHz.

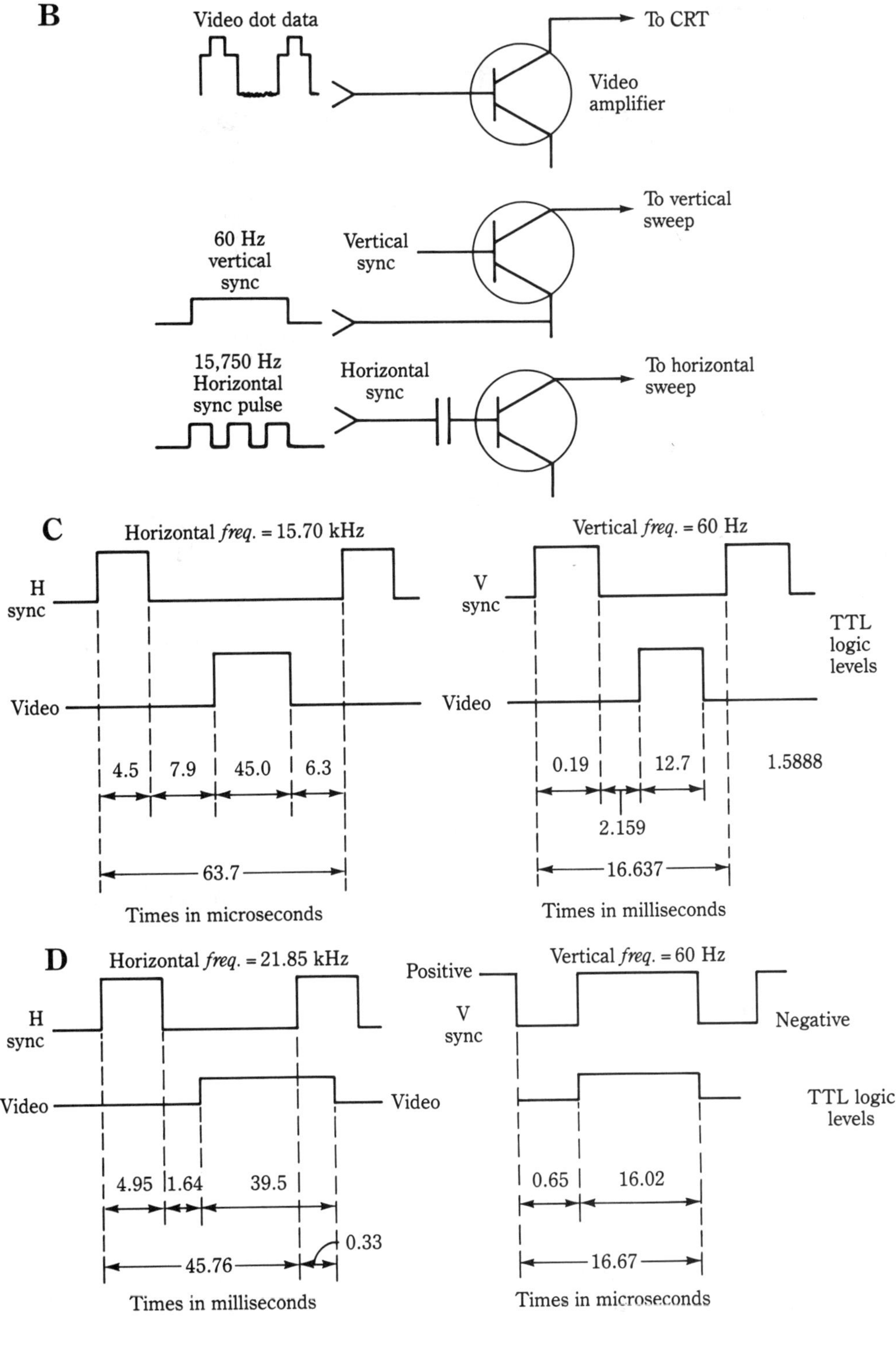
B
Video dot data
To CRT
Video amplifier
60 Hz vertical sync
Vertical sync
To vertical sweep
15,750 Hz Horizontal sync pulse
Horizontal sync
To horizontal sweep
C
Horizontal freq. = 15.70 kHz
H sync
Video
4.5
7.9
45.0
6.3
63.7
Times in microseconds
Vertical freq. = 60 Hz
V sync
Video
TTL logic levels
0.19
12.7
1.5888
2.159
16.637
Times in milliseconds
D
Horizontal freq. = 21.85 kHz
H sync
Video
4.95
1.64
39.5
0.33
45.76
Times in milliseconds
Vertical freq. = 60 Hz
Positive
V sync
Negative
Video
TTL logic levels
0.65
16.02
16.67
Times in microseconds

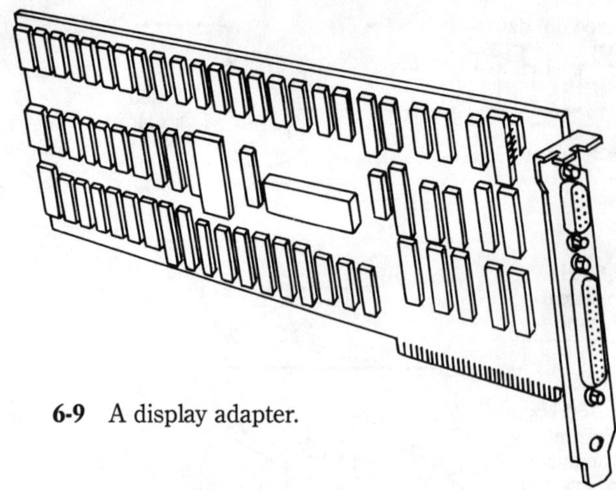

6-9   A display adapter.

(Fig. 6-10). It is the main chip for converting the digital bits from the computer to the image on the monitor. Other support chips are on the board including 4K of static RAM and an MK-36000 character ROM.

This RAM is a part of the system memory map. It acts as the video RAM. On the monitor screen of 80×25 characters, a total of 2,000 characters is present. Each character needs two bytes of RAM to function. One byte contains the ASCII code for the character and the second contains control bits for features, such as blinking of the character, high or normal intensity and normal or reverse video. The address of the video RAM ranges from hex B0000 to B0F9F, starting at the upper left-hand corner of the screen and ending at the lower right-hand corner with the last RAM address. The video RAM is constantly scanned and the contents of each byte are used to turn the dots on and off.

The monochrome adapter uses a 9-pin connector (Fig. 6-11). The functions of the pins are as follows:

Pin 1   Ground
Pin 2   Ground
Pin 3   Not used
Pin 4   Not used
Pin 5   Not used
Pin 6   Intensity
Pin 7   Video
Pin 8   Horizontal sync
Pin 9   Vertical sync

The CRT controller receives address, data, and clock signals from the computer. In the controller chip, the address information is used to access

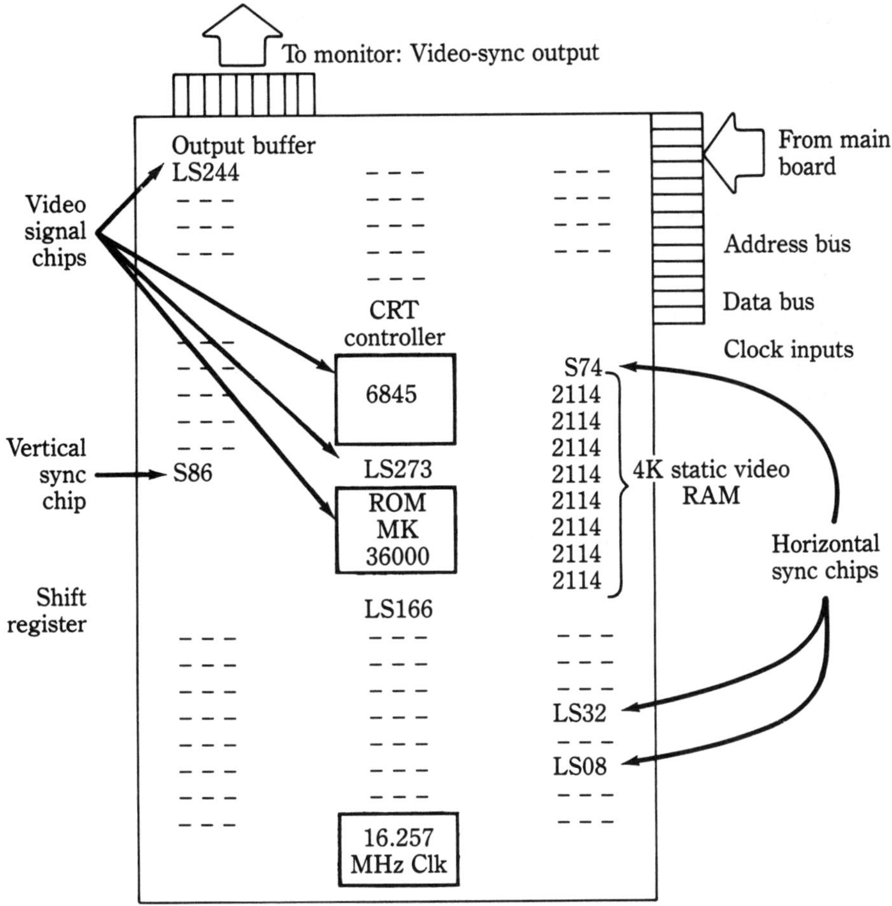

6-10 IBM monochrome adapter layout.

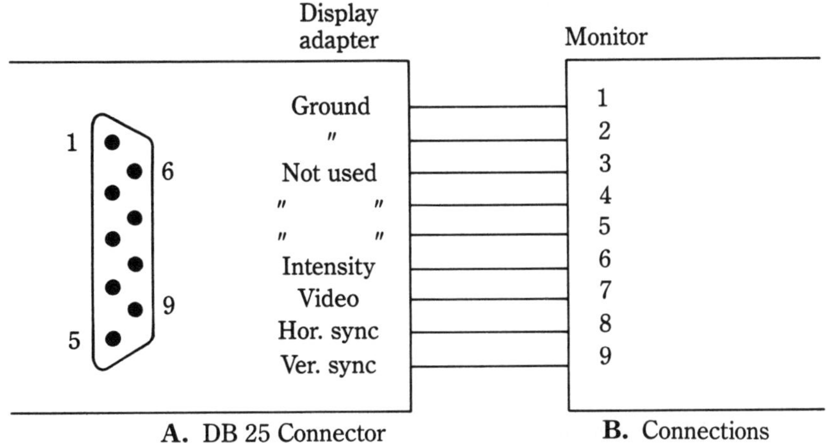

A. DB 25 Connector   **B.** Connections

6-11 Monochrome monitor connections.

the video RAM and the data bits are sent to the video RAM. The controller uses the system clock information to generate the horizontal and vertical sync signals.

The CRT controller acts as a video processor. It uses the video RAM to update the dot information on the screen. It reads the video RAM data and sends this information to the MK-36000 character-generator ROM. It is in the character ROM that the actual character generations is done. As the ASCII-coded byte arrives at the ROM, it is coded into the proper character byte.

The character bytes are sent to a 74LS166 shift register, which converts the parallel byte to serial format. This signal is conditioned and sent to the video output (pin 7). The CRT controller also provides the horizontal and vertical sync information through pins 8 and 9.

The output signals of the card can be checked with a TV servicing scope. Figure 6-12 illustrates the typical signals that should be present. Differences from these signal indicate problems with that particular function.

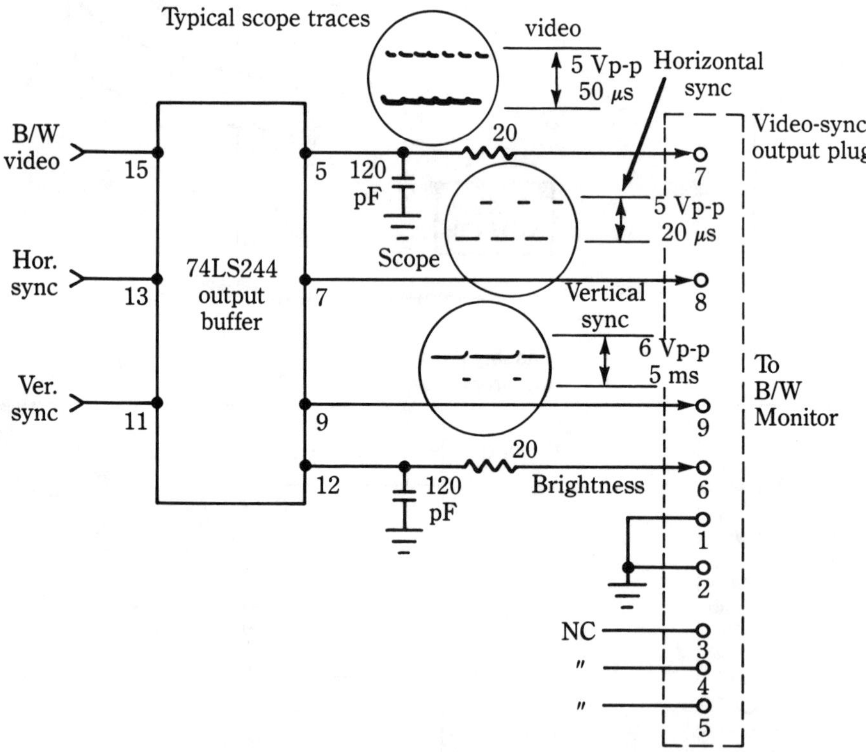

6-12   Troubleshooting monochrome card video-sync outputs.

Color/graphics cards

A *color/graphics card* requires the same type of circuits as a monochrome card, plus the color and graphics circuits that are needed. Various cards are made for the IBM PCs from other manufacturers. These can have different features, but the basic operation is the same. The card that IBM provides uses the circuits shown in Fig. 6-13.

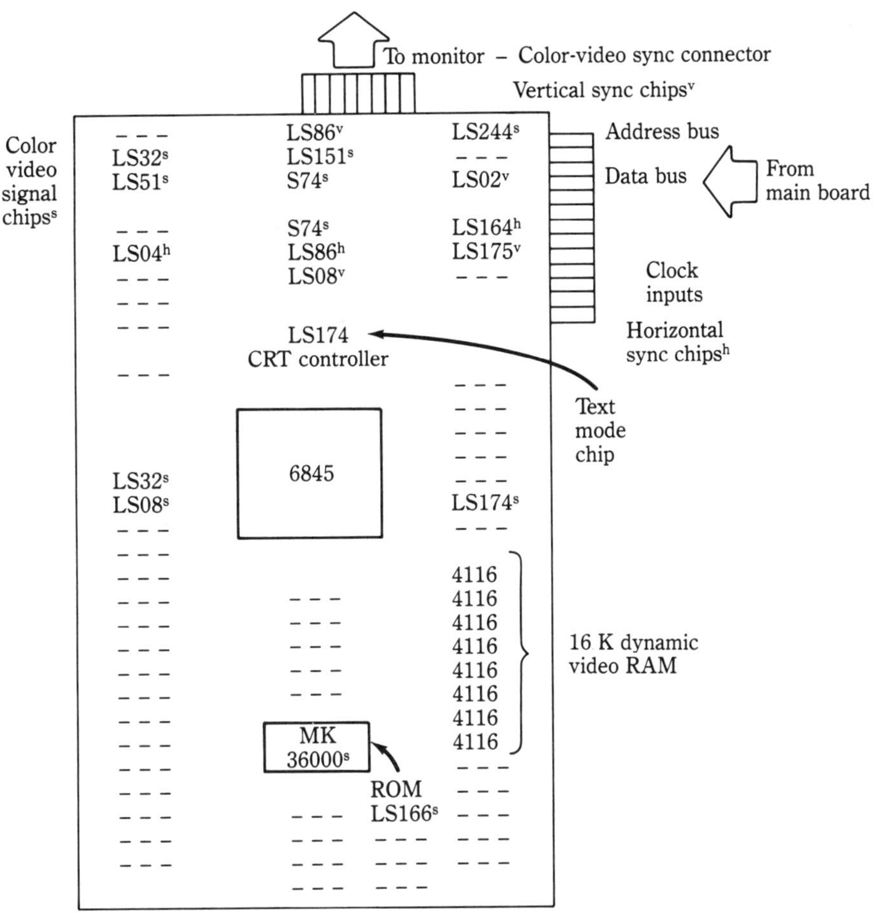

6-13   IBM color graphics adapter layout.

A 6845 CRT video processor is used to control the input from the computer. The video RAM is dynamic rather than static and it holds 16K. It uses 14 address lines, A13 through A0, with a starting address of B8000. The locations are accessed through multiplex chips. The dynamic RAM sends its contents to an MK-36000 character ROM. The ROM outputs are conditioned and sent to the 9-pin DIN adapter connector. The following pin functions are used:

Pin 1   Ground
Pin 2   Ground
Pin 3   Red
Pin 4   Green
Pin 5   Blue
Pin 6   Intensity or brightness
Pin 7   Unused
Pin 8   Horizontal sync
Pin 9   Vertical sync

In addition to these signals for the monitor, the color/graphics adapter might have additional output connectors. Sometimes, an RCA-type jack is

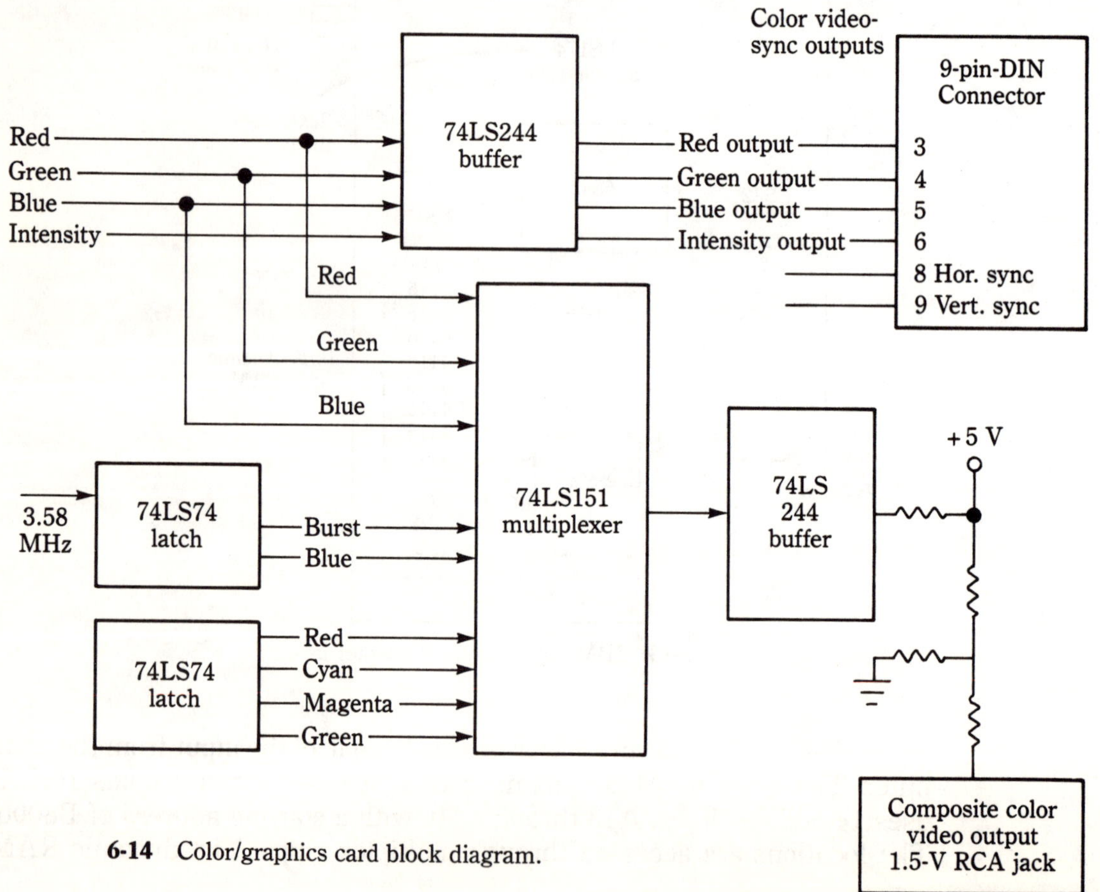

6-14   Color/graphics card block diagram.

used to provide a composite video signal. The three color outputs, the color burst, and clock signals are combined using a 74LS151 multiplexer chip, buffered with a 74LS244 or similar chip, then sent to the RCA jack.

Another optional output that is found on some older adapters is on a 4-pin Berg-type strip. This provides the same outputs as the RCA jack, plus a connection to the +12-V power supply. This can be used to connect the PC to a television. An RF modulator is also required. It will use channel 3 or 4 of the commercial broadcast band. The RF modulator provides the

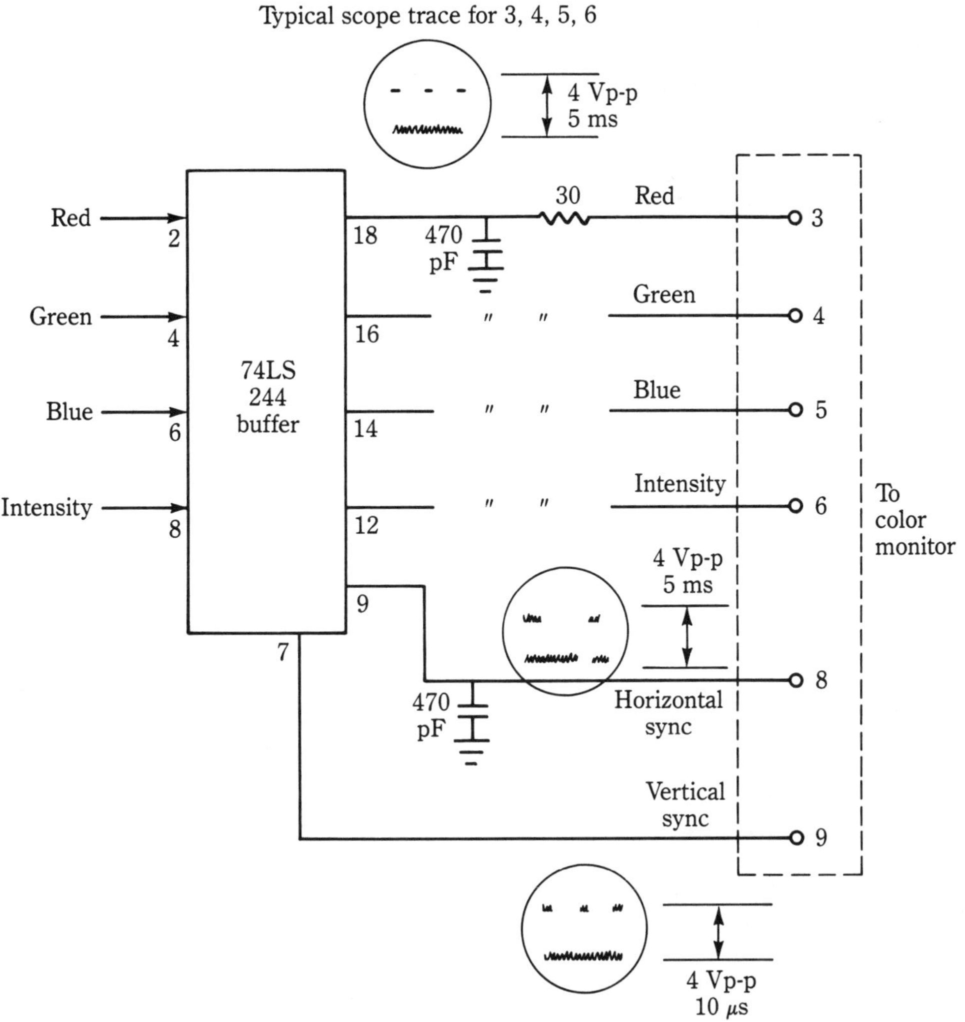

6-15 Troubleshooting color/graphics card video-sync outputs. These types of displays indicate that the video operation is ok and that the problem is in the digital circuits of the computer, processor RAM, ROM, and I/O. Often the screen will appear to lock up and not accept commands.

modulation frequencies for channel 3 or 4 and the +12 V is used to power the modulator, which modulates the composite signal for a color television.

Troubleshooting color adapters

A television service scope can be used to check the output signals of the adapter. Figure 6-15 shows the typical output traces that should be observed under normal operating conditions.

System shuts down with monochrome card installed If the system shuts down, one of the following ICs on the monochrome monitor/printer adapter could be bad:

U3	DM74LS08N
U35	MC6845P
U45	74LS74APC
U54	DM74S86N
U64	DM74LS244N
U100	74LS32N
U101	74LS74PC

Monitor testers

Monitor testers were designed to be comprehensive. Most of these testers are able to test a wide range of monitors. They can be used to test, align, and repair monitors in the field because many are hand-held. They can be especially useful for troubleshooting LANs because they eliminate the need to disconnect and carry the monitors in to the service depot for testing.

To use these testers, plug the monitor under test into the tester, select the mode, and start testing. The unit generates video, intensity, RGB and

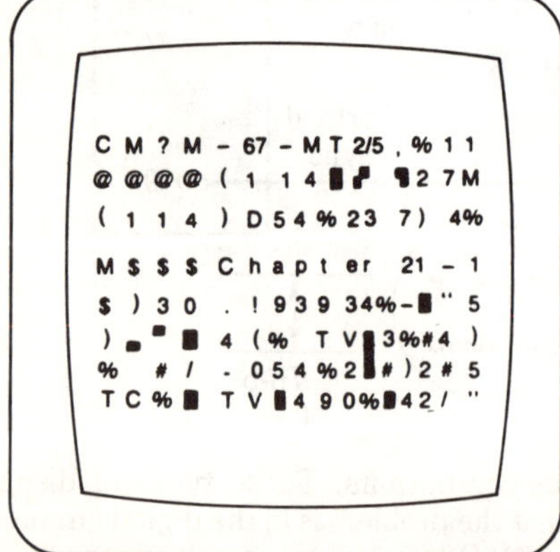

6-16 (A) Garbage text, normal borders. (B) Blank display, normal borders.

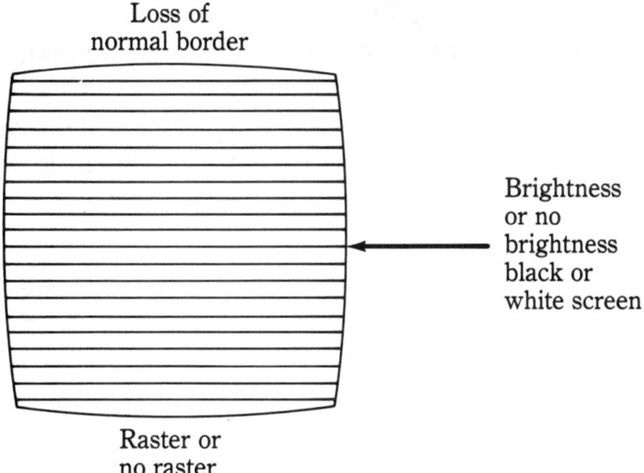

6-17   A loss of border with or without a raster usually indicates a problem in the video circuits.

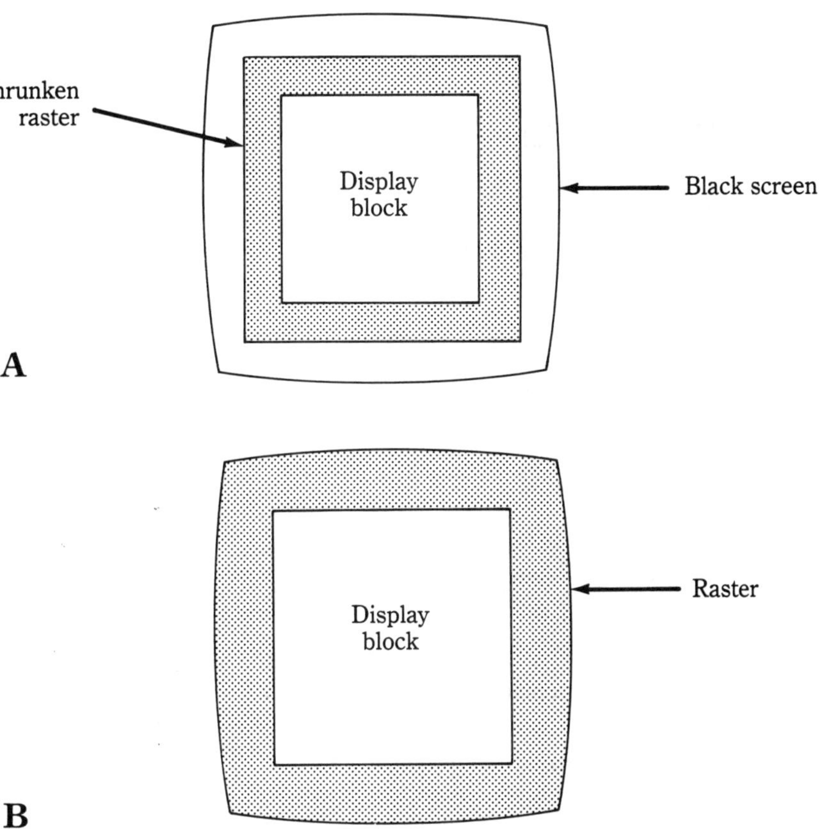

6-18   (A) Typical power-supply failures. (B) A four-sided shrinkage of screen. (C) Bends in pictures with some shrinkage.

horizontal/vertical sync, and TTL signals in four patterns. The units are available for testing IBM PC and AT&T PC6300 compatible color and monochrome monitors.

Sometimes the monitor display will provide characteristic clues as to where the problem is. Figures 6-16, 6-17, 6-18, and 6-19 show some typical display symptoms and their usual causes.

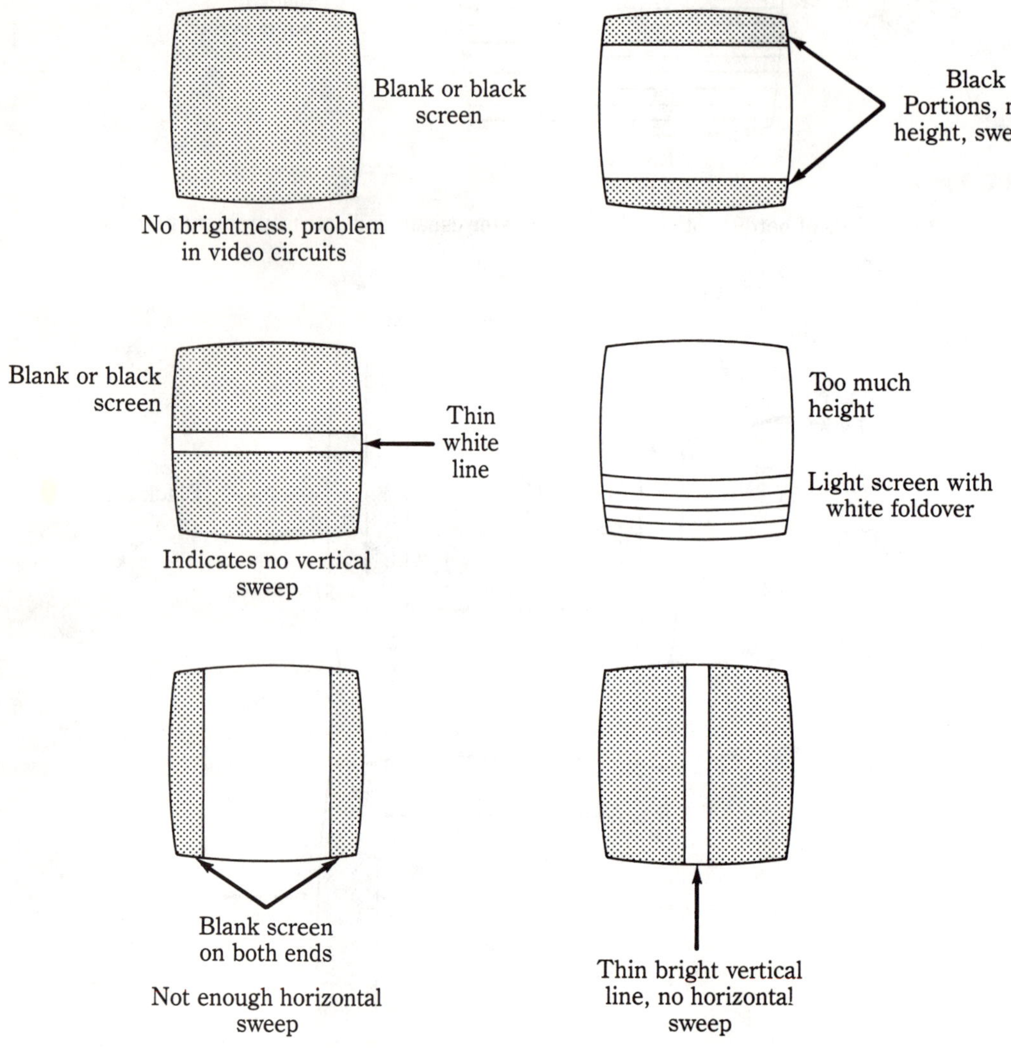

6-19 Several examples of sweep circuit problems.

7
Types of printers

Dot-matrix impact printers

Dot-matrix impact printers create the character by selectively moving tiny pins to form dots in the shape of the desired character. The dot-matrix printing mechanism does not rotate, but it prints using a vertical array of the wire pins. Typically, 7 to 9 pins are used in lower resolution printers and 18 or 24 are used in higher resolution printers.

The characters to be printed are stored in ROM, which determines which pins in the array are to strike the ribbon and imprint the character on the paper. The more wire pins the unit has, the more closely the printing mechanism approximates the print quality of fully-formed characters.

The impact process used is the traditional way to transfer ink to paper. It involves compressing the paper, type element, and inked ribbon. Impact printers press the character element (or pin) against the inked ribbon, which makes an impression of the character on the paper.

The serial impact dot-matrix printer in Fig. 7-1 consists of a printhead with 7, 9, 18, or 24 solenoid-operated print wires. The printhead is moved across the printing area by a shoe that engages in the slot of a cylindrical cam. The single-groove cam ensures vertical linearity by eliminating the crossover that is found in a multi-grove cam (Fig. 7-2).

Two stepper motors drive the print mechanism: one is used for moving the print head, while the other is used to advance the paper (Fig. 7-3). The two motors operate independently and are controlled by a microprocessor. Two methods of paper feeding are used, either a pressure roller driving the paper with friction, or tractors. Paper can be *fanold* (with or without tractor

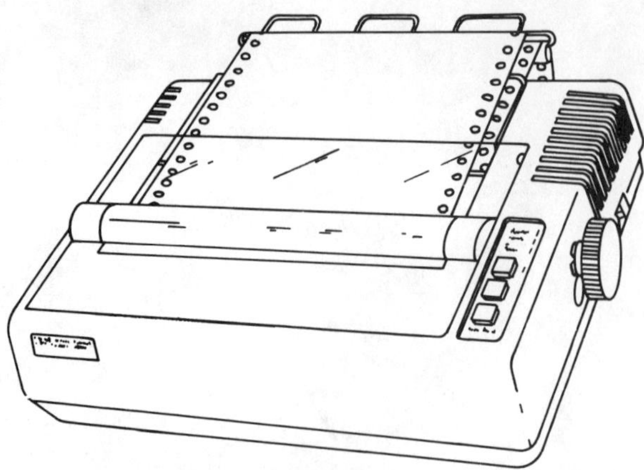

7-1   A dot-matrix printer with tractor-folded paper.

holes), rolls, or single sheets. Optional roll-paper holders and single-sheet feeder assemblies are available for many machines. The inked ribbon is usually self-contained in a cartridge and is easily replaced by opening a lid on the printer case.

Nonimpact printing

Nonimpact printing can be divided into plain and coated-paper technologies. Among those that use plain paper are the *ink-jet printers*, in which tiny droplets of ink are forced onto the paper, and *electrophotography*, which uses a laser writing on a drum.

Coated-paper processes include the following techniques:

1. **Thermal**   Heated elements write on thermally sensitive paper.

2. **Electrosensitive**   Electric charges burn off a thin metallic coating to reveal a black undercoat.

3. **Electrostatic**   The coated paper is selectively charged by a stylus, which then passes through a toner that is attracted by the charged area.

Nonimpact printers that create matrix images include the thermal-matrix printer (Fig. 7-4). The printhead moves across the print line and forms characters by heating chemically treated paper at the desired locations. Print rates typically range from 20 to 120 cps. With this printer, 5- × -7 dot-matrix characters are printed one at a time, in serial fashion.

Electrosensitive-matrix printers use an aluminum-coated paper that changes color when a voltage is applied. The printhead contains electrodes that are pulsed on when a dot is to be formed. The electric charge goes

A. Interior view of dot matrix printer.

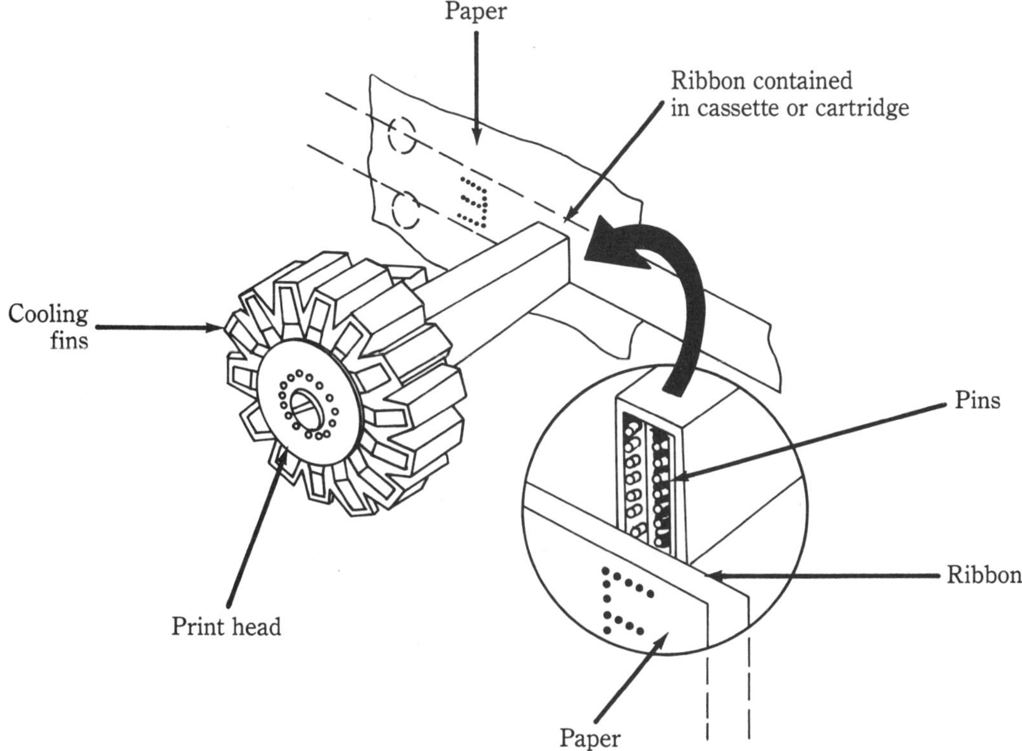

B. Print head operation

7-2   Matrix printing.

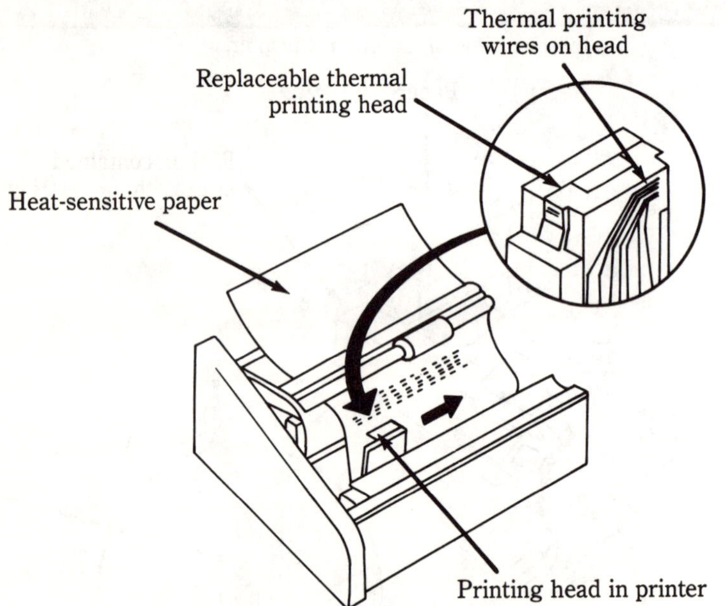

7-3   A typical layout of impact dot-matrix printer.

7-4   Nonimpact thermal printing.

through the paper to a metal plate behind the paper. The plate is at ground potential and it completes the current path (Fig. 7-5).

Line printers

Line printers form characters for a complete line, one line at a time, and are rated in terms of *lines per minute (lpm)*. This rating makes them much

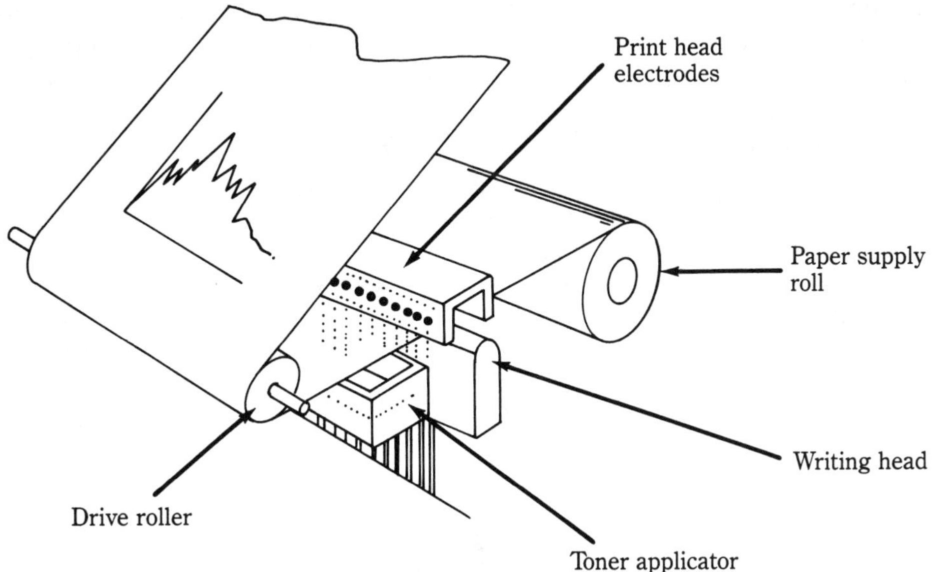

7-5 Electrosensitive printing.

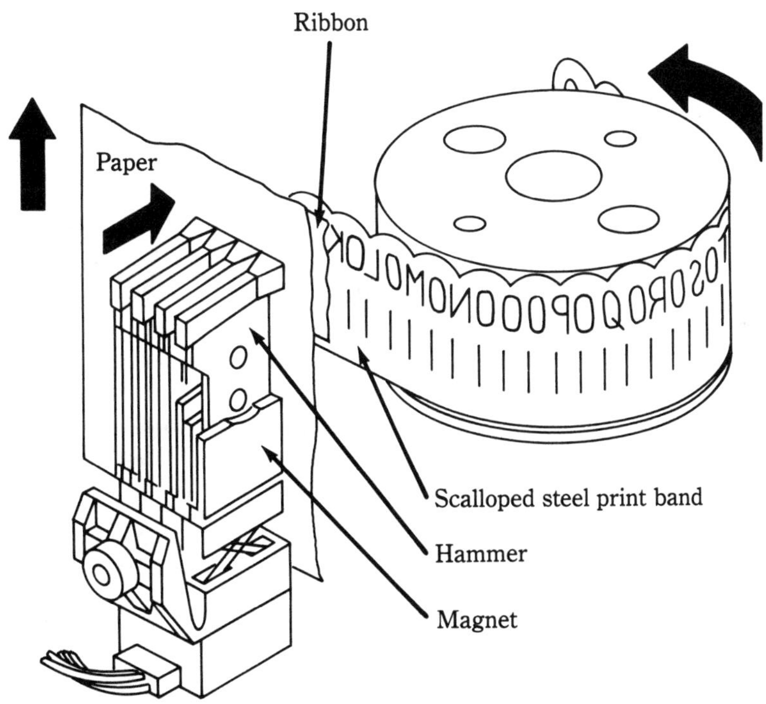

7-6 A solid-line printer using band technology.

faster than serial printers, which generate only one character at a time. These printers use a type-element array, such as a drum, chain, train, cylinder, belt, or band (Fig. 7-6). Some line matrix printers use a shuttle comb or bank of print elements. Multihead matrix printers have multiple solenoid-operated printheads.

Impact line printers include band, drum, and chain types that use a hammer to force the paper (from behind) against the ribbon and a moving-type element. The drum printer (Fig. 7-7) has a complete set of characters embossed against the circumference of a horizontally rotating steel drum. One full set of characters and one hammer is made for each print position.

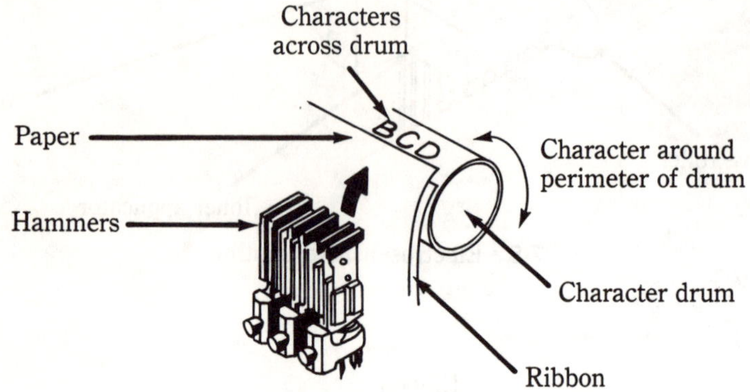

7-7   A line printer using drum technology.

Characters to be printed are transferred to a receive-data memory, one line at a time. The data memory is scanned and coupled to the rotating drum. As the character to be printed rotates into position, a HAMMER-ON signal is issued and the hammer strikes the paper, which forces it into the ribbon and drum. The print rate for this type of mechanism is determined by a combination of drum speed, character set size, paper-movement time, and data-transfer rate.

Figure 7-8 shows a line printer that uses a single-hammer system and a cylinder with a series of raised letters. The carriage movement, the motion of the hammer, and the revolution of the cylinder must be synchronized. This synchronization is done with the mechanical construction of the hammer, cylinder drive, platen, and a dot sensor (which counts raised dots on the cylinder). The relationship between the hammer and the position of the raised dots is tracked and controlled by the dot-sensor signal.

Daisy wheel printers

Solid printing, also called *formed printing*, produces whole solid images at one time. The character to be printed is selected from an array of type ele-

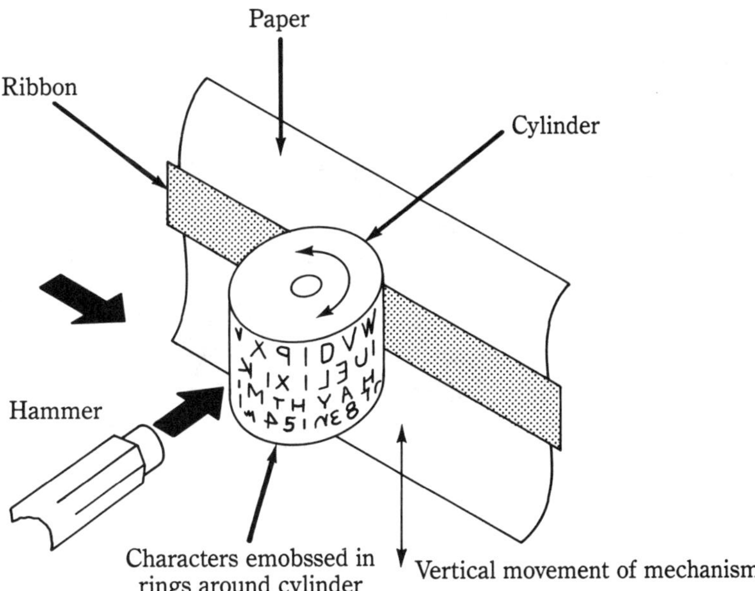

7-8 A printer using cylinder technology.

ments, which are located on an IBM Selectric type ball, a daisy wheel, or a thimble. In the daisy wheel printer, the printing mechanism consists of a steel or plastic disk that rotates in a circle, and moves the proper pedal or finger-like type implement to the area where the print hammer can strike it. Typical printing speeds for daisy-wheel printers range from 30 to 80 characters per second. The printing mechanism is easily removed to change type styles (Figs. 7-9 and 7-10).

Printer characteristics

An important printer factor is speed. Several factors are involved: print rate, throughput, and input data rate. The *print rate* is measured in cps and tells how many characters can be placed on the paper in a second. With line printers, *throughput* refers to the number of lines printed per minute (lpm). The *input data rate* relates to the interfacing of the printer with the computer.

The three interfacing methods are: 8-bit parallel, RS-232C, and Centronics-compatible. Regardless of interface type, however, the input data rate relates how fast the printer can process characters and therefore determines how frequently the printer and computer must handshake.

Noise is an important consideration. Impact printers generally exhibit noise figures that range from 50 dBa (adjusted decibels) to as high as 75 dBa. Dot-matrix printer heads make a buzzing sound, but this is usually

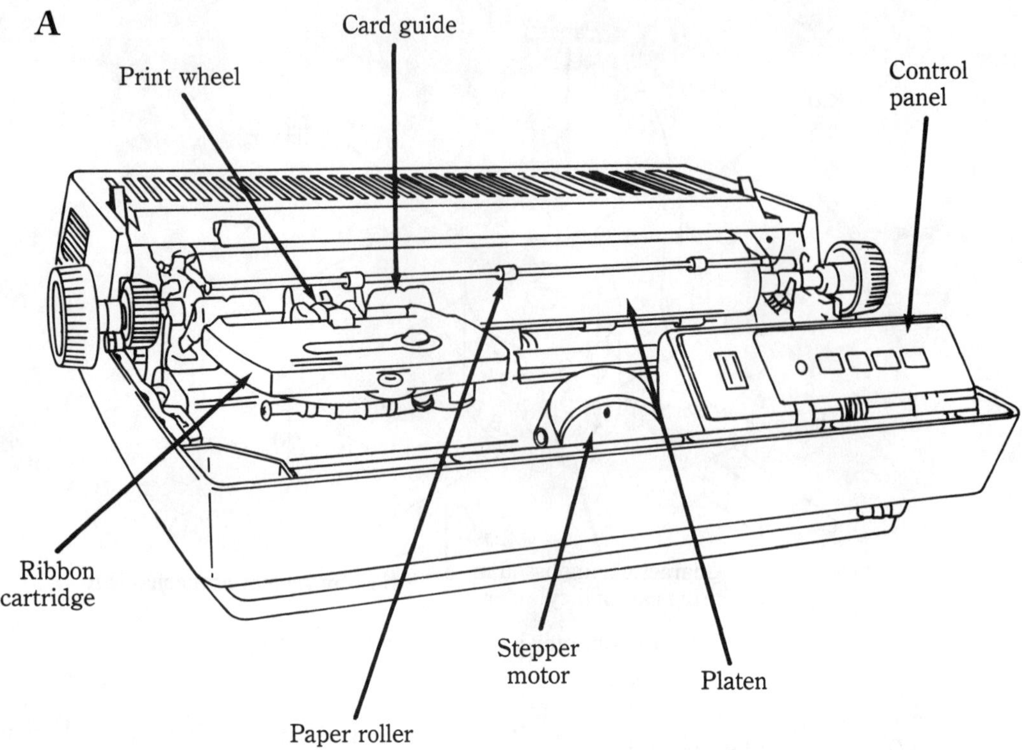

7-9 A daisy wheel printer. (A) A printer with major components. (B) A view of print wheel and ribbon cartridge area.

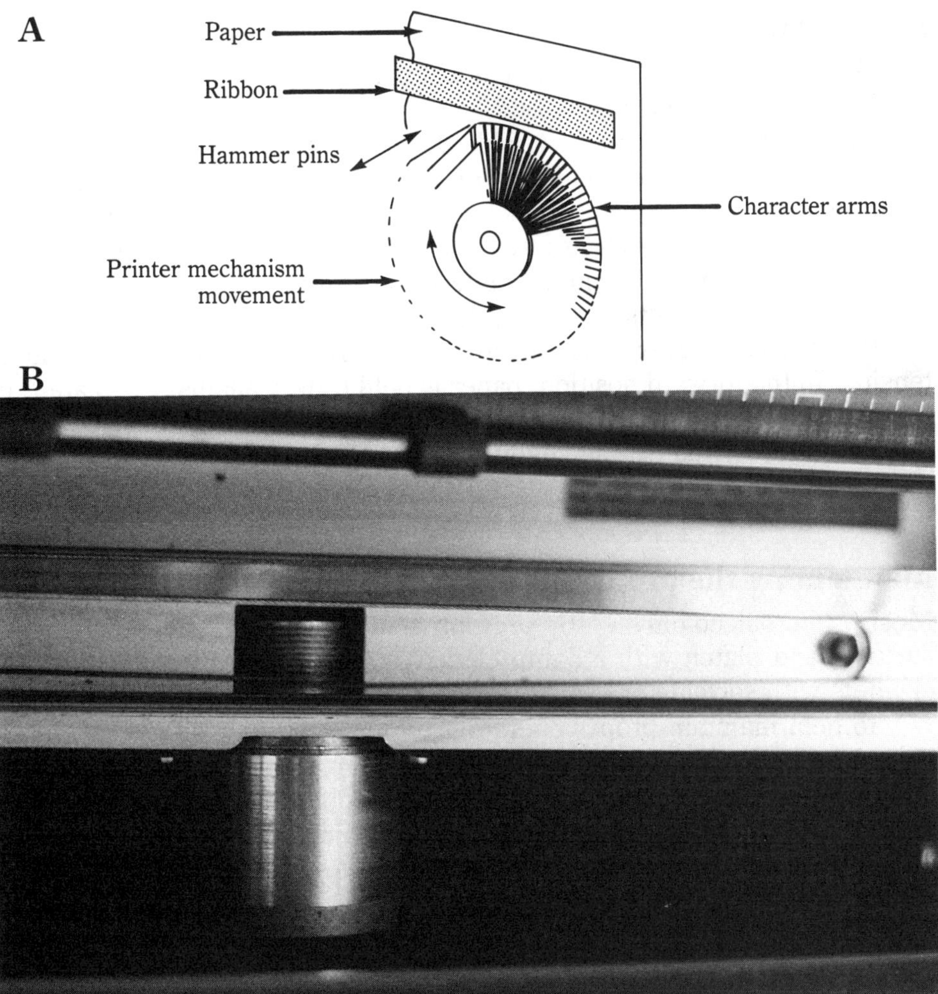

7-10   A daisy-wheel method of serial printing. (A) Hammer and print wheel method operation. (B) View of print wheel carriage stepper motor with cable drive.

something you can live with. You can always cover the unit with a noise-dampening cover.

Printer problems

Certain problems are unique for each of the previously discussed printing techniques. Line printers, for example, must be adjusted properly, or the characters will smear or misregister. Vertically moving character sets, such as drums, can vertically misregister or produce wavy lines. Horizontally moving character sets, such as bands and belts, can horizontally misregister or produce uneven spacing between the characters on a line.

Printer controls

The following controls are found in most printers; their proper operation is essential to most printer functions.

Paper bail   The *paper bail* holds the paper against the platen. Marks on the bail help you position paper on the platen and locate the horizontal printing position. The paper-thickness lever adjusts the printhead position to allow for different printing-form thickness. The lever should be close to the platen for normal printing. The lever should be farther away from the platen for thicker sheets and multicopy forms.

Paper-release lever   The *paper-release lever* controls paper that holds tension. In the forward position, paper is held tightly against the platen. In the backward position, the paper is free to be positioned or removed. With the platen knob, you can manually control the platen to insert and change the paper's vertical position.

Maintaining the printer

Most printers need only a little preventive maintenance. You can clean the surfaces and platen with a damp cloth. You should be careful to not use cleaners with solvents or excessive water.

To help maintain proper operating temperatures inside the printer, it should be kept away from extreme temperatures, such as direct sunlight and direct air flow from room heaters and air conditioners. Paper clips, coffee, matches, cold drinks, and other small objects and liquids should be kept away from the printer.

Paper loading   Select the right paper for the job and always make sure to position the paper squarely and set it tightly around the platen. Also, make sure that the paper-thickness lever is in the correct position. To remove paper from the printer, use the form-feed switch or turn the platen knob.

Printhead and ribbon cartridge replacement   Samples of early printouts can help you know when to replace both the printhead and ribbon cartridge (Fig. 7-11). Use only quality ribbon cartridges in your printer. Other cartridges might not give the same performance and could damage your printer. Store printheads and ribbon cartridges in their containers—in the same environment as the printer.

Troubleshooting dot-matrix printers

The checklist shown in Table 7-1 should be helpful in locating most printer problems. Before trying to correct the trouble, always turn off the printer.

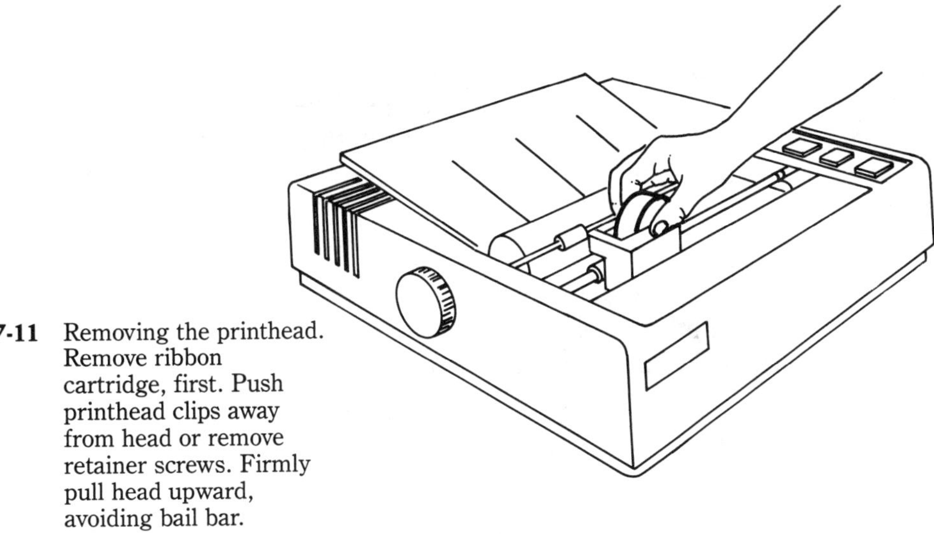

7-11   Removing the printhead. Remove ribbon cartridge, first. Push printhead clips away from head or remove retainer screws. Firmly pull head upward, avoiding bail bar.

Table 7-1.   Dot matrix printer troubleshooting

Trouble	Probable cause	Corrective action
Printer does not start when power is turned on.	Power cord not functioning	Check power cord connections; check power cord for damage.
	Power connection fault	Check internal power connections.
	Fuse open	Make sure fuse is in place. Replace fuse if open. See Fig. 7-12.
No printout.	Printer out of paper	Reload paper and press the READY button.
	Access cover	Close cover and press the READY button.
Light print.	Paper thickness lever set incorrectly.	Reset paper thickness lever to a position closer to the platen.
	Ribbon worn	Replace ribbon cartridge.
Carriage moves, but no printing.	Paper thickness lever set wrong	Reset paper thickness lever to a position closer to the platen.
	Printhead fault	Replace the printhead. Refer to Printhead Replacement.
Paper jams.	Paper path obstructed	Clear paper path.
	Paper thickness	Reset paper thickness lever to a position away from the platen.
Pinfeed paper jams.	Tractors positioned incorrectly	Release and reposition the tractors. Avoid pulling or compressing paper.

Printer confidence test

The *printer confidence test* allows you to send a message to the printer and verify that the printer received your message. The test needs you to input the following information. You can often check this information using a set-up procedure under the printer heading and make a note of the values selected before running the test.

1. Baud rate
2. Number of stop bits (1 or 2)
3. Number of bits per character (7 or 8)
4. Parity enabled/disabled, even/odd

After you enter the information, the test might request you to input your message. The message is then sent to the printer.

Printer problems

When printing ceases (or never begins), like the video output, you have three possible sources for the problem: the system board, the adapter card, or the printer itself. One of the few preliminary tests that you can accomplish, is to conduct a printer self-test to see if the printer itself is functioning properly.

Printer self-tests   Most printers provide a self-test to indicate correct operation. This self-test allows the operator to analyze problems. The self-test is usually invoked by setting a self-test switch or holding one of the printer switches, such as Line Feed or NLQ down while the printer is switched on. The printer might execute the self-test by testing ROM, RAM, and the printing capability of unit. Typical self-tests include the following:

SIGN ON   This test prints a message, such as Printer Model XXX...Self Test..., which indicates the basic printer function.

ROM TEST   This test prints the status of the ROM. The result is zero (0) if the ROM is coded correctly. A ROM BAD condition might prevent the execution of additional tests.

RAM TEST   This test prints the status of the RAM. A RAM BAD condition aborts the test.

PRINT TEST   This test is the basic self-test used in most printers. The printer will print a certain amount of repeated text, which gives a visible indication of the unit's printing capability.

Cleaning print wheels   Print wheels used with carbon-film ribbons seldom need to be cleaned. If cleaning is required, it is to best remove the print wheel and clean with Fantastik™, Formula 409™, or a similar product. You should rinse with water and dry. You should not soak the print wheel in water. Dry the print wheel quickly. Be sure that the reflective coded segments on the back or character side of the print wheel are shiny. You can use a soft cloth to clean these. When cleaning a print wheel be careful not to bend the petals.

Cleaning the platen and roller   The platen and paper rollers are made of rubber. They require periodic cleaning to cleanse and renew their surfaces for more positive friction drive. You should periodically clean the platen, paper rollers, and pressure rollers (you need to remove the platen for access to these). Use soft tissues or cloth wipers and a commercial platen cleaner. Be careful not to get platen cleaner in the unit.

Cleaning the guide   Most printers use a plastic or metal guide to hold paper flat as the printhead moves across the paper. The guide moves with the head. Usually, you will have to remove the ribbon cartridge to get at and raise the paper bail. You might be able to grasp the plastic card guide firmly on each end and pull straight up to remove the guide if it is held in place by spring clips. You can clean the guide using soft tissue or a soft cloth, Fantastik™, Formula 409™, or another commercial product.

Do not use alcohol to clean plastic print wheels or to clean the platen or other rubber parts because it hardens the surface. Periodically wiping the exterior of the printer with a soft, damp cloth will keep its appearance looking newer. Periodic wiping and dusting of the interior should be done to remove large accumulations of paper dust and other foreign matter. Lubrication is best done as the printer is reassembled; a drop of light machine oil can be placed on each bearing surface after it has been wiped clean with a soft cloth.

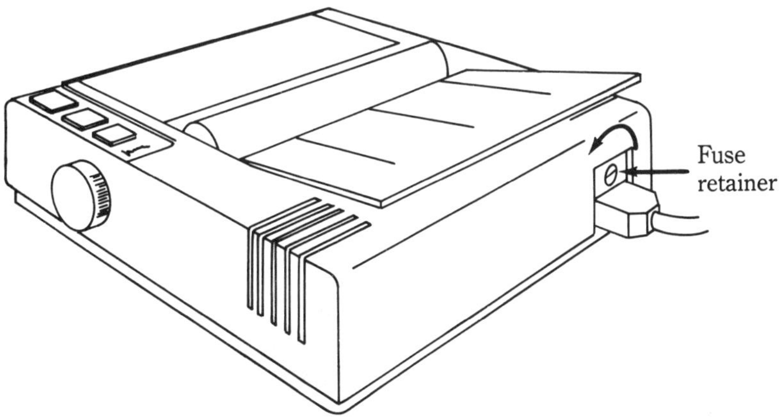

7-12   The fuse is often located next to the power cord.

Laser printers

The laser has become one of the most widely-used technological tools of the present age. *Laser* is an acronym for *Light Amplification by Stimulated Emission of Radiation*. All lasers share the following features: the frequency and phase of light are fixed, and the beam of light generated is coherent (sharply defined) and intense. The laser can use a gas, liquid, or solid to produce the light beam. The *semiconductor laser* is a type of solid laser used in computer printers. It is driven by simple control signals, has a compact size, and consumes less power than other types of lasers. In the laser printer, the laser beam is controlled by the printer signals from the computer. The main components of the laser printer are shown in Figs. 7-13, 7-14, 7-15, and 7-16.

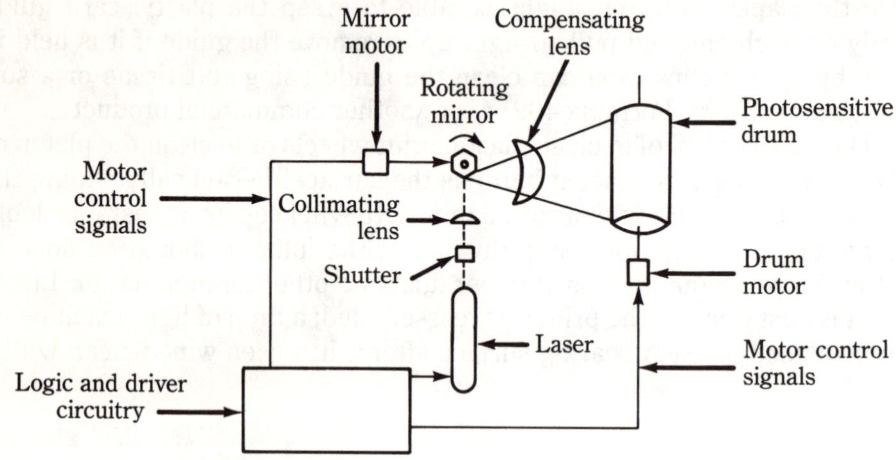

7-13   Main internal components of the laser printer.

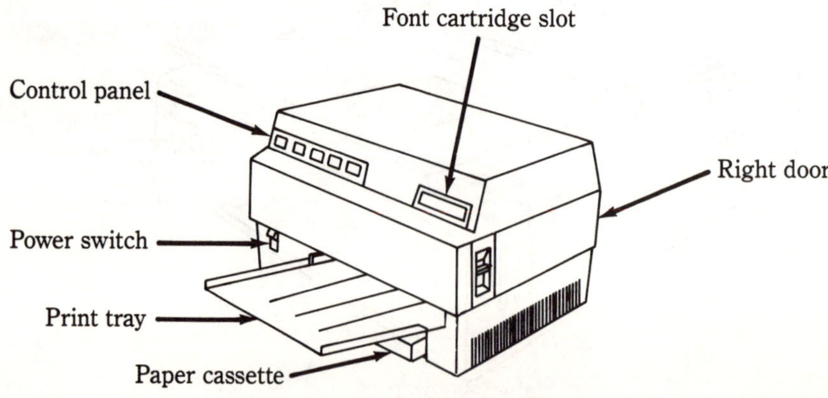

7-14   A laser printer (frontal view).

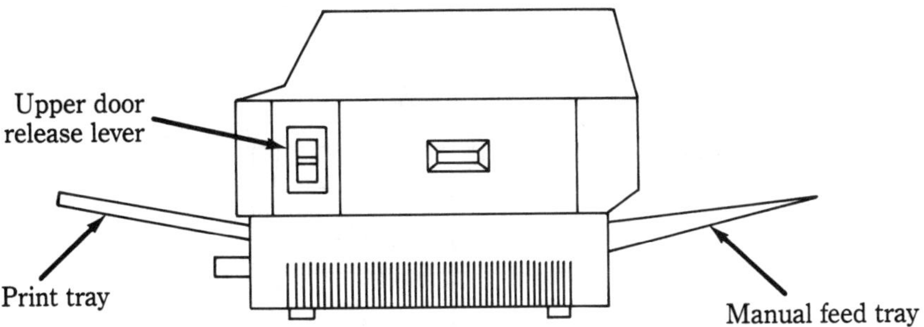

7-15 A laser printer (right side view).

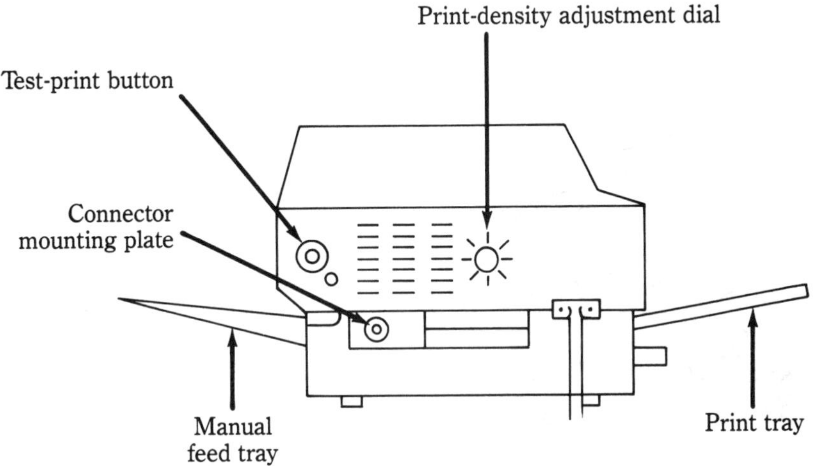

7-16 A laser printer (left side view).

Laser problems

Several types of problems are unique to laser printers. To keep print quality high, it is necessary to clean and maintain the printer.

Paper jams When paper is jammed in the printer, an error code will appear on the status display. Paper moves through the printer from right to left (Fig. 7-17). The printer will have a cassette feed area, a manual feed area, a feeder area, and a fixing assembly area, as shown.

When a jam occurs, the following procedure can be used to locate and clear it.

1. Open the unit and search for jammed paper around the fixing assembly area. Remove the paper carefully (Fig. 7-18). If no jammed paper is found, proceed to the feeder area.

2. Search for jammed paper around the feeder area, and remove it carefully (Fig. 7-19). If none is found here, proceed to the next area.

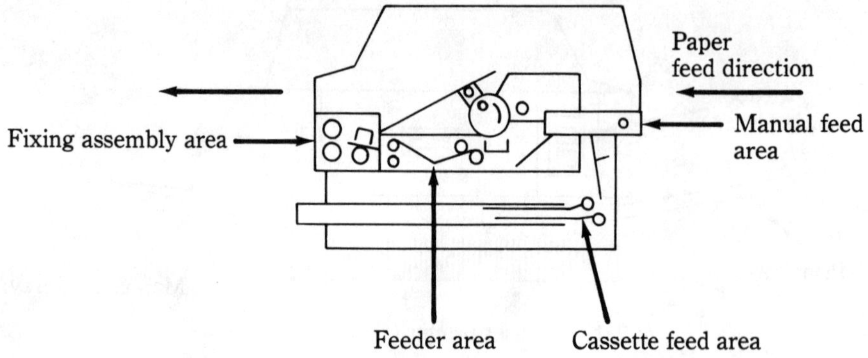

7-17   The paper path through the printer.

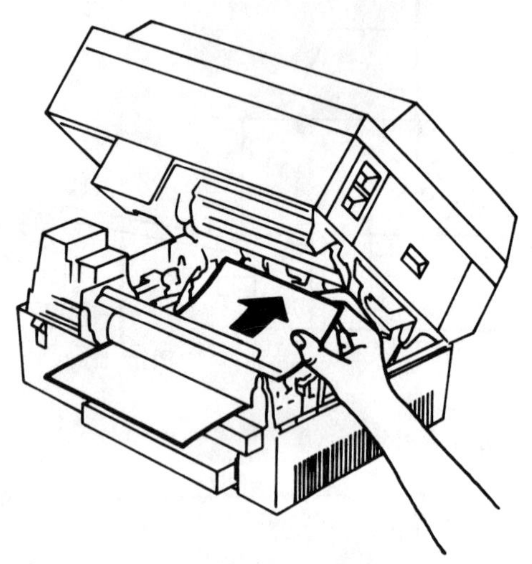

7-18   Open the unit and carefully pull any jammed paper through the fixing assembly area.

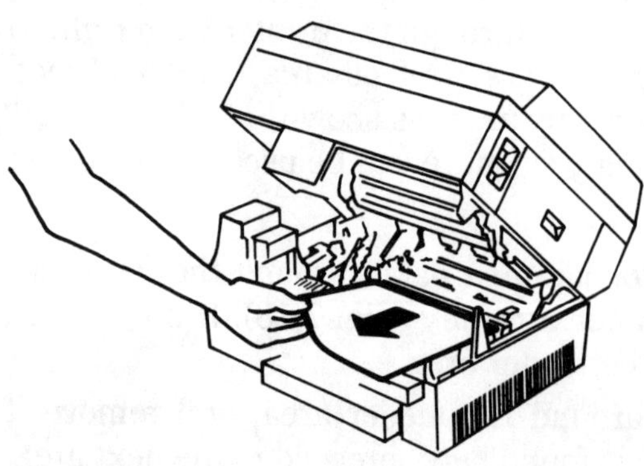

7-19   Carefully pull any jammed paper through the feeder area.

3. Open the rear door and check for jammed paper. Pull any paper out of the printer and close the rear door as shown in Fig. 7-20. If no jammed paper is found here, proceed to the paper cassette.

4. Remove the paper cassette and check it to see that the paper is placed in correctly.

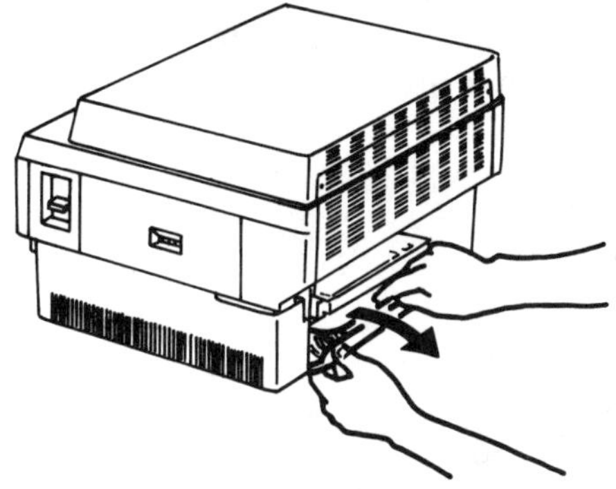

7-20 Open the rear door and pull any jammed paper through slowly.

After checking these areas, the paper jam should be cleared.

Faint printout or white stripe problems If white or light lines or stripes appear on the printout, check the print capacity indicator on the toner cartridge. If it indicates a low condition (usually red) replace the cartridge. If the indicator is not completely red, you can distribute the toner by rocking the cartridge (Fig. 7-21).

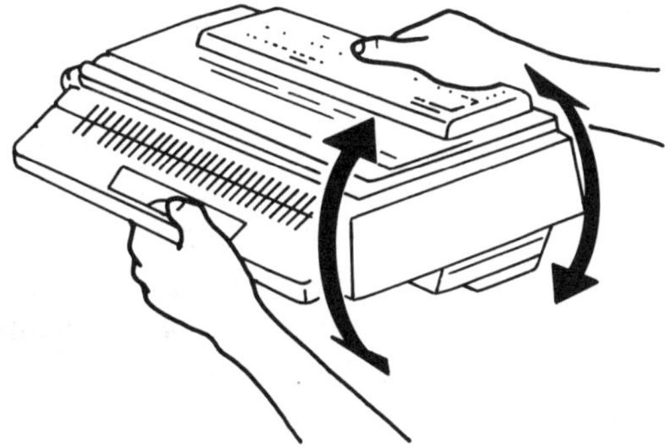

7-21 Grasp the toner cartridge with both hands and rock it gently to distribute the toner.

Moving the cartridge too vigorously can leak the toner and stain the printing. Make a few test printings to check this. If toner stains appear on the printout, the primary corona wire, transfer corona wire, or transfer guide probably need to be cleaned.

Black stripe problem If dirty stripes/toner stains appear on the print-out, it is necessary to clean each of the following parts. Be sure that the power cord is unplugged from the wall outlet before starting these cleaning operations.

To clean the primary corona wire, open the printer and remove the cartridge. The standard Cannon engine uses a special wire cleaner, which is inserted into a slot in the cartridge (next to the shutter) (Fig. 7-22). Move the wire cleaner back and forth in the slot. The special wire cleaner will displace a thin protective plastic sheet in the cartridge.

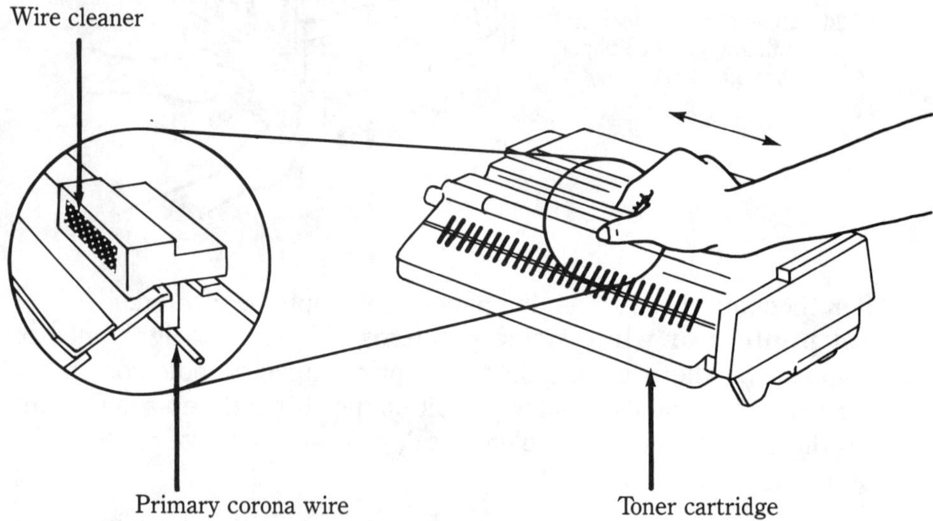

7-22 To clean the primary corona wire, insert the wire cleaner in the slot in the toner cartridge and move it back and forth.

To clean the transfer corona wire, remove the cartridge. Then, move a cotton swab up and down the corona wire carefully (Fig. 7-23). The transfer guide can be cleaned using a damp, clean cloth to wipe the transfer guide as shown in Fig. 7-24. The separation belt (Fig. 7-25) should be checked if a black line appears on one side of the printed sheet. If the front or rear of the belt is dirty, it can be cleaned with a cotton swab or a paper towel.

Separation belt replacement If the separation belt breaks, it can usually be replaced by following this procedure. Open the unit up to get at the separation belt. Open loop A on the separation belt with a screwdriver (Fig. 7-26). Hang loop A on the separation belt from the right side of the upper transfer guide. The indentation on the separation belt should be on the right side. Then, pass the separation belt over the transfer roller, and under the separation pinch roller. Hook loop B on the separation belt to the under-

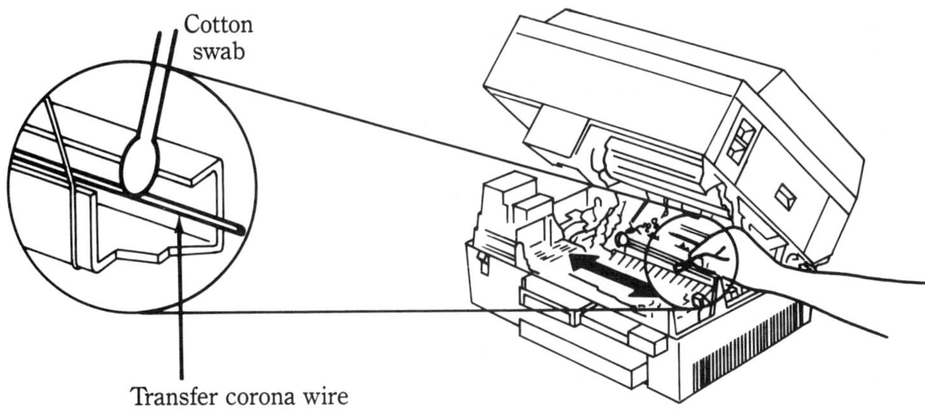

7-23 The transfer corona wire can be cleaned with a cotton swab.

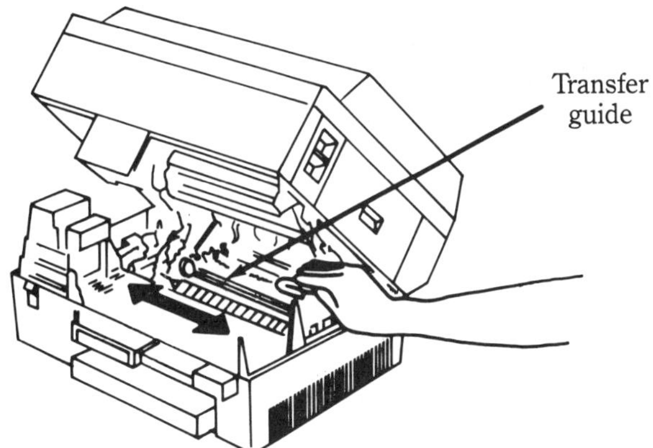

7-24 The transfer guide can be cleaned with a damp cloth.

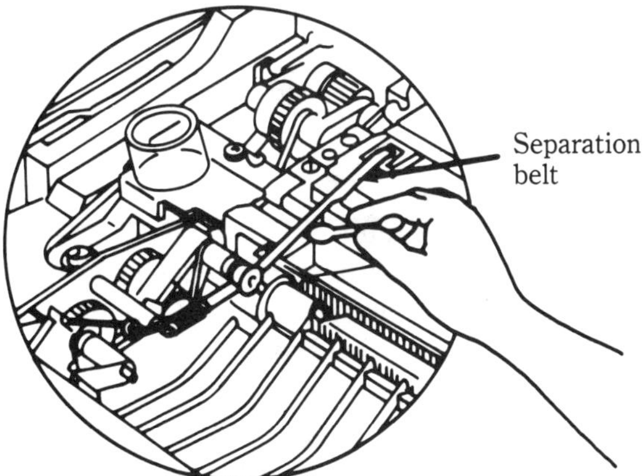

7-25 The separation belt is found on the left side of the internal mechanism. It can be cleaned with a cotton swab if it is dirty.

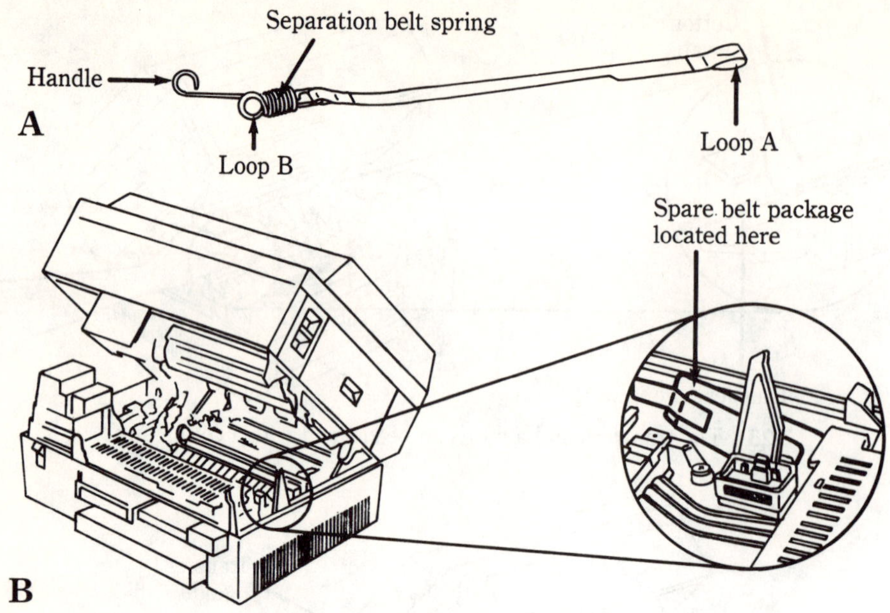

7-26   Separation belts can break, so a spare belt is usually taped inside the printer case. (A) A separation belt. (B) The spare belt location.

side of the spring suspension side of the spring suspender. The following items should be checked after installing the separation belt:

1. The indentation should be on the right-hand side.
2. Loop A should be securely hung from the upper transfer guide.
3. The belt should pass over the transfer roller.
4. The belt should pass between the separation roller and the separation pinch roller.
5. The separation belt spring should be hooked securely to the underside of the spring suspension side of the spring suspender (Fig. 7-27).

Replacing the cartridge   Determine when the cartridge needs to be replaced by looking at the color of the print capacity indicator, which is visible through the window. As the drum rotates, the color of the indicator will change to indicate the usable service life of the cartridge (Fig. 7-28).

Each cartridge contains enough toner to make about 3,000 letter-size prints with 5% toner image in the effective image area. If many originals with high-toner image ratios are printed, toner is used up more quickly, and white stripes can appear on prints before the printing capacity indicator turns red.

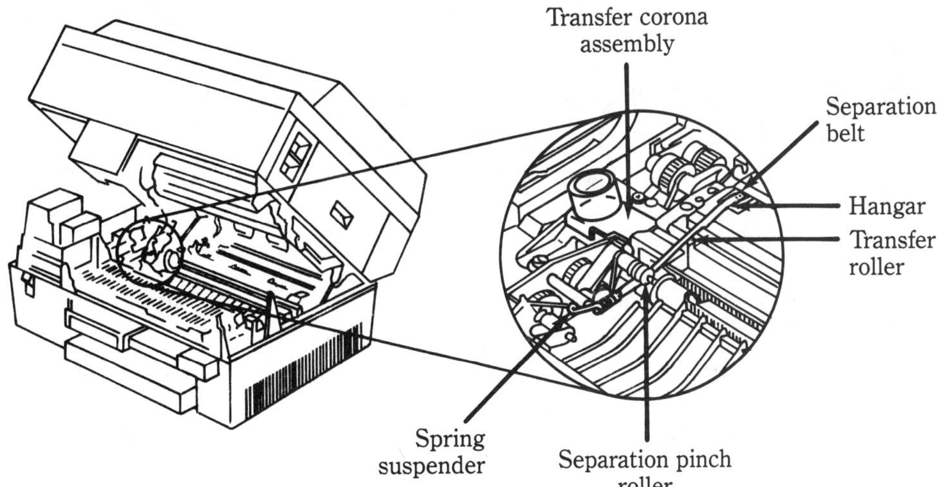

7-27 Installing the separation belt.

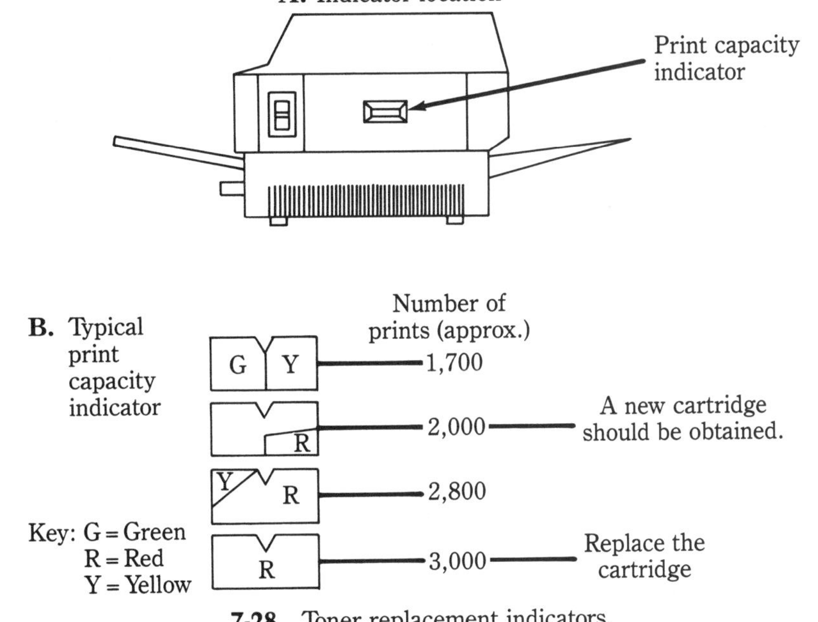

7-28 Toner replacement indicators.

The number of prints is based on an assumed average of 4.5 drum revolutions per print. The fixing roller cleaner felt in the fixing assembly should be replaced and the transfer corona wires cleaned with a cotton swab when the cartridge is replaced.

Storing and handling cartridges   Avoid storing cartridges under the following conditions:

1. Direct sunlight, near windows or outdoors.
2. High temperatures and humidity.
3. Areas where the air is dusty.
4. Do not leave cartridges inside a car for an extended length of time.
5. Areas where corrosive gases or salty air is present.

You should not stand cartridges on end or turn them upside down. The caution label or the handle should always be up. Do not try to modify or disassemble the cartridges or open the drum protective shutter. Do not expose cartridges to direct sunlight or light of more than 1,500 lux. Do not use cartridges for at least an hour after moving them from a cold environment to a warm one. Always use your cartridges before their stated expiration date. The copy quality could deteriorate if you use outdated cartridges.

The following list of typical laser printer problems could occur:

Problem	Solution or recheck procedure
Paper out	Install the cassette after you refill it.
Printer power off	Close the unit correctly and press the Online switch.
Paper jam	Remove the paper causing the jam and press the Online switch.
Cartridge not installed	Install the cartridge and press the Online switch.
Request for manual paper feed	Insert the correct size of paper into the manual paper feeder.
Request for font cartridge setting	Reset the font cartridge and press the Online switch.
Page buffer overflow	Reset the error using the Error Skip switch and press the Online switch.
Print overrun	Reset the error using the Error Skip switch and press the Online switch.
Receiving buffer	Press the Error Skip switch and press the Online switch.
Download overflow	Reset using the Error Skip switch and press the Online switch.
Paint memory overflow	Reset using the Error Skip switch and press the Online switch.
Vector graphic reject	Cancel job.

Work memory over	Reset using the Error Skip switch and press the Online switch.
Communication error	Reset using the Error Skip switch and press the Online switch.
Print check request	Reset using the Error Skip switch and press the Online switch.
Fixing assembly fault	Turn off the power switch, wait for 10 minutes and turn it on again.
Beam defect fault	Reset the Error Skip switch.
Laser temperature control fault	Turn off the power switch, wait for 10 minutes and turn it on again.
Main motor fault	Reset using the Error Skip switch.
Printer control	Reset using the Error Skip switch.
Bus error	Power reset.
Program ROM check	Power reset.
Built-in font ROM	Power reset.
Dynamic RAM error	Power reset.
Scan buffer error	Power reset.
Dynamic RAM control fault	Power reset.

Printer communications protocols

Communications protocols are needed to prevent print buffer overflow when print data is being received faster than the printer can empty the print buffer. A communications protocol is usually needed at baud rates above 300, and in some cases at 300 baud and below.

RS-232-C printer communications   Three protocols are commonly used for printer control. These are the DC1/DC3, Printer Ready, and ETX/ACK protocols. In addition to printer buffer control, the DC1/DC3 and Printer Ready protocols can also be used to respond to error conditions.

ETX/ACK protocol   When the ETX/ACK protocol is used, the computer is required to transmit a string of data that is smaller than the printer's buffers size, followed by the control code, ETX. The computer will then stop transmitting. The printer withdraws the data from the buffer at a rate that is determined by the print speed of the printer until the last character, ETX, is removed. Then, the printer generates the control code, ACK, which is sent back to the computer. The computer will start transmitting data again on receipt of the ACK code. This process is used to protect data from being lost as a result of buffer overflow. When this protocol is used, the computer must keep the data string transmitted from exceeding the capacity of the printer buffer.

DC1/DC3 protocol In this protocol, when the computer begins to transmit a data string, the printer responds with the DC3 character when the printer buffer is almost full (usually within 64 bytes) or when the printer is in check. This protocol requires the computer to monitor the printer for an indication of printer status. The printer will transmit the control code, DC3, when its buffer is close to being full. The computer will stop transmitting at this point while the printer works on the data in its buffer. When the buffer is almost empty, the printer will transmit a DC1 code, which asks the computer to resume transmitting data. A DC3 code will also be transmitted if the printer is in check. Either of these conditions will cause a NAK control code to be transmitted following the DC3 code. The printer must be in check or a DC1 will be sent to the computer by the printer when the printer buffer is nearly empty.

Printer ready protocol The PTR/RDY protocol uses the +DTR interface line. This line will go low (false) when there is a printhead or wheel restore error or when the printer buffer is nearly full. The DTR signal will go true (high) when the printer buffer is nearly empty and when all other conditions are corrected. Table 7-2 shows the RS-232C interface signals that are typically used for the printer operation along with the telco and CCITT designations and the usual pin assignments for the DB 25 connector.

Table 7-2.   RS-232-C serial interface signals

Signal name	Telephone designation	Pin (DB 25)	CCITT designation
Protective ground	AA	1	101
Transmit data	BA	2	103
Receive data	BB	3	104
Request to send	CA	4	105
Data set ready	CC	6	107
Signal ground	AB	7	102
Data terminal ready	CD	20	108

Centronics parallel communications protocol The Centronics printer interface is an 8-bit parallel connection with relatively simple handshake signals. This interface does not support device addresses so that only one device can be connected to the host output port. The typical timing chart (Fig. 7-29) will help you troubleshoot the timing relationships of the hand-

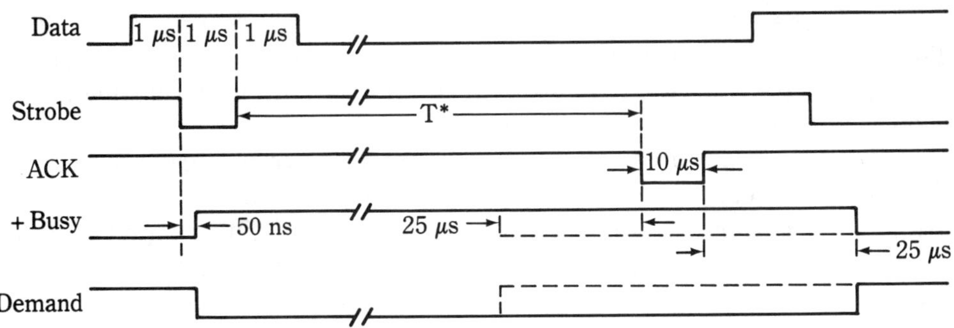

*Depends on the program loop time.

7-29 Typical Centronics timing.

shake signals, which serve as the communications protocol for printers that operate with this type of interface.

In operation, when the printer is ready, the BUSY signal is low. The computer places the data on the data bus and sends a pulse to the Strobe line. The BUSY signal goes high and the computer reads in the latched data, places the data in the print queue and outputs an ACK pulse. The BUSY signal then goes low after the ACK pulse. The DEMAND signal is the inverse of the BUSY signal. The printer will activate the Fault line if the printer detects a printhead or print-wheel restore error and is in a check condition.

The following is a description of the Centronics signals:

Signal	**Function**
STROBE	This starts the reading of data, it is initiated by the computer.
ACK	This indicates that the printer has received data and it is ready to accept the next data.
BUSY	This indicates that the printer cannot receive data.
PE	This indicates that the printer is out of paper.
SELECT	This indicates that the printer is online.
DEMAND	The inverse of the BUSY signal.
INPUT PRINT	A pulse from the computer that initializes the printer.
FAULT	This indicates that the printer is in the error mode.

STROBE is a signal line from the computer that indicates to the printer that the data lines have valid information on them. The data should be valid at least one microsecond before the negative-true STROBE is asserted. Data must be held valid at least one microsecond after STROBE is negated. The length of time STROBE is asserted can range from 1 to 500 microseconds. The trailing edge of STROBE causes the printer to assert ACK. In Centronics printers, the delay between the negation of STROBE and the assertion of ACK is on the order of 2 to 10 microseconds.

These times are for a normal data transfer. Centronics calls the hand-shaking sequence: Normal-Data-Input Timing (Fig. 7-30). For Centronics printers, normal transfers occur when the printer is filling an internal line buffer and is not printing or performing some other operation. If one of these operations is being performed, a BUSY condition exists.

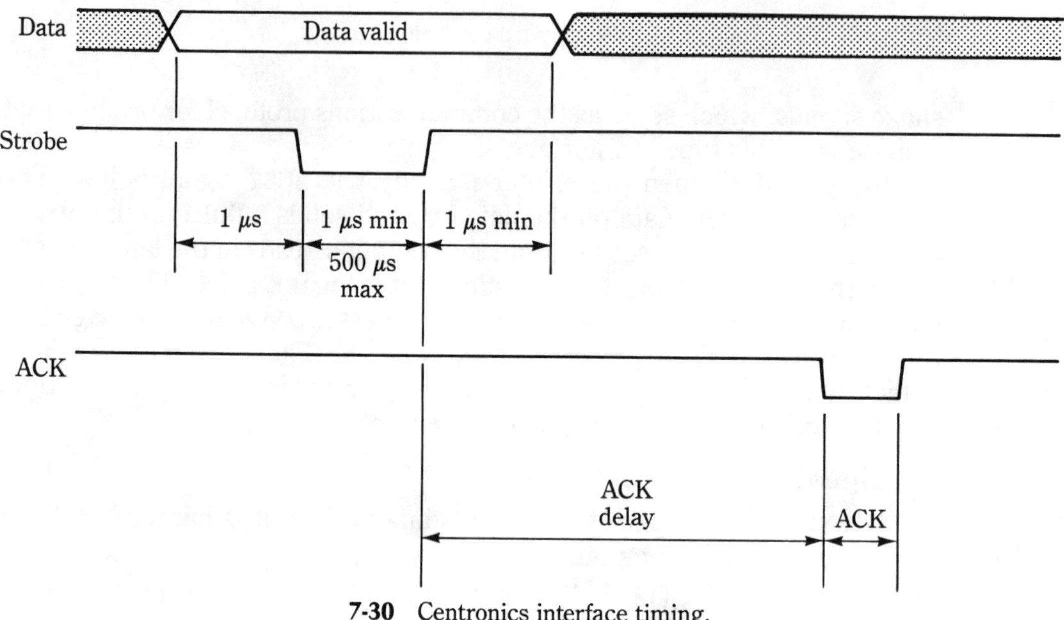

7-30   Centronics interface timing.

A BUSY condition occurs when the printer is given a command to print the line in the print buffer (carriage return), or when a vertical tab, form-feed, line feed, delete, bell, select, or deselect character is sent. The receipt of one of these special characters causes the printer to perform some mechanical operation that takes considerably more time than a few micro-seconds. In these cases, the handshake changes to BUSY condition timing.

The handshake mechanism during a BUSY condition is as follows. After STROBE is negated, BUSY is asserted instead of ACK. This signal indicates that the printer is BUSY and cannot complete the handshake until it is fin-ished. Centronics printers can be BUSY for durations of 2 to over 300 milli-seconds.

After negating BUSY, the printer asserts the negative-true ACK line.

This occurs after a few microseconds and ACK is asserted for a few microseconds. The busy-condition timing ends with this negation of ACK, as does the normal-data-input timing. Figure 7-31 illustrates the busy-condition timing for the Centronics parallel interface.

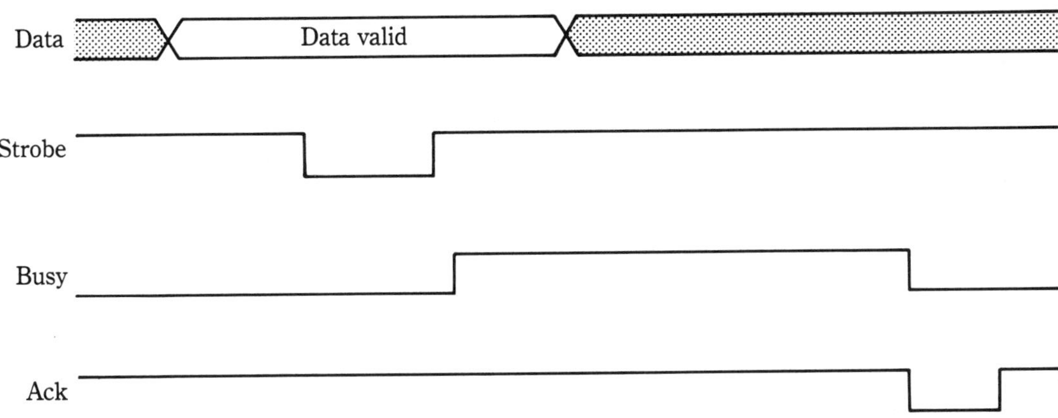

7-31 The timing diagram for the Centronics parallel interface-BUSY-condition timing.

Some printers do not use BUSY because both normal and BUSY protocols end with an ACK. Other printers use a switch to implement either ACK or BUSY. The switch allows the end user to decide which handshake signal is used.

Some printers that use the Centronics interface require the data to be valid for 0.5 microsecond before STROBE is asserted and to be held valid for 0.5 microsecond after STROBE is negated. The STROBE needs only to be asserted for 0.5 microsecond. These times are all half of the original Centronics specification. Any computer interface that is designed for a Centronics printer can also drive this printer with some margin. The BUSY and ACK signals might also be a little different.

BUSY can be activated on the falling edge of STROBE instead of on the rising edge, and negated after ACK is negated. The original Centronics specification requires that ACK not be asserted until BUSY is negated, if a BUSY condition exists.

Some interfaces for Centronics printers assume that the rising edge of ACK is the end of the transfer. This is not quite right, because the negation of BUSY will follow the negation of ACK by another 5 microseconds. If the computer responds to the completion of one transfer cycle with another after 5 microseconds, this printer interface will work with Centronics printers—even though the signal timings are different.

Table 7-3 lists the conductor signals for Centronics interface printers. All of the signals are not used by all printers—especially the newer

Table 7-3. Pinout for the Centronics parallel interface

Signal name	Positive-or negative-true	Signal pin number	Associated ground wire pin number
Data Strobe	Negative	1	19
Data 1	Positive	2	20
Data 2	Positive	3	21
Data 3	Positive	4	22
Data 4	Positive	5	23
Data 5	Positive	6	24
Data 6	Positive	7	25
Data 7	Positive	8	26
Data 8	Positive	9	27
Acknowledge	Negative	10	28
Busy	Positive	11	29
Paper out	Positive	12	None
Select printer	Positive	13	None
Signal ground	–	14	None
OSCXT (OSC out)	–	15	None
Signal ground	–	16	None
Chassis ground	–	17	None
+5 V supply	–	18	None
Input prime (Printer reset)	Negative	31	30
Fault	Negative	32	None
Line count	Negative	34	35

printers. Figure 7-32 shows the Centronics 36-pin connector at the rear of the dot-matrix printer. Next to the connector are two dip switches that are used for setting printer parameters. Figure 7-33 shows a typical parallel printer port card, which provides the Centronics interface signals.

Data meters

Data meters are useful if you are trying to get one computer or peripheral to talk to another. They provide most of the information you need to know about RS-232 data transmission settings, but cost less than the more expensive data communications analyzers. They can be used to test both DCE and DTE devices. Some can generate test patterns and receive data transmissions to give you baud rate, word length, parity, and stop bits. Single-button operation lets you select from menu options, such as Read, Parameter Scan, Parameter Selection, and Print.

1. *Read* can be used to determine the serial protocol being sent from the RS-232 device and displays.

2. *Parameter Scan* sends protocol combinations to the device being

tested. It generates random characters until the correct protocol is found. The correct parameter settings are then printed out.

3. *Parameter Selection* allows the selection of serial protocol for output.

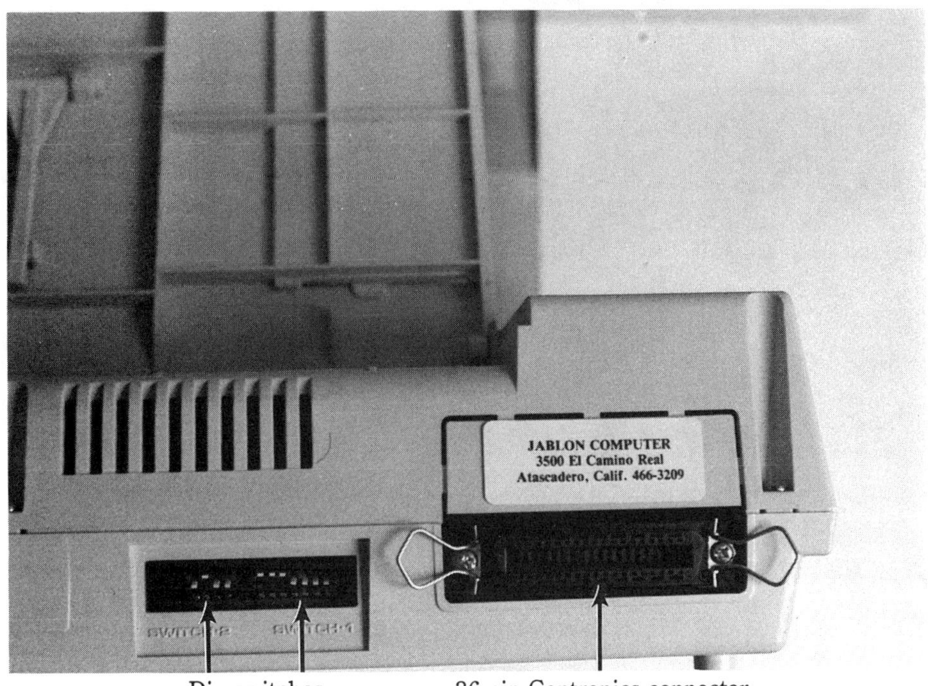

7-32   The rear of dot-matrix printer showing 36-pin Centronics connector and dip switches for changing printer parameters.

Printer exerciser/testers

Printer exerciser/testers exercise and test parallel printers. They are designed as field diagnostic instruments that go beyond the printer's self-test. They can be used to identify problems on site and can be used to test the most popular dot-matrix and daisy wheel printers or any printer that can emulate one of these. Most testers use the parallel (Centronics) interface and work independently, in place of the computer, so that the printer does not need to be connected to any other device while under test. Thus, it is useful for field testing as well as depot repair.

LED status indicators are used to simulate printer conditions, such as BUSY, paper out, or a fault. A bank of dip switches is used to set up the configuration of the different printers and for special conditions, such as

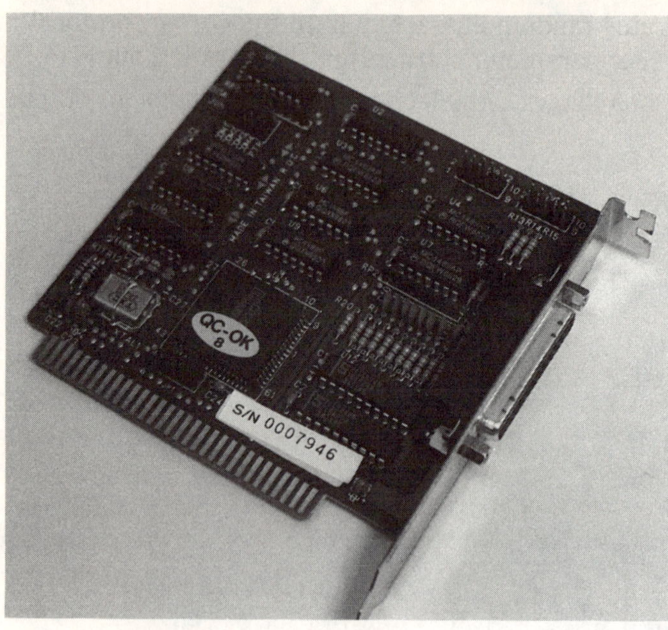

7-33 Parallel printer port card for providing Centronics interface signals.

handshaking, autoLF, force carriage, and wide carriage. The following tests can be performed: paper drift, platen roll, carriage movement, form feed, and special functions, such as underlining, bold and pitch changes, head movement, daisy wheel servo motoring, daisy wheel characters printing, and dot-matrix printheads checking. It also provides the ability to send continuous ASCII characters and test for dot-matrix pin firing with each pin individually.

8
Network problems

What is a LAN?

A *Local area network (LAN)* lets you connect PCs and other devices so that you can share their resources. With a LAN, you can share files or disk storage. You can communicate with other people on the LAN by electronic mail and reduce or eliminate the need for letters and memos on paper. You can also share peripherals, such as printers and CD-ROM drives.

Local Area Networks are limited to a confined area, usually a building, although they can run to nearby buildings. LANs generally use electrical cables, but other wider networks use microwave, telephone, or satellite communications.

Types of LANs

LANs can be distributed (peer-to-peer) or centralized. Both types can use file servers. These are PCs that coordinate access to shared files. The file servers store files and process all incoming requests for files. *Centralized LANs* generally use dedicated file servers. These PCs are committed to central storage and retrieval. They only perform file serving tasks and cannot be used for other tasks, such as for data processing. Processing occurs at the local workstation. Dedicated file servers require a fast CPU, a large hard disk, and plenty of RAM.

Distributed networks, in contrast, allow any or all of the networked PCs to share resources. As a user, you can publish your resources for other users to access. In a centralized LAN, the only shared resources are on the server's hard disk. For example, suppose you have two PCs (#1 and #2) and file server (#3). PC #1 can access the file server (#3), but it cannot access PC #2. In a distributed LAN, PC #1 and PC #2 can access each other's hard disk.

Although distributed LANs can also contain dedicated file servers, their file servers are typically nondedicated. A nondedicated file server can be used as both a server and a workstation. A PC can also be designated to coordinate requests for service to a printer or other device. A PC designated as a print server acts as the conduit for all print jobs. Like file servers, print servers can be dedicated or nondedicated.

Centralized-server LANs are often used for heavy traffic or security reasons. Distributed LANs are usually less expensive and are used on smaller networks.

LAN components

A LAN requires both hardware and software. The *network operating system (NOS)* coordinates the LAN's hardware activity, just as DOS coordinates the hardware activity on an individual PC. The NOS intercepts the data you enter at your PC and passes it along.

The NOS does not replace the PC's regular operating system. The individual PCs will still use DOS as their operating system to run applications at the local PC. The NOS is the bridge to the local PC to the network. LANs require additional hardware. The following is a summary of LAN-specific hardware components.

Network interface cards (NIC)

The *network interface card (NIC)*, which is also called a *network adapter* or *LAN board*, is installed in one of the PC's expansion slots. The NIC provides the connection between the PC and the cabling system. It works with the network software and allows the PC to communicate on the network.

The cabling system

Cables are necessary to hook up the *nodes*, which are the individual PCs, in most cases, although any device can be a node. The cabling system provides the path for data through the network. The several types of cabling systems depend on the type of network used.

A working LAN is more than hardware and software. *Protocols* and *topologies* are other vital LAN components, which also affect how LANs work. Protocols are sets of rules that govern how LANs communicate and topologies are the actual physical layout, the way the PCs are hooked up to each other.

Network technologies can be grouped into three basic types: PBX, cable television broadband, and the baseband types. PBX is most suitable for terminal-computer networking.

Broadband networks *Broadband networks* use cable television technology to provide up to 400 MHz of bandwidth. These different network technologies can coexist, with each serving a different set of needs in the organization. Interfaces are available between the various technologies. Broadband technology supports tree and bus configurations, and uses single or dual 75-Ω coaxial cable. The different devices or user groups that are connected to the network are assigned frequency ranges, called *bands*.

These networks provide the high bandwidth necessary to support hundreds of voice, video, and data channels within the network. Broadband is especially suitable for facilities with a number of buildings in a campus-like environment. The broadband networks, with their large bandwidths and high transfer rates, can support most types of communication, and allow multiple data channels for data and video.

Broadband local networks offer the highest bandwidth capacity, but they are also the most costly for initial implementation—even though the technology is based upon community antenna television hardware. Broadband networks are cost-effective for users with a high volume of voice, video, and data communications. All broadband local networks require separate transmit and receive paths for bidirectional operation.

PBX networks *PBX-based local networks* generally use star or tree configurations with in-place wiring as the signaling medium. These networks are suitable for installations that have been renting telephone equipment. The PBX acts like a large automated switching matrix. Time-division sampling techniques are used to sample each conversation and convert the analog signal into a digital representation. By synchronizing the paths of the digital signals from the various extensions, the PBX establishes a virtual circuit connection.

Microcomputers connected in a PBX network can be switched to a local host computer, another local microcomputer acting as a file server, or an outward-dial trunk on the public switched telephone network. PBX local networks are best suited to low-speed and low-volume traffic, such as communicating word processors, communicating copiers, microcomputers, interactive minicomputers, terminals, and printers.

Baseband networks *Baseband networks* are generally used for a small population of microcomputer workstations. The microcomputers are typically provided with baseband transceivers in the form of expansion boards. Baseband local networks allow a mix of more types of traffic and applications than is possible with PBX networks. The cost of baseband technology is similar to that of broadband technology, depending upon the data rates and station configuration. They are limited in maximum cable distances, and have less growth capacity than broadband networks.

Baseband local networks use a time-division scheme to apportion the single stream of high-speed digital bits among the users. The network typically uses a ring topology. Telephone wiring supports only a star topology, which is rarely used for baseband networks.

Access methods

The different access methods include token-passing, and the different versions of carrier-sense multiple access (CSMA): collision detection (CSMA/CD) and collision avoidance (CSMA/CA). The CSMA methods are best used for networks with an aggregate network utilization of less than 30 percent, and device utilization of between 10 and 40 percent. Carrier-sense multiple-access local networks are best for asynchronous applications and should not be used for synchronous communications applications higher than 30 percent, or for supporting digitized voice applications mixed with any type of data traffic.

Token-passing access is used for applications with use rates greater than 30 percent. Token passing is not sufficient when a small group of devices is highly utilized in a network.

Token passing origin The expression "token passing ring" originated on British railroads in the 19th century. On single sections of track in which trains travelled both directions, a token was needed to switch the track from one direction to the other. The token was a lead block about four inches on a side that contained the insignia of the railway company. It had to be physically put into the switch for the direction to be changed.

Once the signal was switched, the signalman would put the token in a canvas bag. The bag was then hung from a large brass ring, the token passing ring, which itself hung off a pole next to the track. As the train driver passed, he stuck his arm through the ring, taking the ring and token. Upon reaching the end of the track section, he handed the token over to the next signalman, who would reverse the track with the token and then hang it back on the ring for the next driver.

Novell NetWare *Novell NetWare* includes a proprietary network as well as a software operating environment, which is used on top of other vendors' local networks. The NetWare/S-Net is a star-based baseband network that connects up to 24 microcomputers using dual twisted-pair cable (Fig. 8-1).

IBM PC network *IBM's PC Network* is a broadband network that uses one frequency channel for the transmit signals, and a second frequency channel for the receive signals. The network uses the CSMA/CD technique. The IBM PC Network allows IBM microcomputers to be networked

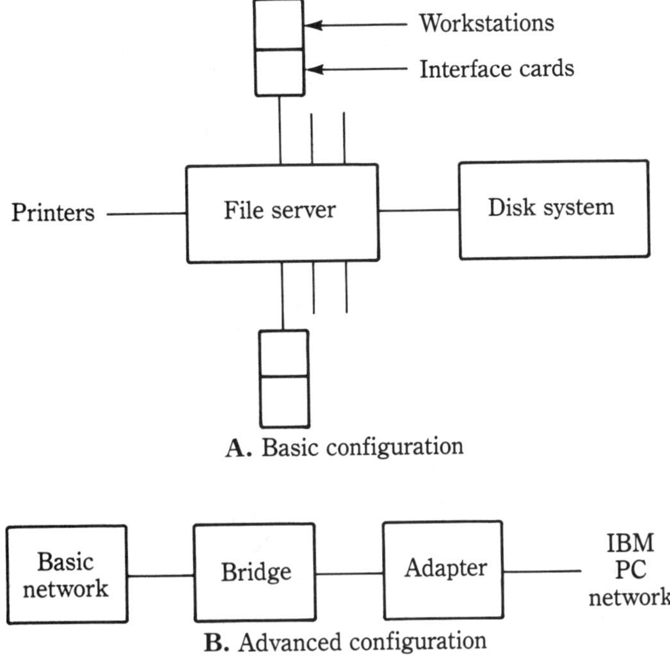

8-1 Novell Software/S-Network

together, with an AT acting as a shared file server as well as a stand-alone device (Fig. 8-2). Devices that act as file servers or have shared printers attached to them must have a hard disk. Other microcomputers need only a floppy disk drive because they use the network as a virtual hard disk.

AT&T ISN *AT&T Information Systems ISN* is an office communications architecture that is based on twisted-pair wiring. The network uses AT&T's Premises Distribution System (PDS) as the signaling medium. PDS can support voice, data, video, and facsimile. PDS can be used with almost any PBX switch product. An adapter on the ISN packet controller supports IBM synchronous communications (Fig. 8-3).

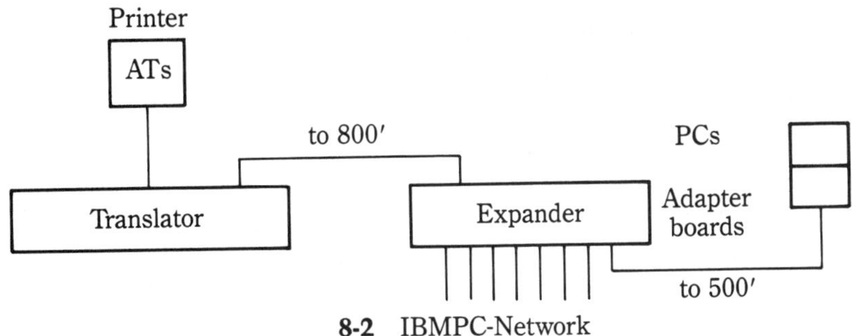

8-2 IBMPC-Network

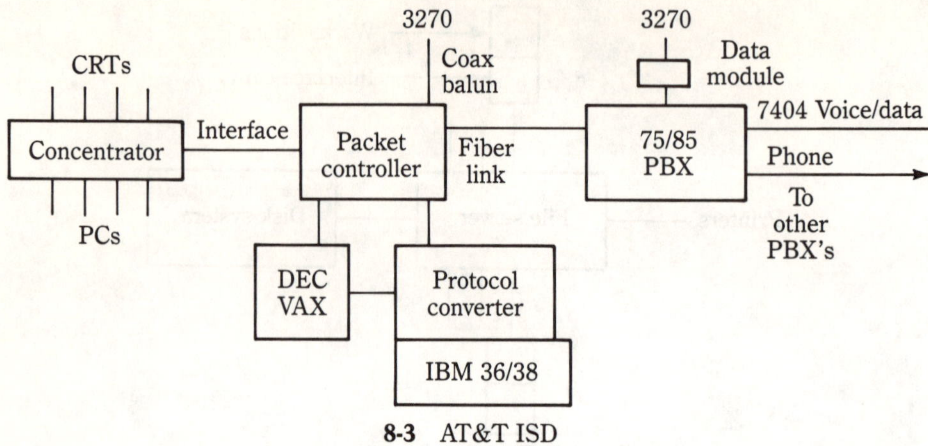

8-3 AT&T ISD

Arcnet *Arcnet (Attached Resource Computer),* is a token-passing bus network. A token determines who has access to the media. Only the PC holding the token can broadcast onto the cable. Arcnet is usually a physical star, but it can be a physical bus.

Every PC on the network is numbered sequentially. The token passes incrementally from PC to PC, by number. When it reaches the last PC in order, the token returns to the beginning and forms a logical ring. To transmit data or a token, each PC broadcasts its data out onto the network. The data moves to every PC. Only the PC that is next to receive the token or to whom the data is addressed can listen to the broadcast.

Arcnet cards The *Arcnet card* consists of four sections. The controller implements the Arcnet protocols and controls access to the card's packet buffer. It also decodes addresses and acknowledges packet reception. A transceiver retimes the signal so that the controller knows when to accept the data. The third component (called the *hybrid*), moves data to and from the cable to the card. It converts the cable's analog signal to the card's digital signal. An impedance transceiver is needed for bus topologies. The other component is the packet buffer, which holds 2K. It can hold up to four packets of information at any one time. When data is received by an Arcnet card, the hybrid action converts the analog signal to a digital signal. The signal is retimed and sent to the controller chip.

With these actions completed, the controller can operate on the packet. Arcnet packets have less than 512 bytes of data. The first four or five bytes are overhead. They contain the ID of the sender, the ID of the receiver, the length of the information, and a protocol identifier that identifies the type of network operating system. The controller strips away the preliminary data and leaves the message's text. The text is shipped off to the packet buffer for temporary storage.

After storing the data, the controller posts an interrupt to the CPU. The interrupt notifies the host of the packet's reception. It requests permission to move the data from the card to the host's memory. When permission is granted, the data is moved into the host's memory, where it is processed.

Arcnet LANs are easy to install because a few configuration rules exist. Workstations need to be within 2,000 feet of the hub, but daisy chaining the hubs extends the distance between nodes to four miles. The thin coax, RG-62, is easy to work with and twisted-pair cards make Arcnet even easier to install. When a cable fault occurs, it is easier to isolate a problem than with a bus or with ring topology. Most Arcnet cards come with diagnostic lights. See Table 8-1 for a summary of LAN technologies and characteristics.

Data recovery

Data from a crashed server disk can often be recovered using an outside service. These firms generally perform data recovery along with rebuilding disks in a clean room facility. Many of these firms handle DOS, NetWare, and other network operating systems.

A typical problem that can occur with NetWare disks, include *controller card failure*, where the card (because of SFT NetWare's disk mirroring feature) writes data improperly to the first drive and the same improper data gets written to the second drive. In this case, the controller card must be repaired or replaced and the affected directories must be rebuilt. If the

Table 8-1.   LAN technology

	Ethernet (IEEE 802.3) thick net standard ethernet	ARCnet (802.4 modified)	Token ring (802.5)
Speed	10 Mbps	2.5 Mbps	4 Mbps
Media access method	CSMA/CD	Modified token passing	Token passing
Topology	bus	Star or bus	Ring
Cabling	standard ethernet (thick cable)	RG-62/U (Coax) or twisted pair	IBM type 1 (AMP) or IBM type 3 (UTP)
Max. nodes per segment	100	255	
Max. distance per segment	500m/segment	2000 ft	300m station to MAU (Multi-station Access Unit) 200m MAU to MAU
Typical NICs (Network Interface Cards)	8-bit 8K SRAM 16-bit 16K SRAM	Coax star Coax bus Twisted pair	MAU

master boot record is destroyed, the boot record must be rebuilt byte by byte.

In some cases, NetWare's Vrepair utility can attempt to rewrite data improperly. A disk running SFT NetWare will crash because of the redirect area filling. Sometimes when Vrepair is run on these disks, it has destroyed the directories and file allocation tables. Vrepair should only be used for small disks of no more than 50M bytes.

Other hardware problems can be solved by replacing the interface board (in the drive) or the controller card. If the stepper motor has burnt out, it must be repaired or replaced before the data can be retrieved. If the heads have truly crashed into the surface of the platter, iron-oxide particles will be removed from the platter, physically destroying data. However, if a crashed drive is quickly put out of service, it is still possible that some or most of the data can be retrieved.

Ontrack network utilities

Several disk management utilities are offered by Ontrack Computer Systems. The *Disk Manager-N* is a disk installation software package for Novell NetWare-based LANs. It allows you to install a nonstandard disk subsystem under NetWare. There can be a considerable savings over the expense of a Novell-compatible drive.

Using Novell's Compsurf formatting utility, a 117M disk can require over 30 hours to format. Using Disk Manager-N, the process can be done in 75 minutes. A 72M drive can require over 20 hours with NetWare; Disk Manager-N can complete it in less than one hour. Compsurf does not retry on soft errors, and it needs to be sure that it has found all of the bad sectors during installation. The Ontrack package uses retries. It also allows you to create custom disk partitions to meet specific requirements and to select an interleave factor that optimizes the performance of the software that operates from each partition.

Another Ontrack package for NetWare users is *Netutils*, which is designed for maintenance and data recovery. The program allows you to scan all data on both a disk and file basis. You can move through the disk, partition by partition, or scroll through the sectors, head, and cylinders. You can check each byte and get a hexadecimal/ASCII representation of your data, as well as search for specific characters that you wish to modify. This can also be done on a file by file basis. Data on both the hard and floppy disk in a NetWare network can be examined.

Netutils also lets you retrieve data from the server—even when it's down as a result of network hardware failures. As long as the workstation and hard disk continue to function, you can retrieve data from a server that is down. Netutils prevents the loss of data by locating bad spots on the disk, deallocating them, and moving the data. The directory is rebuilt, along with the file allocation tables. Ontrack's Dosutils is the DOS version of these utilities, for DOS-based network operating systems, such as 3+ and PC LAN.

Before your server has a chance to go down, you can run another Ontrack program, *Disk Manager Diagnostics*, to find potential problems. This program uses diagnostic tests to detect and isolate disk, controller, and media problems. These tests include a controller test, a nondestructive write/read test and error correction code test, a nondestructive scan test, a random-read test, and a seek test. If these are used during installation or reinstallation of the disk drive, they can be used to ferret out problems in cabling and jumper selection.

Cheyenne network utilities

NetBack is a set of utilities for Novell NetWare users. The program allows you to reconstruct the server and its bindery using information that was previously stored in a storage utility. This utility, called *VaultFile*, extracts information from the current server and creates a file for storing bindery data, login scripts, system autoexec files, and printer definitions.

A corrupt server can be reconstructed before data files are reloaded. If you need to set up a new network server, you can set up the new server, based on information from another server's VaultFile, regardless of its NetWare version. If you need to restore trustee rights, NetBack can do it— even if the directories no longer exist. NetBack also generates reports on system usage, trustee assignments, and disk usage reports.

Network errors

Network performance is often a function of error conditions on the network. A frame-check sequence or cyclic redundancy check verifies that the +bits in the frame were transferred correctly. A misalign error occurs when a frame is received with a frame-check sequence error that shows a total number of bits that is not divisible by eight. Errors can be caused by several conditions.

Illegal-size frame errors can be of two types. Frames of less than minimum or 64 bytes are known as *runts*. Runts are usually caused by collisions on networks over large distances. This problem occurs on large networks when one node begins transmission and another node physically distant from the first begins transmission and collides with the first. Runts occur because of the propagation delay on the network which allows the first node to transmit enough of its frame onto the network to be recognized as a partial packet.

Frames longer than a maximum of 1,514 bytes are sometimes called *jabbers*. Jabbers are normally caused by hardware failures. The presence of runts indicates potential problems. Hosts and file servers tend to be the concentration points for such traffic. In the locating of specific nodes, the suspect nodes are those with high levels of incoming and outgoing traffic. The activity of a particular node can indicate where problems can exist.

Collisions on some types of networks are a part of the access technique. In light traffic situations (under 5%), collisions occur as a function of the randomness of the data.

Network loading

Network loading information has several important uses. It facilitates the pinpointing of potential problems. Each frame sent from a given source gives a number at the intersection. The number indicates the frequency of traffic. The important factors are data and error rates, as well as frame-size activity.

Activity can change rapidly, depending on user activity, but often a few connections generate most of the traffic. These sites are usually the source of any problems.

Network testing

Many protocol and network standards use special commands and responses for testing protocols and software. In addition to loopback testing procedures for the upper-layer protocols, several local area network standards include loopback procedures. Examples of such test facilities are the Ethernet Configuration Testing Protocol (CTP) and the IEEE (Institute of Electrical and Electronic Engineers) 802.2 Test Command and Response.

The Ethernet CTP allows single or multiple-hop loopbacks. With this test facility, a frame can be sent to a node, then either returned or forwarded to a third node, and finally returned to the originating node. The IEEE 802.2 test facility sends a Test command frame to a node. If the command is the proper format, the node will return a TEST RESPONSE, which contains an information field that is identical to the original test command. These facilities can be used to test for the proper functioning of the network interface.

Delay measurements

Delay measurements show how performance varies with network usage and give a good indication of potential performance and capacity problems. To measure the propagation delay, it is necessary to compare the time that the message is successfully placed on the network to the time that the response message is successfully received.

The remote node processing time is subtracted and the remaining time represents the round-trip propagation delay for the network. You can measure this variation over time under a variety of network loads to indicate the network's contribution to transaction response time.

Propagation delay measurements are particularly useful at gateways and bridges. By taking the measurements over long periods of time, it is possible to determine how performance varies with network usage and to flag potential performance and capacity problems.

Network baseline

To effectively measure network characteristics, it is necessary to establish a baseline of information about the network. The *network baseline* consists of the network performance information. Baseline characteristics can include ongoing utilization, peaks, and error rates. The network baseline can serve many purposes. It can provide a basic reference of data to explain the general network characteristics. It can also be used as a reference for troubleshooting performance problems.

One network traffic parameter that can influence errors and waste network capacity is the burstiness of the traffic. When a network node receives a large number of packet bursts, it is possible for that node to miss some packets. This problem occurs when the node or its interface is not able to process the incoming packets fast enough. These errors are masked from the user by the upper-layer protocols. Protocols retransmit the data one or more times until it is properly received.

Protocol analyzers

A *LAN protocol analyzer* is a type of instrument that can be used to provide an independent, controlled network load. The analyzer can be used to observe the effects on network performance parameters. Simulating traffic and measuring its effects will provide information on the impact of network changes. Modeling the traffic target for (or addressed to) specific devices and measuring their response is useful for identifying the limitations of such devices as bridges and gateways.

When a simulated traffic load is used, it should have the same characteristics, including the distribution of frame size and burst rate. Adding traffic with representative characteristics makes it possible to predict performance error rates and collisions.

Local area network analysis can provide you with the following:

- What channels are most active.
- What types of errors are occurring.
- What the network loads are at any particular time.

Some products, such as Excelan's LAN analyzer and Hewlett Packard's HP 4971s, provide network performance statistics and can be used to run tests on individual stations and review the results. They can analyze high-level protocols, such as Transmission Control Protocol/Internet Protocol and Xerox Network Systems. They cannot simulate a terminal to perform extensive testing, nor can they remove faulty products from the network with this type of analyzer.

Most products of this type interface with the local area network and provide menus that permit the operator to establish test parameters, take measurements, and evaluate the results. Different packaging approaches allow several alternatives. Some controller boards fit into an expansion slot in an IBM Personal Computer, XT, AT, or compatible with at least 512K of RAM. Packaged systems might consist of an AT type of personal computer with 640K of RAM, a 20M hard disk, and the controller board installed. Local-network control software is also available separately on diskettes.

Units are available with a communications and statistical facility. Some work only as analyzers and others can function as node or standalone personal computers when not being used for network analysis. Most analyzers provide similar types of tests and levels of information. Operators can name the channels or individual terminals to be tested and the types of errors to be sensed and collected. Users can also specify their own specific bit-pattern triggers.

Most products allow data to be simultaneously displayed in hexadecimal or ASCII formats. The displayed information can indicate the source and destination address, length, and the type of errors detected. These units allow the operator to scroll through the entire buffer or go to selected source and destination addresses within the buffer or to the packets on disk.

Traffic loading

The network management capabilities of most testers are restricted to measuring the traffic loading on each channel. Most testers allow users to inject packets into the network data stream to test how well the system reacts to increased traffic. These analyzers allow users to view the traffic-level loading in real time.

The screen display might show:

- The channel loading in the form of a bar graph.
- The percentage of errors occurring by error type.
- The number of packets transmitted with and without errors.
- A count of individual error types that occurred on each channel.
- The number of complete packets received.
- The source and destination addresses of user-selected channels.
- The volume of packets set by one address to another.

Bar graphs showing the traffic periods that are measured according to interframe-spacing time provide a view of the traffic patterns in real time. The display can show absolute time, acquisition time, the percent of deferred requests, collisions, and percentage of aborted attempts.

Most products can measure traffic, provided that the volume stays below 40% of network capacity. Above that, they tend to lose packets. Packets can be lost in special applications, such as setting traps for specific bit patterns. Because setting data traps is used for fault packets can be a problem.

Bar charts that show network loading during specific periods can provide the average packet size gathered over a specific test period. If 95% of the packets had 64 bytes, this information can be displayed with the peak traffic rates. Performance statistics can include the number and types of errors that occur during the measurement period. In addition to analyzing local networks, many products can be used to control measurements at remote locations. Software packages, such as Meridian Technology's Carbon Copy, can be used to control the remote site.

Although most units provide similar facilities for monitoring and measuring local network performance, some screens incorporate more performance statistics, and some units can be used as a network node for other applications, when not being used for analysis. Figure 8-4 represents screens that illustrate some features of a typical protocol analyzer.

Other troubleshooting tools

A number of testing tools can be used for troubleshooting networks. Typical of these is the Pair Scanner from Microtest. This unit is hand-held and battery-powered and it works with virtually any cable type. The Pair Scanner solves many of the difficult problems that are associated with twisted pair cabling systems. It helps network managers and systems installers who work with Ethernet, ARCnet, Token Ring, and all forms of telephone wiring systems that are used in network communications. These often

Frame number	Time since previous frame	Destination	Source	Highest protocol

Previous frame next frame new capture	Options

8-4   Protocol analyzer screen features.

complex topologies present performance and reliability challenges that protocol analyzers and Time Domain Reflectometers were not designed to solve. The Pair Scanner fills this need.

Like the other types of scanners, the Pair Scanner (Table 8-2) uses TDR (Time Domain Reflectometry) or "cable radar" to locate and/or measure cable shorts and breaks, length, resistance, and electrical noise (interference). The Pair Scanner includes all of the standard scanner functions,

Table 8-2.   Scanner types

Function feature	Pair scanner	Cable scanner	Quick scanner
Prevents network downtime	X	X	X
Locates faults, shorts or breaks in cabling	X	X	X
10BASE-T hub tests	X		
Isolates "intermittent" problems	X		
Monitors Ethernet networks	X	X	X
Monitors Token Ring networks*	X		
Maps network wiring	X	X	
Certifies compliance with specifications	X		
Special twisted-pair features	X		X
Hard copy report/printouts	X	X	
Includes wire trace capability	X	X	
SCOPE mode support for TDR displays	X	X	

plus it measures signal loss, generates a link-bit for hub testing (10BASE-T), supports alarm programming, and includes a built-in relay for rapid switching between transmit and receive pairs. You can use the Pair Scanner to locate and repair problems in your LAN cabling system quickly and accurately. It even can be used to isolate intermittent problems. Network installers can use the Pair Scanner's certification capabilities when installing even the most complex systems and print out hard copy reports for clients.

The Pair Scanner Kit comes with the Pair Scanner Unit, the 10BASE-T injector, printer cable, 2RJ45 adapters, Token Ring adapter cable, and 10BASE-T adapter cable. Also available are an operations manual and a durable hard-plastic carrying case that is able to house an array of additional accessories (injectors, adapter kits, and testers).

Injectors for the pair scanner

Microtest has developed a series of injectors to enhance the testing capability of the Pair Scanner. By injecting a specified frequency into the cable, the Scanner can identify errors and certify that the wiring meets the manufacturer's specifications.

Multiline injector The *Multiline Injector* can be used with the pair scanner or with another Multiline Injector. By pulsing each wire sequentially, it identifies mismatched pairs, short circuits, breaks, and inverted pairs by simply visually inspecting the red/green LEDs on the Pair Scanner display.

Type III injector The *Type III Injector* is used in conjunction with the Pair Scanner to help you certify that your twisted-pair wiring works, as per the IBM Cabling System Type III specification. By injecting four precisely calibrated frequencies, it will determine dB loss at 256 kHz, 512 kHz, 776 kHz, and 1,000 kHz.

The Pair Scanner provides the following troubleshooting functions.

1. Locates breaks, shorts, bad crimps, etc. in wiring.
2. Isolates faulty Token Ring MAU's and connectors.
3. Locates fault in all LAN cabling systems.
4. Certifies that wiring lengths are within specification.
5. Automatically identifies LAN terminators.

10BASE-T injector The 10BASE-T Injector certifies that your twisted-pair wiring meets IEEE 10BASE-T specifications. It calculates dB loss by injecting a precisely calibrated 5- and 10-MHz signal into the cable. This injector is included in the Pair Scanner Kit and it does not need to be ordered separately.

Quick scanner   This troubleshooting unit:

1. Pinpoints faults in LAN cabling using cable radar.
2. Displays results in plain English.
3. Tests all twisted-pair and coax cables.
4. Is menu driven so that it is very easy to use.
5. Monitors Ethernet network activity.

The Quick Scanner is the easiest-to-use member of this product family. It tests virtually all coax and twisted-pair cabling for the most common LAN wiring faults instantly. It is designed for network installers and administrators with small- to medium-size networks. This hand-held, menu-driven scanner will help you install your LAN and keep it up and running properly with minimum time, effort and training. Because of its small size and low cost, the Quick Scanner is often the best solution for troubleshooting LANs in the field.

The Quick Scanner makes network troubleshooting easier. Just turn it on, attach the cable, and hit the [Enter] button. It automatically scans the systems and instantly reports any faults in your network cabling. If no problem exists, the Scanner indicates this and toggles into network monitor mode to display network traffic statistics (IEEE-802.3 networks only) in any easy-to-understand graphic format. Quick Scanner is the first scanner to be completely menu driven, which makes it even easier to perform standard diagnostic tests. Press the [up arrow] or [down arrow] button and the menu screen changes. When you arrive at the menu option you want, simply hit [Enter], and it runs the test, and it displays such results as OPEN AT 300 FEET, SHORT AT 110 FEET, or NO FAULTS FOUND.

The Quick Scanner Kit is supplied with the Quick Scanner Unit, a quick test adapter for twisted-pair cable scanning, and an extensive operations manual. With the proper accessories, the Quick Scanner can troubleshoot all major LAN systems including; Token Ring, 10BASE-T, ARCnet, and all twisted-pair and coaxial systems.

Cable Scanner   This troubleshooting unit:

1. Locates breaks, shorts and bad crimps.
2. Monitors Ethernet network activity.
3. Determines when a repeater is needed.
4. Finds missing or bad terminators.
5. Detects electrical interference.

Cable Scanner is a hand-held network diagnostic tool that is designed for people who install, service, troubleshoot, or manage LANs. It uses a form of "cable radar" to locate and/or measure cable shorts and breaks, length, resistance, and electrical noise (interference).

Cable Scanner supports thin Ethernet, ARCnet, Token Ring, twisted-pair, TV cable, coax, and 10 user-defined cable types. Whatever your network cabling system, Cable Scanner's technology does the work for you by eliminating the problems that often plague network administrators, thereby significantly reducing network downtime. Installers can use Cable Scanner to help produce "as-built" diagrams of LAN cable installation and print system-quality reports or determine if existing cabling will support data transmission.

Cable Scanner can monitor LAN traffic and graphically display or print out a 24-hour daily activity log. Connected to an oscilloscope, the scanner's precision, high-speed, pulse-generating circuitry offers installers a detailed view of the entire LAN, including the transceiver, terminator, and multiple faults at a fraction of the price of a traditional TDR. Cable Scanner can also be used to determine how many feet of cable are on a spool before installing it in your facility.

The Cable Scanner kit comes with the Cable Scanner unit, the Cable Tracer accessory, an ac adapter/charger, a printer cable, a three-cable adapter, an extensive operations manual, and a PC diskette. With the proper accessories, the Quick Scanner can accurately troubleshoot all major LAN systems.

Cable Scanner adapters Several adapters have been developed to expand the capabilities of Cable Scanner. 10BASE-T and Token Ring testing can be easily performed with the use of these special adapters.

The Token Ring adapter (BNC) allows you to use the scanner to test Token Ring networks that use IBM data connectors. The adapter has two BNC connections to an IBM Data Connector so that the wire pairs are open and data can travel through the connection and into the cable for scanning.

The 10BASE-T adapter kit provides a connection from twisted-pair wiring with various RJ-style connectors to a Microtest Scanner. The 10BASE-T adapter kit includes an RJ-11 to scanner adapter, two RJ-45 to scanner adapters, and a RJ-45 female-to-female coupler.

The Ring Scanner is a Token Ring Tester and MAU Analyzer that:

1. Detects shorts, breaks, and miswires.
2. Automatically switches between 4/16-Mbps.
3. Provides intentional ring fault test.
4. Verifies MAU port and relay.
5. Replaces the IBM Token Ring Cable Tester.

The Ring Scanner finds cabling problems, isolates defective MAU's, and verifies the proper installation of both 4 and 16 Mbps Token Ring networks. It was also designed to generate the phantom voltage necessary to test data connectors and MAU's. The Ring Scanner is a dual-purpose device; as a standalone Token Ring tester, it performs the same diagnostic functions as IBM's standard Token Ring cable tester, but it can also be used as an accessory to the Microtest Cable Scanner, Quick Scanner, and/ or Pair Scanner for even greater functionality. When interfaced with any of these scanners, the Ring Scanner can provide a graphical display of network traffic that will help pinpoint problems with excess traffic on the LAN. When used with the Cable Scanner or Pair Scanner, it also allows network activity and test results to be printed out or saved in the scanner's memory. The Ring Scanner is supplied with the necessary cable, connectors, and an extensive operations manual.

Transceiver Monitor The Transceiver Monitor provides diagnostic capabilities for thick Ethernet and IEEE 802.3 networks. It also enhances the diagnostic capabilities of the Pair Scanner and Cable Scanner when used with these two networks. By using the Cable Scanner or Pair Scanner to monitor network activity, you can monitor activity in real time, save a record of activity over time, and print out activity reports.

With the Transceiver Monitor you can monitor total network activity on the Transceiver Monitor's LEDs; verify that a network transceiver (also called a *Media Access Unit* or *MAU*) is receiving power from a network workstation; connect your Cable Scanner or Pair Scanner to the transceiver to monitor and record activity over time; print reports; and scan the transmit (TX), receive (RS), and collision (COL) wire pairs of your AUI (Attachment Unit Interface) cable for faults. The collision signal pair is often referred to as the *control-in (CI) pair*.

The Transceiver Monitor kit includes the Transceiver Monitor unit, a three-foot workstation attachment cable, and a scanner connection cable.

Telco Adapter The Telco Adapter kit provides LAN installers and administrators who use twisted-pair cable, everything they need to ensure network wiring quality. With the Telco Adapter kit, you can check the wiring data transmission efficiency, find faults, and monitor network activity. The Telco Adapter kit is a combination of Microtest's various twisted-pair adapters in one convenient and cost-effective kit.

The Telco Adapter kit includes: RJ-45-to-alligator clip unterminated cable adapters, an RJ-45 female-to-female coupler, RJ-45 to RJ-11 adapter cables, 100- and 120-Ω terminating plugs, a shorting plug, a 66 punchdown block adapter, a 100 punchdown block adapter, an RJ-45 "Y" adapter, a connecting cable for punchdown block adapters, and a Smart-T, all packaged in a convenient plastic case.

Coax Interface The Coax Interface kit provides LAN installers and administrators of coaxial-based LAN systems with the accessories needed to both diagnose problems and maintain network quality. Used with one of the scanner units, this coax kit enables the LAN technician to find most typical coax cable problems, including opens or shorts, exposed shields, and improper connections. It also adds increased functionality to the scanner products. If twisted-pair cabling is used, the coax to twisted-pair adapter is required to use the scope feature of the Pair Scanner. The Token Ring to BNC adapter allows for scanners to test Token Ring networks using IBM data connectors.

The Coax Interface kit is a combination of Microtest's various adapters. The coax kit includes: an RG58 male-to-male adapter cable, a BNC male-to-male coupler, an N-Series adapter (#3570-05), a BNC female-to-male adapter, a BNC female-to-female adapter, a coax-to-twisted pair adapter, a coaxial "T" Adapter, and a Token Ring-to-BNC adapter.

Network probe Network Communication's Network Probe family consists of four instruments (Table 8-3). Each of these network testers can be used at remote field sites to perform maintenance operations. Their data line monitoring capabilities are designed for end-to-end communications networks and can be used for installation, maintenance, and performance measurements. The Network Probe is a: bit error-rate tester, digital voltmeter, speaker/monitor, SNA protocol analyzer, up/down line load utility, V.35 protocol monitor, data line monitor, asynchronous terminal, RS-232 status monitor, X.25 protocol analyzer, Baudot protocol monitor, and DDCMP protocol analyzer.

All models are compact, with a simple menu and laptop design. The user can program (in English) up to 7 transmit strings with the 6610. Figure 8-5 shows the display screen. A mass-storage disk drive option is also available. The 6620A has a nonvolatile internal memory (64K RAM). This instrument can also act as both a speaker/monitor and as a digital multime-

Table 8-3. Network probe specifications

Model	6610	6620A	6630	6640
Internal memory	32K	64K	64K	128K
Baud rate	56Kbps	56Kbps	72Kbps	256Kbps
BERT/BLERT	19.2Kbps	19.2Kbps	64Kbps	128Kbps
Program strings	7	7	16	16
dB meter		X	X	X
Ohm meter		X	X	X
Vac/Vdc meter		X	X	X
Speaker monitor		X	X	X
Continuity tester		X	X	X
Permanent backup		X	X	X
Async term memory	none	none	4K	8K
Remote control				X
VT100 emulation				X
Graphic lead status				X

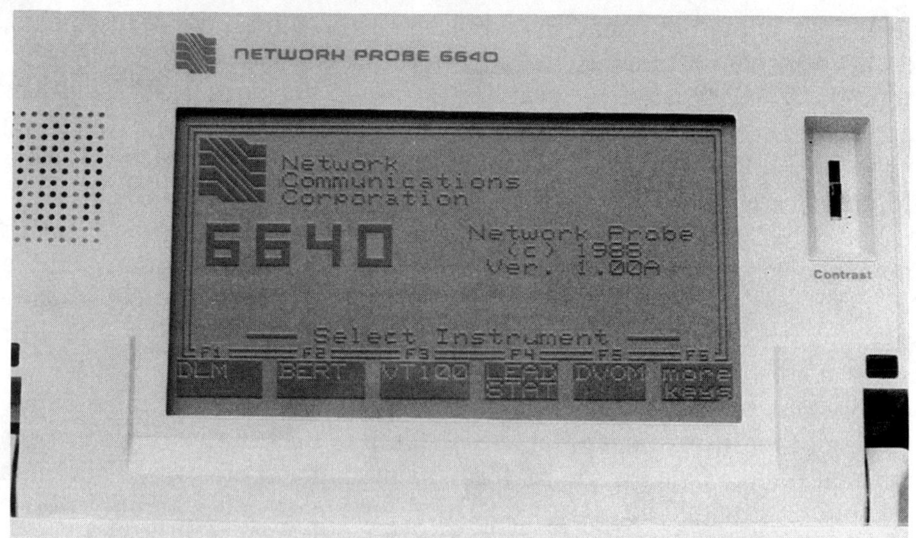

8-5 Network Communication's 6640 Network Probe Network tester.

ter. The speaker/monitor feature allows the user to listen to any irregularities that might occur on the transmission line being monitored. The digital multimeter feature provides the user with an ac/dc voltmeter, a decibel (or level) meter, an ohmmeter, and a continuity tester.

The 6630 allows 72 Kbps monitoring in SNA and X.25 real-time decode. As a BERT tester, it allows transmit speeds of 28,000, 38,400, 48,000, 56,000, and 64,000 synchronous and it can perform error-rate calculations that display the percentage of error-free seconds. When it is used as an asynchronous terminal, the unit has a built-in 4K character capture buffer with a buffer-save feature. The 6630 allows 16 programmable transmit strings (buffers) of 240 characters each.

The 6640 has 128K of nonvolatile RAM and allows monitoring, emulation, and analysis up to 256 Kbps. An auto configuration feature automatically displays line parameters that give the user immediate recognition of line configuration or type. The remote-control feature enables the user to control a slave unit from a master control site. The graphic lead status feature provides a visual display of control-lead and data activity and can program multiple lead alarms. An optional 3$\frac{1}{2}$″ floppy-disk drive can add 800K of real-time mass storage to help track difficult diagnostic problems.

9

Other input devices

Keyboard technology

Many types of input devices can be used, including keyboards. In the common alphanumeric keyboard, each key depression causes a 7-bit code to be stored in a character register in the memory. The code can be determined by the program and sent to the monitor or printer in the form of a character. The key can also have a fixed function, such as insert or delete. The key function could also be determined by the program that is running at that time. Some functions might also require multiple key depressions.

It is also possible to accumulate consecutive characters into a buffer until a termination character is typed, which thereby produces a character-string input. This technique is common in programming applications. Several technologies are used to detect a key depression: mechanical contact closures, a change in capacitance, and a change in magnetic coupling.

A number of factors tend to make one keyboard different from another: key spacing, slope or shape of the keyboard, shape of the key caps, and the contact pressure needed to depress a key. Other differences involve details of the layout, such as separating keys (such as line delete from other frequently used keys) and making frequently used keys easily reachable without the need to simultaneously depress the control or shift keys.

The programmed function keys are provided as a separate unit. This is done in some applications, but usually the function keys are integrated with the main PC keyboard. The function keys differ from the other keys in that they are always prelabeled.

The function keys usually have no predefined character meanings. They are generally used for commands or menu options. Dedicated keys have permanent labels. The function keys can be labeled with coded overlays, on which the command names are printed. The function keys can also report pressure releases, as well as depressions. This will allow you to start an activity when a key is depressed and then to terminate the activity when the key is released.

Another type of input device is a *chord keyboard*, which has keys that are shaped like piano keys. It is operated by depressing several keys at the same time, like playing a chord. It can be used for music or command input. With five keys 31 chords can be generated. Learning the chords requires some training, but users can learn to operate these devices. Chord keyboards are generally not suitable as substitutes for the standard type of alphanumeric keyboard.

Touch panel and tablet technology

Touch panels allow the user to indicate items on it using a finger, rather than by moving a screen cursor to the item. The touch panel is mounted across the face of the CRT and when the user's finger touches the panel, this position is detected using one of several different technologies.

One type of high-resolution touch panel uses two layers of transparent material; one is coated with a thin conductor and the other is resistive. Finger pressure causes a voltage drop on the resistive substrate, which is measured to calculate the coordinates of the pressure point.

Similar techniques are used in digitizing tablet technology. *Graphic pad digitizers* use a flat tablet and a stylus pencil. The tablet provides a flat surface over which the stylus pencil is moved. The position of the stylus is monitored by the computer. The stylus usually incorporates a pressure-sensitive switch, which closes when the user pushes down on the stylus. This switch indicates that the stylus is at a position of interest on the screen and that a menu choice is made.

Most tablets use an electrical sensing system to measure the stylus position. A grid of wires can be embedded in the tablet surface. The electromagnetic coupling between the electrical signals in the grid and in a wire coil changes as the stylus is moved. This induces an electrical signal in the stylus and the strength of the signal is used to determine the position of the stylus on the tablet.

The digitizer senses the position of a pen, cursor, or some other pointer and electronically relays this information to the computer as an x-y coordinate on the pad. A drawing placed on the tablet can be digitized by positioning the stylus over each point or line to be recorded.

Other digitizer technologies are electrostatic and magnetostrictive. The *electrostatic tablets* radiate an electric field, which is sensed by the pen. The system changes the frequency of the radiated field as a function of where the pen touches the surface. This frequency changes for each tablet position. The digitizer circuits translate the frequency changes into x-y coordinates, which are then sent to the computer. Electrostatic digitizers can sense the pen position through most media with a low dielectric constant, such as paper, plastic, or glass.

Electrostatic systems can have problems digitizing accurately in close proximity to metal, or partially to conductive materials, such as pencil lead or some felt-tip inks. Magnetostrictive tablets use magnetostrictive wires that are laid beneath the table to keep track of pen position. A magnetic pulse on one end of the wires produces a small strain wave, which propagates across the tablet. The wave is detected using a pick-up coil in the pen or cursor. The time elapsed from the start of the pulse and the time that the probe senses can be related to the position of the pen.

Magnetostrictive tablets are not sensitive to conductive materials. However, magnetic objects that are near the tablet surface can disturb the magnetic properties and degrade the operation. These tablets must also be periodically remagnetized with large magnets. In the electromagnetic tablets, either the table or the pen transmits a small ac signal, which is detected by receiver circuits. These circuits produce the digital signal that defines the pen location. Electromagnetic digitizers are not affected by conductive or magnetic materials on their surface and generally require no periodic recalibration.

Potentiometric device technology

Several types of input devices use potentiometers. A set of rotary potentiometers (Fig. 9-1) can be mounted in a unit, such as a joystick. Slide potentiometers, in which a linear movement replaces the rotation, are also used in some designs. Potentiometers are sampled by devices whose analog values are converted and stored in registers to be read by the microprocessor. The values read from the registers are then converted to equivalent numbers to be used by the program.

An analog-to-digital converter and a power supply can be used to determine the potentiometer's position by measuring the voltage (Fig. 9-2). The voltage is proportional to the amount of shaft rotation about the axis. When

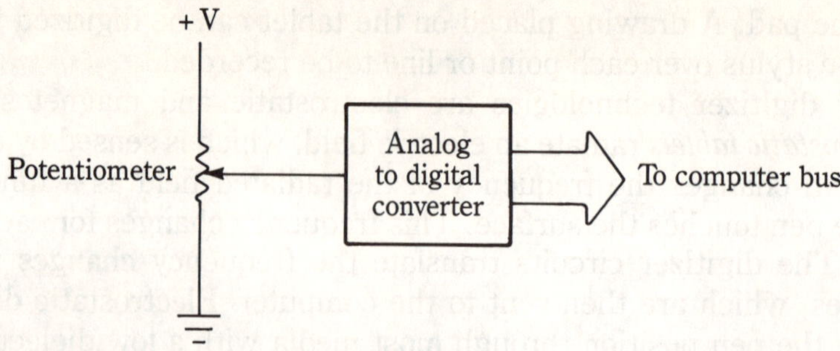

9-1 The potentiometer interface requires a power source for the potentiometer and an analog-to-digital converter to process the signal for connection to the computer bus.

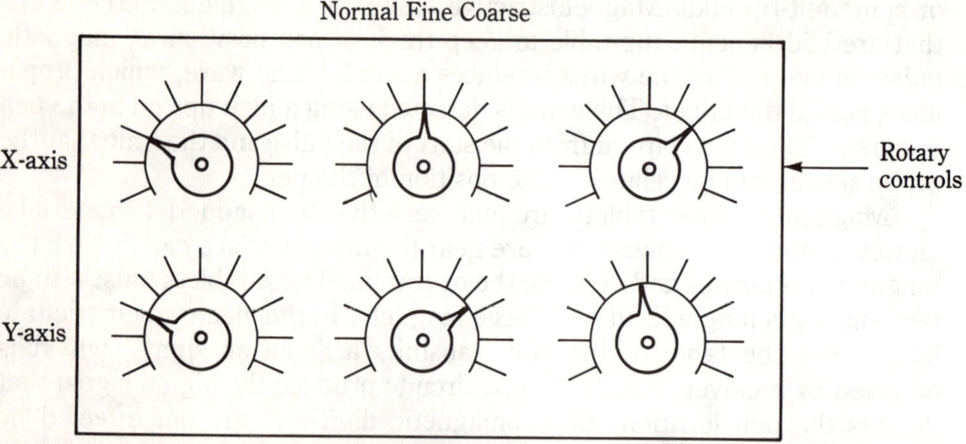

9-2 A set of controls can be used for screen positioning. Two controls are needed for 2-axis positioning. The other controls could be used for fine and coarse positioning.

the converter is correctly adjusted, a zero position will correspond to a digital reading of all zeros and a full-scale position will correspond to all ones.

Trackball technology

Trackball controls are large plastic balls that are mounted with some fraction of the ball surface protruding from the top of the enclosing unit. The ball rotates freely within its mount, and is typically moved by drawing the palm of the hand over it. Rotating the ball can be detected by the computer to move the screen cursor.

Trackballs can be used to select commands that are displayed on the display. The ball positions the cursor to the proper area of a menu. Pushing a keyboard key (usually Return) makes the selection. The computer reads the cursor position at the time when the key is pressed and executes the procedure that is listed in the menu.

Trackballs (which are sometimes called *crystal balls*) are used as shown in Fig. 9-3. The ball's motion turns potentiometers, whose output is converted into digital data for reading by the microprocessor.

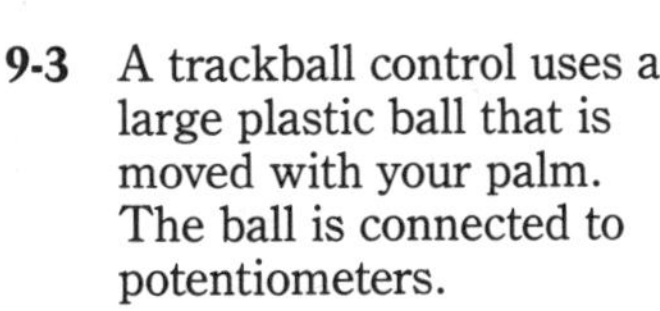
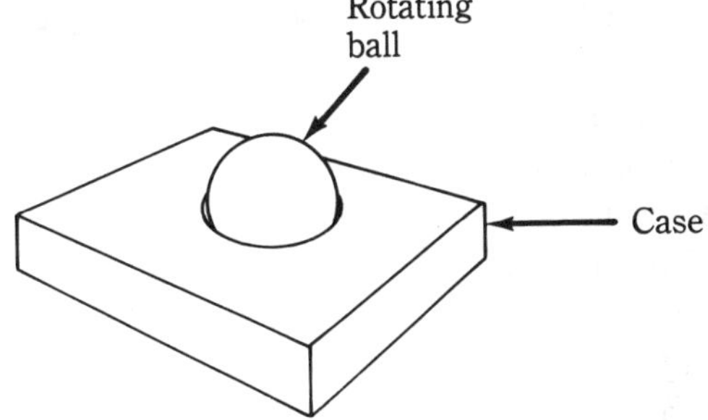

9-3 A trackball control uses a large plastic ball that is moved with your palm. The ball is connected to potentiometers.

Light pen technology

Light pens are used as element-indicating devices. The light pen does not emit light to create lines on the screen. It senses or detects the light from the picture elements on the screen. Some light pens do use a narrow-focused light source, called a *finder beam*, which is directed at the screen to indicate what picture elements are in the pen's field of view.

A hand-held light pen consists of a pencil-sized plastic cylinder with a light sensor in one end. One light pen design is shown in Fig. 9-4. A number of different designs are used. The other end is connected to the computer by a cable. As the user positions the light-sensitive pen tip to select a point on the screen, the light pen sends a pulse when this screen area is bright. The pulse produced by the light pen is then used to calculate the screen position where the pen was.

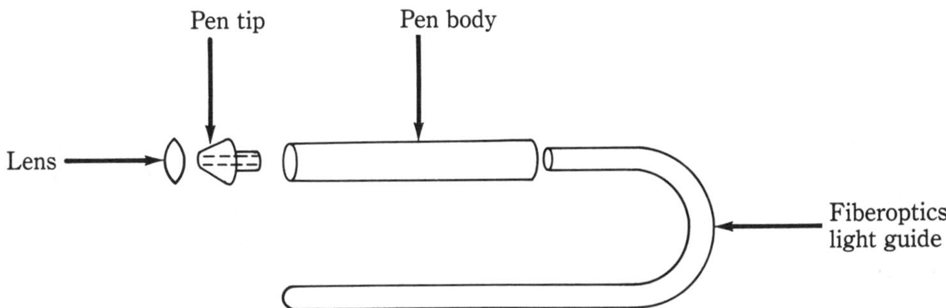

9-4 The basic light pen design uses a lens with a fiberoptic cable.

The pen senses the burst of fluorescent light that is emitted when the electron beam is bombarding the phosphor. This is the light emitted during the drawing of the picture element. The pen's output is usually connected to the system's control logic so that the microprocessor stops executing commands when the pen senses the light. This signal can be correlated with a menu list to detect the particular item being displayed at the time when the light from the pen was detected.

Most light pens also produce a second signal that the user generates by pushing a button on the pen to signal the microprocessor of the user's selection of a point (Fig. 9-5). When the computer is interrupted by the light-pen signal, its instruction counter will contain the address of the next instruction. This address can be used to give the application program the location of the segment that contains the detected element. Using this technique, the light pen acts as a locator for a raster display, which stops the raster scan at the detected pixels. The x-y coordinates provide the locations.

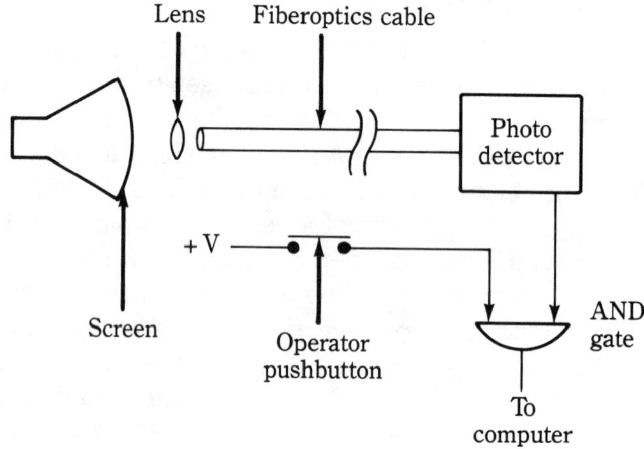

9-5   An operator pushbutton is used as a part of the light-pen function to select a point on the screen.

Several factors can affect light-pen performance. Many CRT screens use bonded implosion shields over the display tube, which leave a gap between the outer glass surface and phosphor. This gap can cause accuracy problems when positioning the light pen. Unless it is properly adjusted, a light pen can detect false points (such as adjacent characters) or fail to detect the desired points.

Joystick technology

A *joystick* is like an aircraft control stick; the user controls the motion of a cursor on the screen by pushing it in the direction of the desired motion. The displacement-type joystick actually moves, but with the force-actuated joystick, the stick is fixed and the force from the user's hand causes the cursor motion.

Force-actuated or *isometric joysticks* use strain gauges on the shaft to measure the deflections caused by the force. Joysticks can also be rotated or pushed on the end to control other variables besides the basic position. The joystick can be moved left, right, forward, or backward (Fig. 9-6). Potentiometers sense the movements. Springs are sometimes used to return the joystick to its center position. Some joysticks offer a third degree of freedom because the stick can be twisted clockwise and counterclockwise.

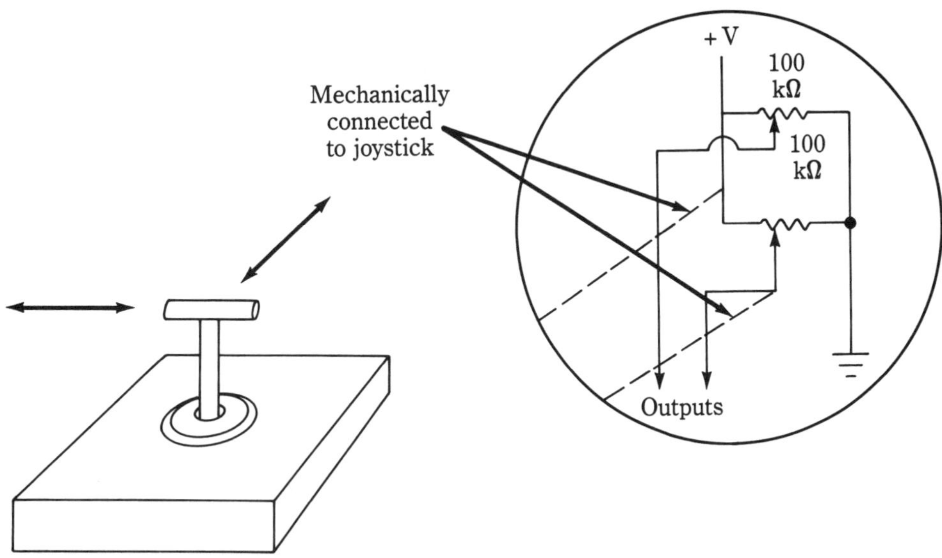

9-6 A displacement joystick acts as a handle to position the cursor. Potentiometers are used to sense the movements.

In an *absolute joystick*, the travel of the joystick will correspond directly to the screen position. Moving the absolute joystick to its upper position places the cursor at the top of the display. Moving it to its lower left position places the cursor at the lower left corner of the display.

In the *rate joystick*, the motion of the joystick imparts a direction of motion to the cursor. If you move the rate joystick to the left, the cursor will move left from its present position. Push it to the lower left and the cursor will move diagonally in that direction. When you return the joystick to center, then the cursor stops. In many designs, by varying how far in any direction the rate joystick is moved, the user controls the speed at which the cursor will move.

The *absolute/rate joystick* is a hybrid design that utilizes both techniques. A switch on the joystick handle is used to select the mode. In the absolute mode, a motion to the upper left corner with the joystick will move the cursor to the upper left corner of the computer display. Once the general target area is reached, the switch is released, and the cursor is positioned using the rate mode.

It can be difficult to use a joystick to control the absolute position of a screen cursor accurately because even a small hand movement is amplified in the position of the cursor. The cursor's movements can become erratic because the joystick does not allow fine positioning. A small dead zone is normally used to allow for drift in the joystick's center position. The relationship of cursor velocity to joystick displacement is generally not linear (Fig. 9-7).

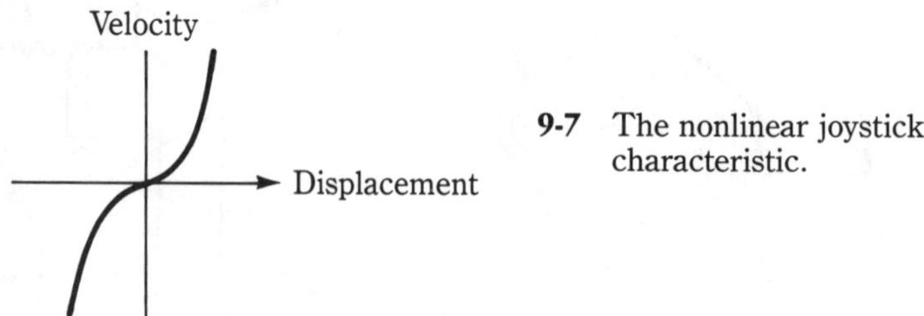

9-7 The nonlinear joystick characteristic.

A variation of the joystick is the *joyswitch*. The joyswitch can be moved up, down, left, right, and in four diagonal directions. A switch allows nine states. In each of the eight ON states, the position of the screen cursor can be changed at a constant rate in that direction.

Mouse technology

Mouses use rollers or an LED and a ruled metal surface. Movement of the unit causes the rollers to turn internal potentiometers or the LED to sense the ruled lines. These voltage changes are, in turn, used to sense the relative movements of the mouse and track the relative position. The motion is converted to digital values and used by the microprocessor to calculate the direction and magnitude of the mouse's movement.

The mouse is normally moved on a flat surface, called a *mouse pad* (Fig. 9-8). The computer maintains a current mouse position register, which is incremented or decremented by the mouse's movements. The mouse usually has one or more pushbuttons, which are used to input commands.

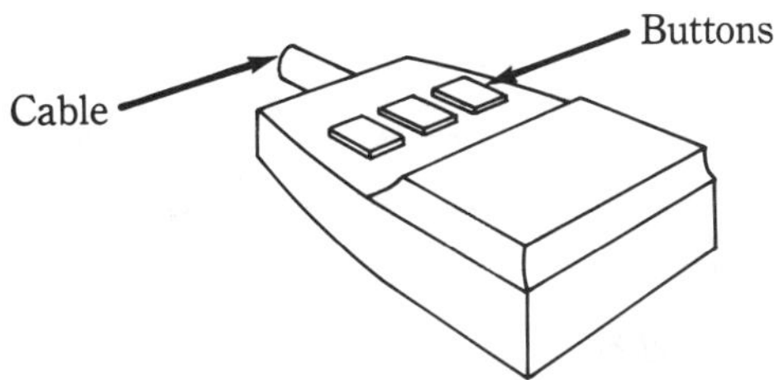

9-8   The mouse is designed so that it will fit the hand. The buttons are arranged so that the mouse will not be moved when a button is pressed.

Mouses are available as optical, mechanical, optomechanical, optical-mechanical, acoustomechanical, or analog-tracking units with one to four buttons. The tracking might depend on or be independent of the rotation of the mouse. The resolution ranges from 20 to 2,000 counts/inches and serial or parallel interfaces are available with relative or absolute-position information in a variety of data formats and at different baud rates.

In general, mouses are designed so that the front of the device is low because that is the way that a hand naturally falls. Mouses are also lightweight because they are frequently lifted up and repositioned on the surface. The buttons are often parallel to the surface so that the mouse won't be moved accidentally when a button is pressed.

Although six different techniques can be used to perform the tracking function of a mouse, only the optical, mechanical, and optomechanical styles are widely used.

Optical mouses

Optical mouses track position by counting the number of line (or dot) crossings on a special mouse pad, much as a bar code wand reads bar codes (Fig. 9-9). Because no contact is between the mouse and the surface and they have no moving parts, optical mouses are reliable. They do not require maintenance, and tracking errors of less than 1 in 100 are typical throughout the life of the mouse. A special mouse pad is needed for optimum performance.

Some optical mouses track motion relative to the orientation of the mouse pad. The mouse cannot be rotated more than 90 degrees in either direction. Other optical units track motion relative to the orientation of the mouse, which is similar to the tracking characteristics of mechanical mouses.

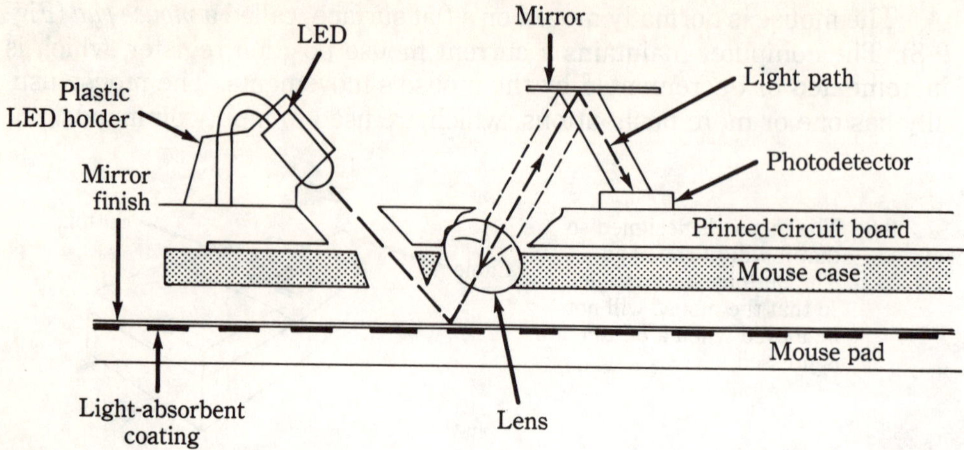

9-9 The optical mouse travels over a grid of lines on the mouse pad. An LED provides a light beam that is either absorbed or reflected.

Mechanical mouses

Mechanical mouses use a metal ball to drive two orthogonal mechanical shaft encoders. This technique is low in cost and lets you track motion on any surface, but these units have a limited lifetime (because of the mechanical switching of the encoders) and require periodic cleaning.

Optomechanical mouses use a ball to drive two orthogonal optical shaft encoders (Fig. 9-10). This technique is low in cost, has a longer life (compared to the mechanical mouse), and lets you track on any surface, but periodic cleaning is required.

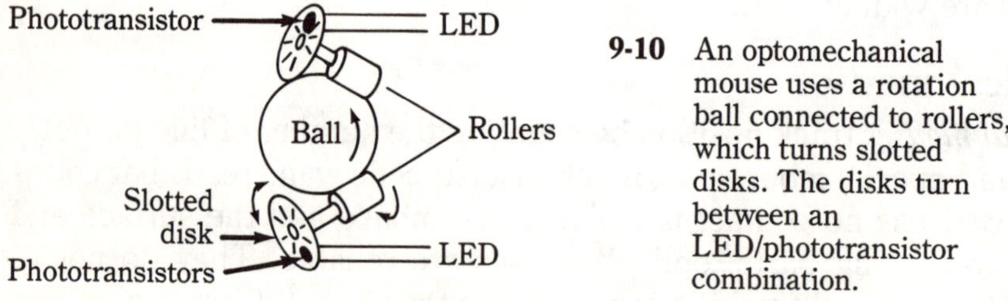

9-10 An optomechanical mouse uses a rotation ball connected to rollers, which turns slotted disks. The disks turn between an LED/phototransistor combination.

Optical-mechanical mouses use an optically sensed spring-loaded plate to determine the direction and to optically count the line crossings on a special mouse pad. These units have characteristics that are very similar to optical mouses.

Acoustomechanical mouses use strain gauges to determine direction and a piezoelectric transducer to determine the magnitude (Fig. 9-11). Acousto-

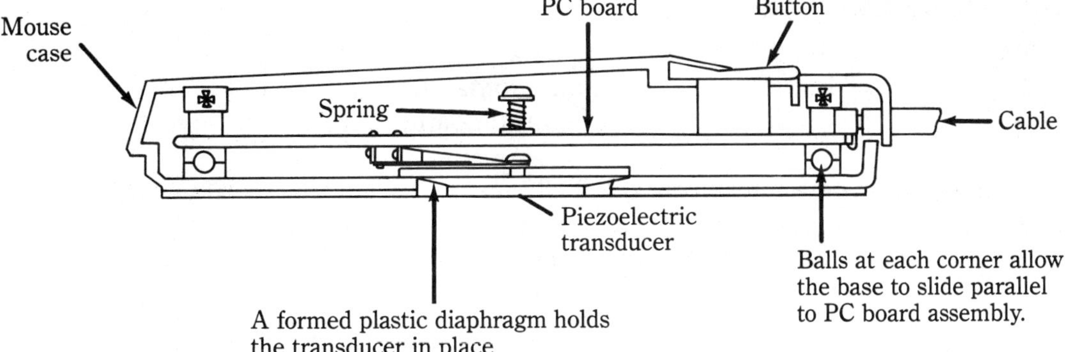

9-11   Acoustomechanical mice determine direction by the pattern of change in resistance in a strain gauge, which is returned to position by a spring action. An A/D converter provides a signal in proportion to the x-y shear. A microprocessor combines this data with velocity information from a piezoelectric transducer to reflect movement by the mouse.

mechanical mouses have no moving parts, no maintenance, and they can track motion on almost any surface; however, the resolution (counts/in.) depends on the type of surface on which the mouse is used and on the downward pressure that is placed on the mouse.

Analog mouses use either a ball or two orthogonal metal wheels mounted orthogonally to drive the shaft of a potentiometer. This technique is compatible with the interfacing schemes that are used by personal computers. The disadvantages are that such mouses have a limited lifetime and a limited amount of travel in any one direction because of the potentiometer. Generally, some kind of pad is used with nonoptical mouses to reduce slipping, audible noise, and to protect the desktop. This pad is often rigid. Most nonoptical mouses do not work well, unless they are horizontal.

The major problems that can occur with mouse input devices are:

1. *Maintenance*   Optical mouses have no moving parts. Because mechanical, optomechanical, and analog mouses require regular maintenance, some mouses have access holes for maintenance.

2. *Slippage*   Optical mouses rarely miss a count, but mechanical mouses can slip on the surface.

3. *Audible noise*   Some mechanical mouses that use a metal ball make audible noise on some surfaces. This noise may increase over a period of time. It is sometimes possible to reduce this noise by running the mouse on a sheet of paper.

4. *Jitter effects*   When a mouse is positioned between two grid points, a type of jitter, called *teasing* might occur. The mouse might jump ahead or back by one count. Teasing might also increase over time. Many devices use hysteresis to eliminate this problem.

Interfacing techniques

The two basic interfaces for mouses are parallel and serial. Parallel mouses generally use quadrature encoding for motion and encode switch depressions as a TTL low voltage. Different 9-pin standards are used by the manufacturers.

Serial mouses are interfaced to RS-232 ports. A wide variety of protocols might be used, but the electrical and mechanical interface is standard. Generally, these protocols send the change in the mouse state (buttons or position) whenever the mouse changes state.

The Mouse Systems serial protocol is typical. It is a 1,200 baud relative-position protocol that provides 48 updates/second with a maximum velocity of 50 inches/second. Information is transmitted only when the mouse state changes. Instead of polling the mouse, the microprocessor uses interrupts to service the device.

Modems

Modems use modulation to translate digital data signals into a signal form that is suitable for transmission over a particular medium, usually telephone lines. Modems can also use demodulation to retranslate the transmitted signals into the original digital data pattern once they reach their destination. Thus, they can be used as both input and output devices. The word *modem* is a contraction of *modulator/demodulator*.

True modems

True modems function like modems, but have advantages over modems in certain applications. Suppose, modems are functionally defined as *devices that allow communication between data devices over media that would not normally allow data transmission*. Based on this definition, a modem might or might not transmit data through modulation and demodulation. Short-haul modems might use techniques, such as current drive and return to zero. True modems use modulation/demodulation techniques.

Modulation and demodulation *Modulation* is a process by which a device generates an analog carrier signal and varies a characteristic of that signal, such as the amplitude, in relation to a digital data signal. *Demodulation* is the reverse process, by which the original data signal is recovered.

At the most basic level, a modem might use only two variations of a characteristic. A frequency-modulating modem might use one frequency or tone to represent spaces (0) and another frequency for marks (1).

Modulation techniques The most common modem modulation techniques are amplitude modulation (AM), phase modulation (PM), and frequency modulation (FM). Some modems might use these techniques in various combinations. Most modems use PM and FM because they are better suited to the requirements of data communications than AM.

AM modems, as the name suggests, vary the amplitude of the carrier signal in relation to the data signal. The number of amplitude levels used determines the amount of information that each level transmits. With two levels, for example, each level transmits either 0 or 1; with four levels, each level transmits either 00, 01, 10, or 11. Thus, modems that use four levels transmit twice as much information within the same time span as modems that use two levels.

Some modems might use AM in conjunction with another technique to increase the speed of data transmission over a given bandwidth. For example, a carrier signal modulated with two phases can transmit a maximum of one data bit per cycle (0 or 1). If that carrier signal was also modulated with two amplitudes, as in *quadrature amplitude modulation (QAM)*, the possible number of data bits per cycle would be two (00, 01, 10, or 11).

Although AM is inexpensive to implement in modems, it is not especially popular because of several problems. One problem is a wide bandwidth requirement, which makes it usable only for very low-speed data transmissions. Also problems from low noise tolerance can cause data errors in data transmissions. Phase modulation has good noise immunity, but it also uses a lot of bandwidth.

A simple example of *phase modulation* is a shift between two phases, and each phase shift represents a single data bit (0 or 1). This technique is commonly called *phase shift keying (PSK)*. In more complex phase modulation, four or more phase shifts might be used to transmit data and each phase shift transmits two or more data bits. This reduces the required bandwidth and allows higher data rates. Shifts of 90, 180, 270, and 360 degrees, for example, could be used to transmit 00, 01, 10, or 11.

The receiving modems in PM will detect each phase shift by reference to a fixed phase or, more typically, to the last phase. The modems must detect each shift as it occurs to order to achieve high data rates. These modems must also be synchronized with each other to allow rapid shift detection and signal decoding. This requirement makes these modems better suited for synchronous data transmissions, which is their primary use. The complexity of the detection and decoding circuitry is relatively high.

FM modems do not need to be synchronized and are a simpler design for operation above the voice band. FM modems typically use a technique called *frequency shift keying (FSK)*, in which the carrier only shifts between two frequencies (tones). FSK modems are usually *phase-coherent*; each new frequency follows the phase of the previous frequency. There is no forced phase shift and the frequency components that would result from such shift are missing. The receiving modem only needs to handle the two data-carrying frequencies. This allows higher data rates because phase-coherent modems can detect these frequencies within a very short period, even within half a cycle.

Some modems use the on-off technique to transmit data. In this case, the modems simply turn the carrier signal on or off to transmit 0 and 1. This technique could be viewed as either FM or AM modulation. Modems and modem-like devices can be grouped into seven basic types: long-haul modems, short-haul modems, medium-distance modems, data-over-voice modems, acoustic couplers, modem eliminators, and line drivers.

Long-haul modems allow the transmission of data over large distances. With a long-haul modem, it is possible to access a computer located across the country or ocean. These modems can be either half-duplex or full-duplex, and some long-haul units have both capabilities. Normally, long-haul modems modulate a voice-frequency carrier signal with the digital data pattern. They are designed to compensate for the variations that occur in the line parameters, such as amplitude and phase delay. In theory, the range of long-haul modems is limited only by the quality of the media over which they are transmitted.

These modems can be divided into two subtypes, depending on the type of lines that they use. Most long-hauls are designed for operation on the *public-switched (DDD) network*. Others are designed for use on *dedicated leased telephone lines* (Bell System Type 3002 voice channels). DDD modems are the most common. DDD modems are typically Bell-compatible and will operate with either Bell System modems or other Bell-compatible models.

All DDD modems require FCC certification (U.S.) or DOC registration (Canada) for direct connection to the public-switched network. Modems that operate on dedicated leased lines do not require FCC/DOC certification, but they might require line conditioning (C1, C2, C4, D1, or D2) to eliminate problems on dedicated leased lines. *Conditioning* controls the frequency response and other channel characteristics to lower the error-rate at high speeds.

Microprocessors are used in most long-haul modems for reliability and flexibility. Most long-hauls for PCs provide complete menu-driven controls with autodialing to store multiple numbers and log-in sequences. Other features include error-detection and control auto answer; autodial, multiport operation, alternate voice/data transmission, and dial backup.

Short-haul modems typically operate at distances of up to 10 miles. Short-hauls are widely used for data transmission within metropolitan areas, in campus environments, and within building complexes. Short-haul modems are used because they are less expensive and provide higher data rates. These advantages allow more efficient use of existing leased lines.

The most common data rate for short-haul modems is 9,600 bps, but some short-hauls operate at much higher rates (256 Kbps). Most short-hauls, which are also known as *local data sets*, operate on privately owned metallic circuits or leased lines. The distances at which they operate are limited by the transmission speed and the diameter of the wires over which they transmit.

Generally, short-haul modems do not require dc continuity. In addition, the communication line for a short-haul is isolated from the modem through a transformer, which helps protect the modem from damage and disturbance from transient signals (lightning, for example) on the line. Short-hauls also provide high reliability and lower bit-error rates.

Many short-haul modems are not true modems in the sense of having a carrier signal that they modulate. These modems are actually line drivers that send the digital signal directly over the channel by acting as a signal conditioner. Because the integrity of the digital signal depends on the speed and distance involved, these short-hauls have a very limited range. The smaller short-hauls measure less than 4 inches in length, weigh only a few ounces, and plug directly into an RS-232 connector.

Medium-distance modems fall between short-hauls and long-hauls. They can operate at separation distances of up to 200 miles. These devices are true modems because they generate a carrier signal and modulate it. They do not require all of the complicated long-distance circuitry of long hauls. Medium-distance modems include synchronous and asynchronous models.

Data-over-voice modems are sometimes known as *local-area data transports (LADTs)*. They allow simultaneous voice and high speed, full-duplex data communications on a single pair of two wires of existing telephone wires for up to several miles. DOV's are true modems. They generate carrier frequencies and modulate them with the digital data pattern. Frequency allocation and a sophisticated filtering system prevents the voice and data channels from interfering with each other. Available models are PCC certified, but are not designed for use on the public-switched network or leased lines. Some models work as 2-wire modems on private telephone lines or other metallic circuits.

In addition to long-haul, short-haul, medium-distance, and data-over-voice modems, several other types of modems and modem-like devices are used. These units are used in specialized applications, where conventional modems are not practical or cost-effective.

Acoustic couplers, for example, are found in portable applications. These devices acoustically provide a data path to the switched network directly through a telephone handset. In general, acoustic couplers do not operate at speeds greater than 600 bps. They are low priced and do not need FCC/DOC certification.

Modem eliminators are another example. They are used when the distance is very short (200 feet) or when a clock source is needed to permit communications over a very short distance. These units extend the possible separation distance between two data devices. Each modem eliminator serves as a substitute for two modems by regenerating the data and control signals and by providing the necessary crossover and clock source.

Line drivers, like modem eliminators, are alternatives to conventional modems in very local applications. These devices, which usually require dc continuity, run on customer-owned (private) twisted-wire pairs or coaxial cable. The line is not isolated from the equipment, which makes line drivers susceptible to damage and interference from transient signals. Line drivers are usually not Bell-approved for use on telco lines. As discussed earlier, some so-called short-haul modems or local data sets are actually line drivers. Because of the limitations of line drivers, they cannot be used as a replacement device for an application that requires the capabilities of a short-haul modem.

Depending on the number of dedicated communication lines involved, the cost of using multiple modems can quickly become unreasonable. In this situation, *multiplexers* are used. Multiplexers combine several low-speed inputs into one high-speed output. As a result, they allow two or more data devices to transmit data simultaneously over a single medium. Multiplexers concentrate data, which would otherwise be routed over many separate point-to-point lines, into a composite stream that is transmitted over one link. Some multiplexers have built-in modems.

The two basic techniques of multiplexing are frequency division and time division. In *frequency division*, the communications channel is split into different frequencies and the data from the different sources is transmitted together. In *time division*, data from each source is put on a schedule, and only one data signal at a time is transmitted. Time division multiplexing can allocate time on either a fixed or a statistical basis.

Modem and MUX testers

Modems and MUX testers are generally microprocessor-based instruments. They can be used to test and monitor a data communications system at the modem-terminal interface. A breakout panel provides access to the conductors of the interface between the terminal and the modem. Synchronous and asynchronous protocols can be used for a variety of tests. Master and remote polling tests can be performed on two- or four-wire systems. An echo test drives received data (RD) back out as transmitted data (TD) to verify message transmission.

Bit error-rate testers   A *Bit Error-Rate Test (BERT)* counts bit errors in different patterns. Transitions can be detected in a steady mark or space pattern. User-constructed messages can be entered and tested. Handheld microprocessor-based testers can perform several tests. A typical BERT tester might be capable of testing synchronous data links to 72 Kbps and asynchronous data links to 38 Kbps. These can perform bit-error testing, % error-free seconds testing, and count positive and negative transitions on any interface lead. They can also generate Fox messages in ASCII, BAUDOT, and IPARS.

BERT/breakout testers BERT/breakout testers function as both a basic BERT tester and a battery-powered breakout box. They are capable of analyzing both the bit error rate of digital data communication channels as well as breaking out and monitoring both sides of the RS-232 interface. They usually have separate transmitter and receiver sections that allow full-duplex tests to be performed in either end-to-end or loopback configurations.

In some units, the transmitter can generate up to four switch selectable dot patterns, including 2,047-bit repeating pseudo-random sequences and an alternating mark-space pattern. The receiver section generates a replica of the selected transmitted data pattern and compares this error-free replica with the received data pattern. The breakout box is line powered and is capable of monitoring both sides of the RS-232 interface.

10
Testing techniques

An important part of testing is what to do if the computer does not work. The goal is to know what went wrong and why. This testing or troubleshooting process requires some knowledge of the computer hardware, in addition, a number of techniques are available for identifying and correcting problems. Problems related to component failure and methods for identifying them are covered. The general troubleshooting tools available to identify and locate these problems will also be described. These include voltmeters, continuity testers, logic probes, signature analyzers, oscilloscopes, and digital analyzers.

Common problems

Typical problems that can occur in a computer system include:

1. Connection faults, open or short circuits.
2. Component failures or, wrong value or type of component installed.
3. Software or disk media errors.
4. Noise or interference errors.

Connection faults

Connection faults can be detected by a resistance check from point to point in the system. Each wire or circuit track must provide a complete connection. Connection faults can be troublesome problems, but they are easily solved (Fig. 10-1). Circuit paths can be buzz-tested using a simple continuity-checker that emits a tone for a connection and is quiet for an open (Fig. 10-2). Such a tester leaves both hands and eyes free to track the wiring.

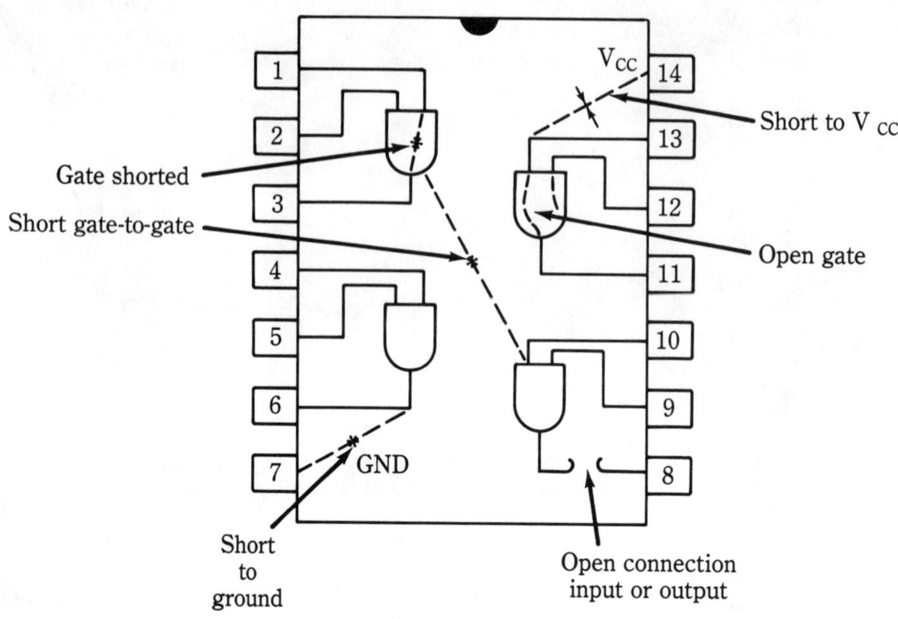

10-1   Typical failures in a small 4-gate IC.

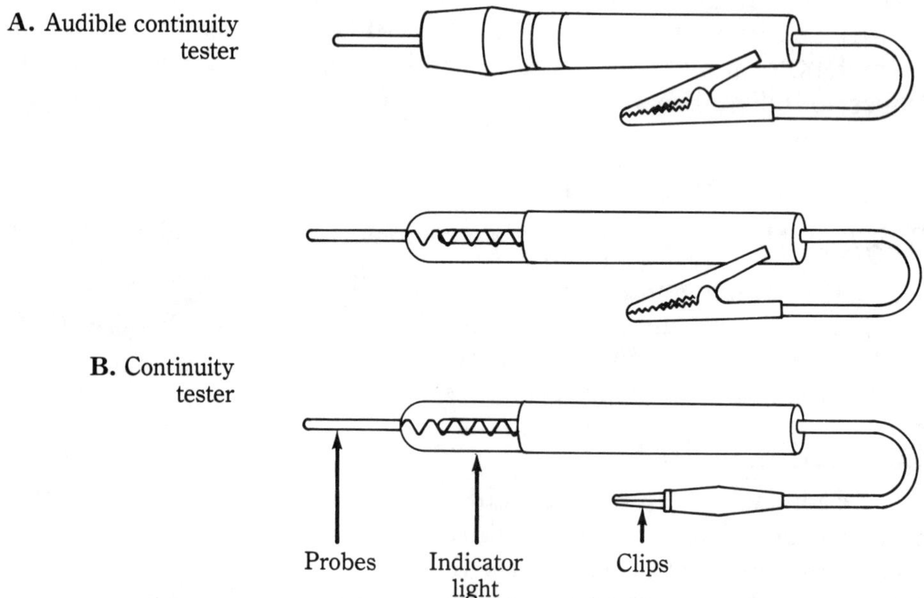

10-2   Audible continuity testers operate with 1.5-Vdc AAA batteries and emit a 70-dB audible signal for a connection of less than 150 between the probe and clip ends. Continuity testers will test for the presence of voltages from 2 to 500 Vac or Vdc.

Component failures

Components such as resistors, capacitors, inductors, transformers, transistors, diodes, integrated circuits, and connectors can all fail. Resistors can open and capacitors can become leaky. Each component can be assigned a figure of merit, known as its *meantime-between-failure (MTBF)*. This statistical prediction estimates (in hours of use) how long an average part will last under typical operating conditions. Table 10-1 lists some typical values of failure rates for good-quality parts and connections. These numbers are often used to estimate those parts that are most likely to fail after a certain period of time. The failure rates are determined from test data and field return data on a large number of parts.

Table 10-1. Average failure rates for typical computer parts and connections

Component or connection	(%/1,000 hr) failure rate
1. Capacitor	0.02
2. Connector contact	0.005
3. Diode	0.013
4. Integrated circuit	0.015
5. Quartz clock crystal	0.05
6. Resistor	0.002
7. Soldered joint	0.0002
8. Transformer	0.5
9. Transistor	0.04
10. Variable resistor	0.01

Some parts will last longer, on the average, than others. These values assume that all parts are properly installed and equipment is operated properly. Because failure rates are defined as 1/MTBF, knowing the failure rate of each component in the computer will provide the failure rate for the complete system. Add the failure rates of all the components in the computer to provide the computer failure rate. The inverse of this number is the system meantime-between-failures.

Electronic components exhibit a bathtub type of lifetime characteristic. This means that many failures occur when the parts are new, most of the other failures occur when the parts are old and fewer failures occur in between. Initial burn-in tests are often used to root out most of the initial failures. This means the computer is left running for a specific period of time, often for several days. Most of the initial failures will occur during this time.

Software problems

Software can be at fault. For example, there might be a routine in a program for restoring data to an internal register during a power interruption. Suppose a mistake was made when copying this program, which restores conditions when power returns. If this routine does not work when the power fails, the unit might go into a foreign state.

Another potential problem could be an arithmetic calculation that causes an overflow and halt condition when an input value exceeds a register's capability. The system might work well until this condition is exceeded. Then, the system might stop mysteriously.

These types of software problems (bugs) can be difficult to identify. You will usually have to contact the software vendor or developer and report this type of problem. They might have a patch or fix worked out already or they might have advice on how to back away from the problem and how to avoid it in the future.

Noise problems

Noise can be a problem in circuits with low-level signals. It is generally kept under control by the circuit design, but drift in components or a break in a shield or ground connection can cause a noise problem to surface. When a current is in a wire, an electromagnetic field is present. Power transformers, motors, and electrical wiring have fields. When these fields become large enough to generate signals in wires or components, they become a problem. Even a small length of wire can act as an antenna for noise.

When integrated circuits switch, they can cause current changes in their power requirements. When many circuits switch at once and the system logic changes are not balanced, the power-supply voltage changes can affect other parts of the circuit. Bypass capacitors are often installed near each integrated circuit to prevent this type of noise. A noise spike can occur from turning on a piece of equipment on the same power line. In a system without noise filters, if that spike occurs at a critical time, data can be lost.

If two wires are close together, a pulse traveling along one induces a pulse in the other, as a result of transformer action between the two wires. This type of induced pulse can cause reflections in the wiring and toggle a logic circuit or cause read/write data errors. To prevent these problems, twisted and shielded lines are often used.

The power supply is always filtered (Fig. 10-3), but a small amount of 60-cycle ripple is always at the output of the filter. If this ripple becomes large enough, it can affect the contents of memory and cause an improper read or write. The power-supply will also have a small droop in voltage under heavy load before actual regulation occurs.

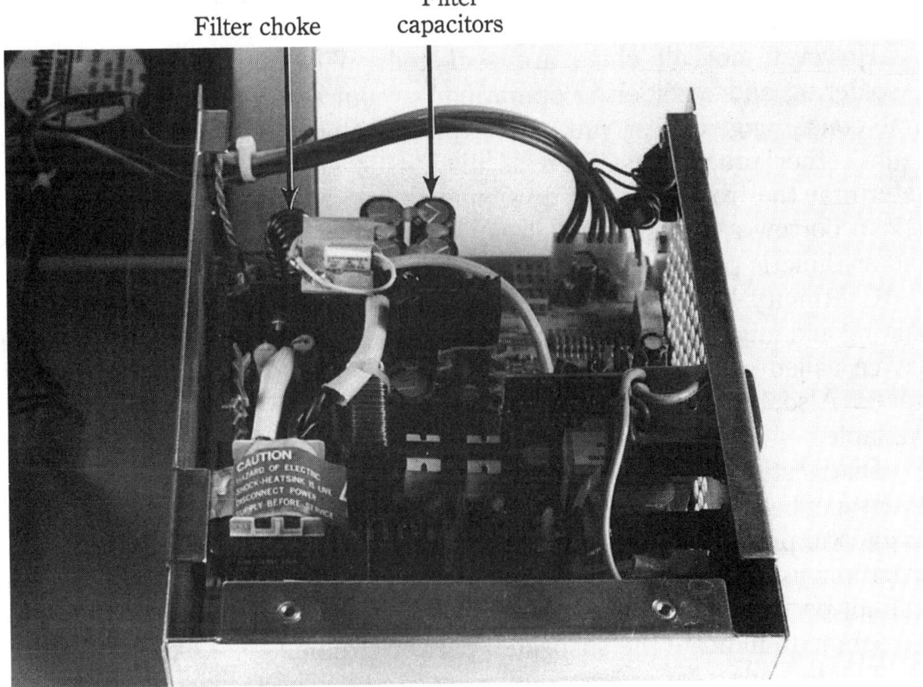

10-3   An XT power supply. The filter components are located at the rear.

Troubleshooting tools

A number of tools can be used to find problems. When you have a problem
with your computer, the first step is to analyze the symptoms of the problem. You must be able to indicate the circuits that are likely to contain the
defect. Thus, you need some tools that will tell you the condition of the circuit.

Typical hardware tools include a low-voltage continuity tester, a logic
probe and a Volt-Ohm-Meter (VOM). The continuity tester can be used to
find shorts and opens. This type of tester is used when the computer is disconnected from power.

The logic probe can be used to check high and low logic levels and
pulses on the pins of the digital circuits. The logic probe is used when the
computer is powered on. The VOM is an all-around instrument that can be
used to measure voltages, as well as to measure resistance and continuity.

A common technique is to make some measurements with the test
equipment and/or run some diagnostic tests. Based on the results of these
hardware or software tests, you can make a replacement of the suspect

part. For example, if the microprocessor is suspected from the results of software tests, you can unplug it and try a replacement.

However, not all chips are socketed. With the microprocessor, a desoldering and resoldering operation is required. This operation can be time consuming. Unless you have experience working with small components, other procedures (such as diagnostic software) are best used to determine the trouble. If you do suspect a socketed chip though, and have or can borrow a replacement, it can be worth a try. Many memory chips and arithmetic processors are socketed.

Continuity, logic, and voltage tests are usually simple, but are time consuming and might not be able to indicate some problems. A signal injection device called a *logic pulser* can be used and another unit is the current tracer. Also, various types of oscilloscopes and frequency counters are available.

Diagnostic software is another important tool for testing. Simple programs can be stored on the ROMs in the computer or on a disk. Specialized diagnostic programs are available for most parts of the computer. These programs usually exercise various circuits in the computer and if a circuit will not perform properly, a special trouble number or code will appear on the screen to indicate the suspected part or circuit.

The following list of test equipment can be used for troubleshooting:

Power On	**Power Off**
Voltmeters	Ohmmeters
Continuity testers	
Oscilloscopes	
Frequency counters	
Logic probes and analyzers	
Digital signature analyzers	
Signal and function generators	
Automatic testers	

Most troubleshooting tools are designed for certain kinds of problems. It is important to know the limitations of these tools. Open conductors and incorrect voltages are among the most common problems and they are also the easiest to detect. An ohm meter can be used to check for opens and shorts and a DVM or VOM can be used to check voltages and currents. If you have the proper schematics and the time, it is possible to make sure that every component draws the right currents and receives the proper voltages. Figures 10-4 and 10-5 show several types of digital meters.

To measure a voltage, a VOM is placed in parallel with the circuit element. Consider the measurement of a power-supply output voltage, the VOM can be used to measure such voltages, but it will not detect excessive

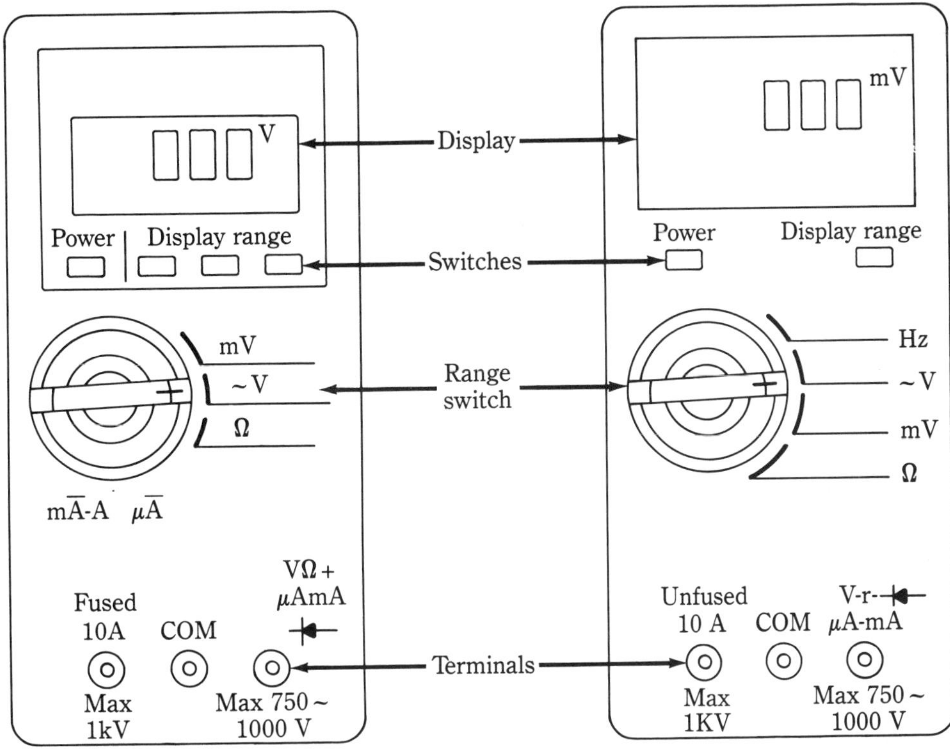

10-4 Two examples of hand-held digital VOMs.

ripple or noise riding on the power-supply outputs. An oscilloscope must be used to measure excessive ripple or noise.

In order to measure a current, the meter must be placed in series with the component. This means the circuit must be broken. It is always possible that some connections can be made, without cutting wires or traces. In the previous power-supply example, the meter can measure the voltage across the load and then by disconnecting the load and reconnecting it in series through the meter, the current can be measured. These measurements should be within the required tolerances. Incorrect values might indicate later problems.

Component substitution

Resistors, capacitors, diodes, and transistors can all be checked against known good devices. They can be measured with the DVM or VOM to determine if they are basically functional. For example, a good diode will have a low resistance in the forward direction, usually less than a few ohms. The resistance in the reverse direction should be much greater (by a factor

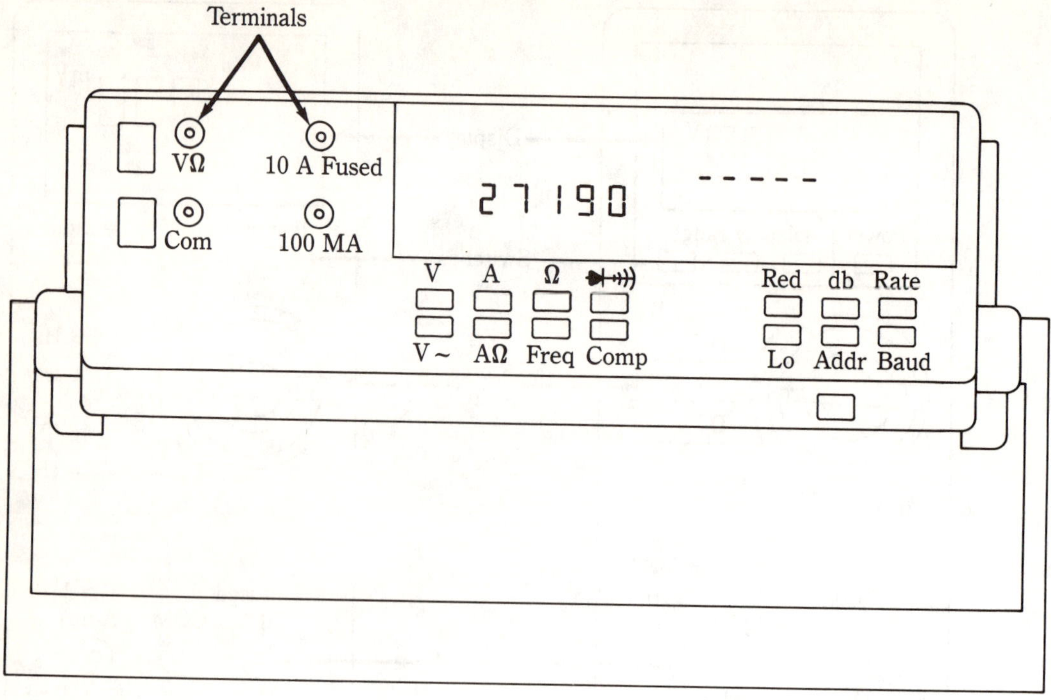

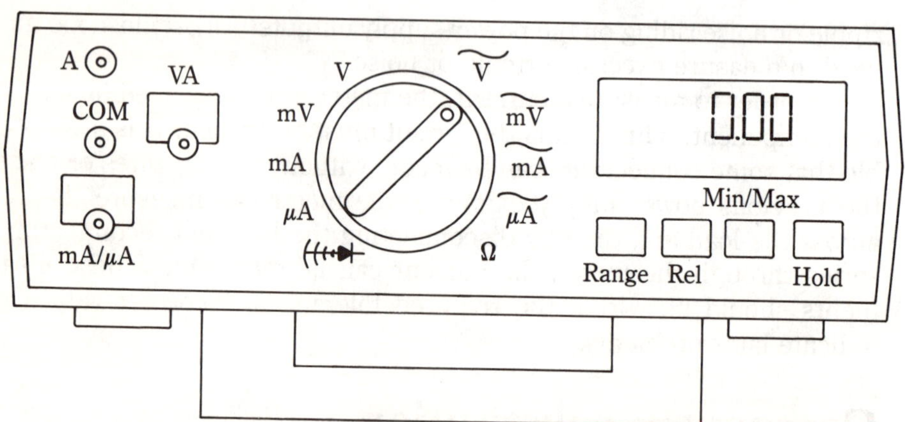

10-5 Bench-type digital multimeters. (A) This model measures frequency to 1 MHz. Dc current accuracy is 0.05% and a dual display allows two measurements from the same signal. (B) This model will measure voltages from 100 to 1000 Vac or Vdc, currents from 0.1 to 10 A (ac or dc) or resistance from 0.1 to 10 A (ac or dc) or resistance from 0.1 to 10,000 MΩ with a relative mode that calculates the difference between the present reading and following readings.

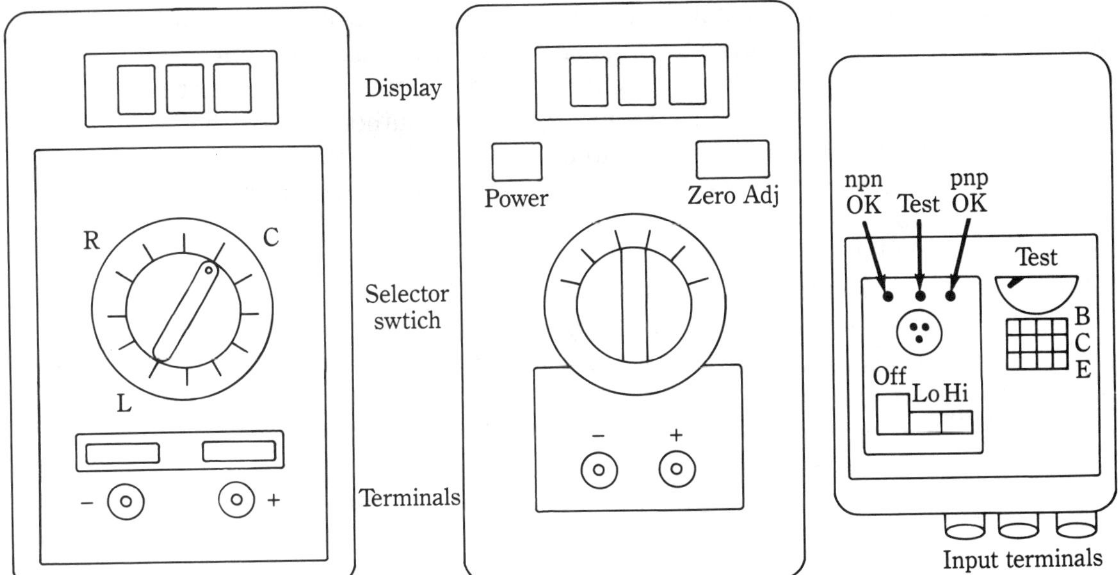

10-6 Hand-held instruments. (A) An LCR meter with 3¹/₂ LCD display. Measures capacitance from 200 pF to 2 mF, resistance from 20Ω to 20 MΩ and inductance from 2 mH to 200 H. (B) A digital capacitance meter with nine ranges from 200 pF to 20 mF, fuse, protection to prevent damage from a charged capacitor and + .5% accuracy. (C) This transistor tester is a GO/NO-GO tester with LEDs to indicate npn-OK or pnp-OK. It can be used to test FETs and SCRs in or out of the circuit.

of 100 or 1,000). A bipolar transistor can be quickly checked in much the same way because it consists of two diodes connected back to back.

Special test equipment is needed to measure the actual device characteristics of diodes and transistors (Fig. 10-6). Integrated circuits can be difficult to test without expensive equipment. It is much easier to have several of each devices available in order to replace a device with a possible malfunction. Intermittent problems are often caused by connector or solder-joint failures. These can be checked first, before going on to other components.

Intermittent problems will generally require an oscilloscope (preferably with some storage capabilities) or a logic analyzer, which stores the logic states that can be used. Static problems are easier to solve.

Voltmeters

The *voltmeter* is versatile and convenient for checking computer circuits. But, be careful when using the ohmmeter in the VOM to check resistance in the computer. The ohmmeter section uses batteries that can apply a dangerous voltage to the component under test. One cell might be used to provide 1.5 V for the low ranges, but the higher ranges could have several cells added together in series to furnish 6 V. A small transistor junction could be destroyed with the higher voltage. The small transistors used in the more complex ICs are even sensitive to the lower voltages, although most have some form of protection on the input. To avoid unneeded problems, use a low-voltage ohmmeter scale. The voltmeter function of the VOM does not furnish any voltage to the components.

When the VOM is used to check the logic states, the negative lead is attached to ground and the logic states can be checked on a pin-by-pin basis. TTL voltage levels are typical. If you measure the voltage levels on TTL devices, a high can range from +2.5 to +5 V and a low will range from 0 to +0.8 V. A voltage between +0.8 and +2.5 V indicates a tristate condition. The test point is in a high-impedance state and a logic probe LED would not be triggered by this voltage.

In a CMOS chip, the voltage levels are similar, but not the same as TTL. A high level is above +4.2 V and the low state is below +1.8 V. The range +1.8 and +4.2 V represents the tristate condition. In both TTL and CMOS chips, the tristate condition could indicate a failure or the chip could be in a normal condition. If you find a tristate condition, check the part number and function of the chip to see if it represents a failure.

Continuity testing

A *resistance continuity tester* will light up or buzz if a complete circuit is present. Many continuity testers use 1.5-V batteries that can damage a sensitive junction. A low-voltage tester can be built using the circuit shown in Fig. 10-7. The circuit, as well as the rest of the tester, can be built from available parts or the circuit can be built or installed to modify an existing continuity tester.

If you are modifying an existing tester, the circuit can use the same batteries and bulb. The additional parts needed are the npn transistor and a CMOS comparator (such as the CA3130). A few resistors are needed to bias the circuit. The transistor switches the bulb on and off and the comparator is used to turn the transistor on and off.

The completed circuit delivers about 0.2 V to the component under test. This voltage is low enough to protect most sensitive junctions and is below the voltage necessary to turn most components on. If a device is switched on during testing, it could cause the computer circuits to change state and indicate a malfunction.

Logic pulsers

The *logic pulser* is a type of signal injector. It has two connections that are made to +5 V and ground. The pulser is touched to a test point and it has a

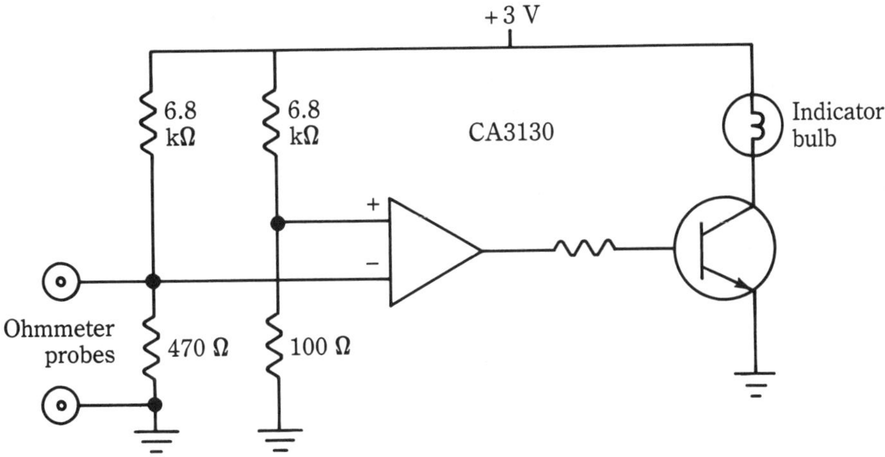

10-7 A voltage limiter for an ohmmeter.

button that can be used to send a pulse to the test point. The pulse voltage
is usually high and pressing the button will cause it to become low, then
high again. These pulses can be used to test digital circuits. A test point
that is low can be switched to a high state.

Current tracers

The *current tracer* is a current-probe device that can be used to detect an ac
current. It has a small magnetic pickup coil in its tip and when this coil is
close to the magnetic field produced by an ac current, an indicator light
glows. The tracer can be used to trace the path of or detect a continuous
pulse train. The sensitivity is adjustable and the detectable current range is
typically a few hundred μA (a very dim indication) to a few mA (fully lit).
The current path must be in line with the pickup coil, if the current flow is
at an angle of 90 degrees there will not be enough coupling for the pickup
to work.

The current tracer is useful when a circuit has several parallel
branches and a problem, like a short, could be in any one of the branches
(Fig. 10-8). In order to isolate the branch with the short, each branch would
have to be disconnected and tested separately. This work would require cutting or desoldering each branch to separate them and then resoldering to
connect them.

The current tracer allows you to test the current in each branch. A
TTL high output would normally have a current of about 40 μA. A TTL
low output will normally have a current of about 1.6 mA. With a short circuit, the high current would be about 55 mA. The normal high current of
40 μA will not light the lamp of the current tracer but a current of 55 mA
would cause a very noticeable bright light. The current tracer can be

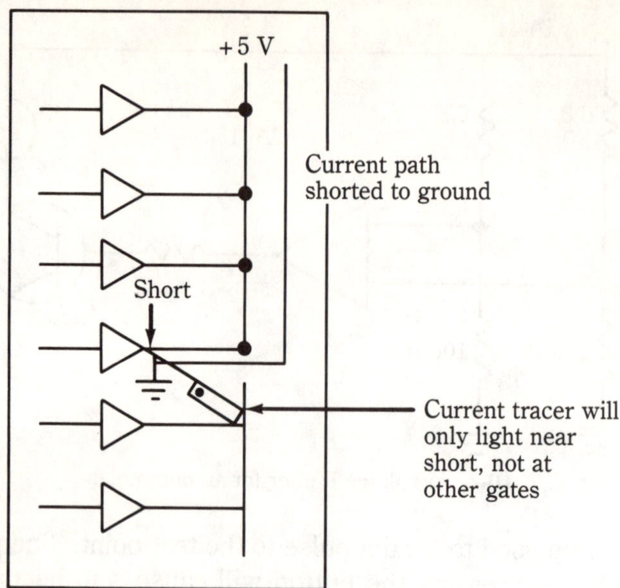

10-8 A current tracer is helpful when many parallel paths exist. It can be used to find the shorted point.

quickly touched to the suspected circuits and the bright light will point to the faulty track or circuit.

Logic probes

The *logic probe* is designed to test digital circuits for the proper logic states. No actual measurement of voltage is made, but the probe will indicate a high, low, or pulse condition. The probe usually has switches to select CMOS or TTL levels and multiple or single pulses. Two leads are connected to power the probe. One connection goes to ground and the other goes to +5 V to provide the power for the indicator lights. The logic probe connection is made by touching the test probe to the IC under test.

The probe usually has at least three LEDs to indicate, high, low and pulse conditions (Fig. 10-9). When only the high LED lights up, a high is at the test point. When only the low LED is lit, a low is on the test point. In either case, no pulsing activity occurs and the duration of the signal is constant at the test point. If both the high and pulse LEDs are lit, there is a series of positive pulses. When both the low and pulse LEDs are lit, there is a series of negative pulses.

You also get an indication of the frequency. Usually, if the frequency of a square wave is less than 100 kHz, all three LEDs will light. The square wave has a 50% duty cycle for both the high and low durations so that both LEDs light. When one state (high or low) has a larger duration, the light for

LED states high　low　pulse	Signal sensed	Explanation
○　○　○	No signal	Open circuit three-state
✹　○　○	5 V ⌐‾‾‾‾‾ ⊓⊔ 1 0 V	High level
○　✹　○	5 V ‾‾⊔⊓ 0 0 V ⌊____	Low level
✹　○　✹	‖‖‖‖ 1	Negative pulses from high level
○　✹　✹	‖‖‖‖ 0	Positive pulses from low level
○　○　✹	⊓⊔⊓⊔⊓⊔	Square wave greater than 100 kHz
✹　✹　✹	⊓⊔⊓⊔⊓	Square wave less than 100 kHz

10-9　Typical logic probe signal sensing states.

that state will light. When the frequency is above a 100-kHz square wave, only the pulse LED will light.

Logic probes are useful for checking logic levels on ICs and they are helpful for isolating static or steady conditions. A quick indication is possible; it will show that a signal is a 0, 1, or undetermined. The undetermined state usually indicates a problem, unless it is a tristate floating output. Figure 10-10 shows several types of logic probes, a logic pulser, and a clip-on logic monitor.

The VOM and logic probe do not indicate time, so they are of limited or little use for dynamic problems. What is needed are devices that can indicate if the timing is correct.

The oscilloscope

In order to obtain timing information, an oscilloscope can be used. By using one or more traces, critical events can be measured as a function of time. A

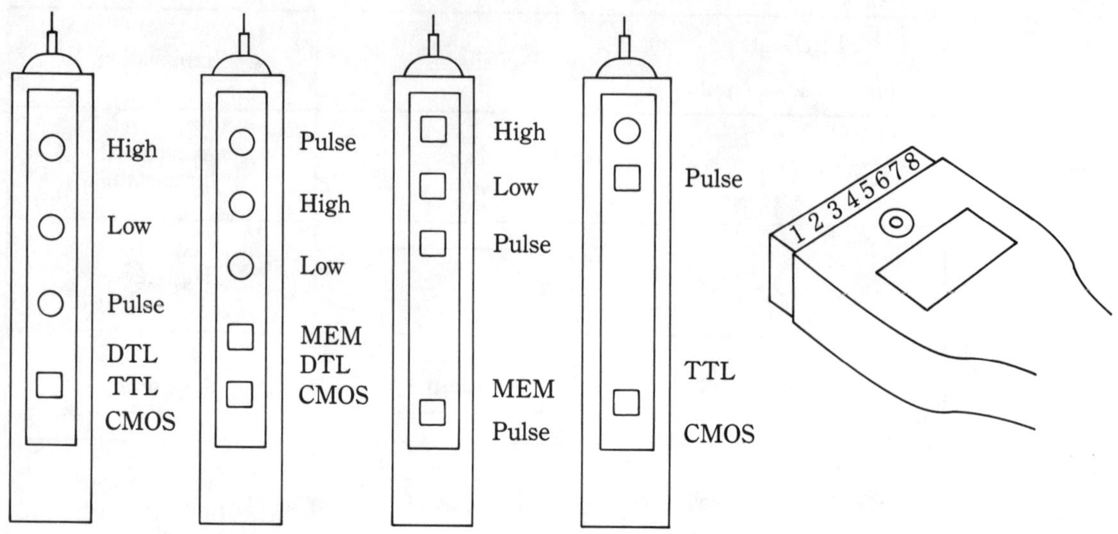

10-10   Logic probes and pulsers. (A) 50 ns to 10 MHz. (B) 50 ns to 35 MHz. (C) ECL 3 ns to 100 MHz. (D) Logic pulser 100 #2 train, 100 ma 1 s for TTL, lo s for CMOS. (E) Clip-on logic monitor, 16 channels for 8-, 14- or 16-pin OCs/ 16 LEDs light for high logic levels.

general-purpose oscilloscope has a horizontal frequency range of about 100 kHz. Thus, it can be used to view and measure frequencies up to this range. The minimum clock frequency of an IBM PC is 4.77 MHz, so one cycle of the clock cannot be viewed. You would see 47.7 complete cycles if the maximum frequency of the oscilloscope is 100 kHz. This would appear as an envelope (Fig. 10-11). You would not be able to recognize individual cycles, but you would know that the clock is running.

Besides the clock circuit, other signals can be tested with a general-purpose oscilloscope, such as the video signals in video circuits. Figure 10-12 shows how to measure the signals of these and other circuits. The multitrace high-frequency oscilloscope can be used to check the timing between critical chips, such as the microprocessor and the memory. This is done using a timing diagram (Fig. 10-13).

In microcomputer systems, events as short as 10 ns might need to be observed. A 10-ns square wave will be filtered and will look like a sine wave on a 10-MHz oscilloscope. A unit with a 50- or 100-MHz bandwidth is needed to see these faster events clearly. Transitions from one logic level to the other would generally occur in less than one μs to avoid noise problems. An oscilloscope can be used to indicate if a logic-level error is present.

Such a measurement, along with the knowledge of the correct logic timing, will indicate to the troubleshooter that a line is at fault. By observing chip-select, control, and bus lines with an oscilloscope loading, timing and noise problems can be found. The logic levels should fall between accepted limits; voltage levels that fall between states indicate problems.

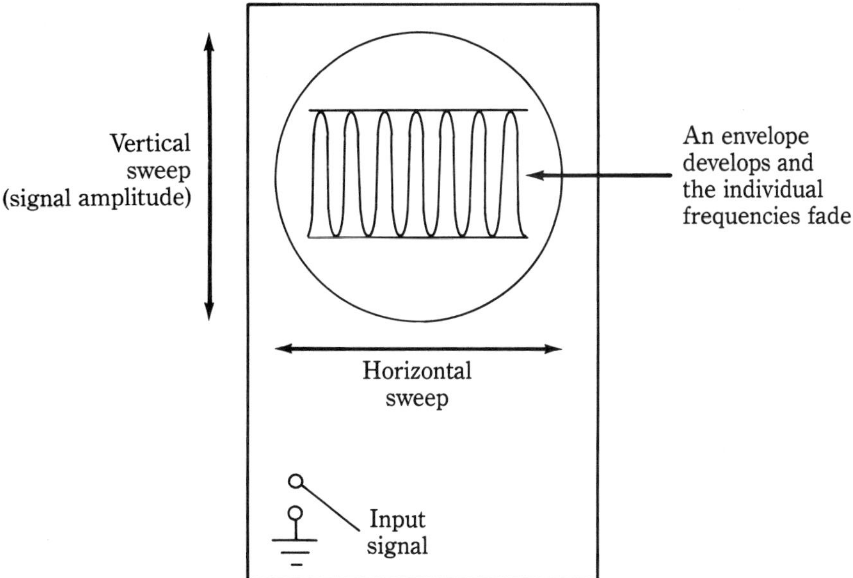

10-11 If the vertical input frequency is much greater than the horizontal sweep, the individual frequencies will be lost with only the outside envelope left.

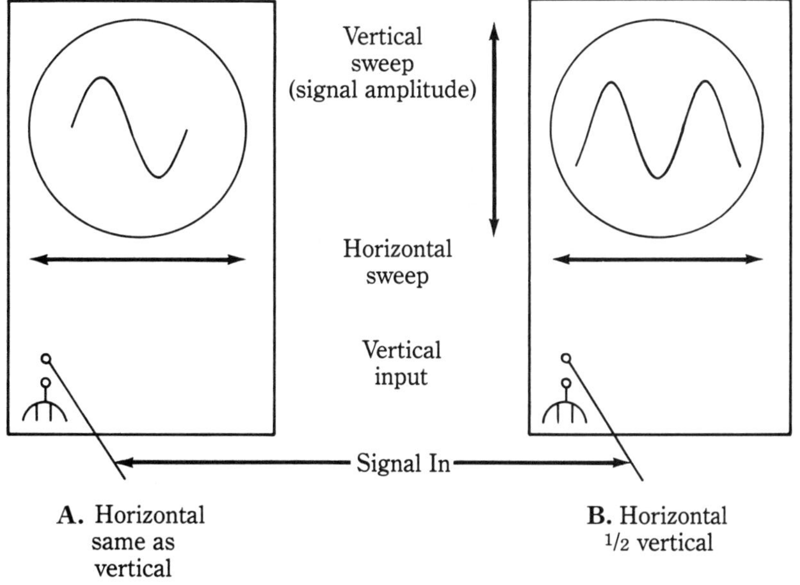

10-12 Using a scope to check signal amplitude and frequency.

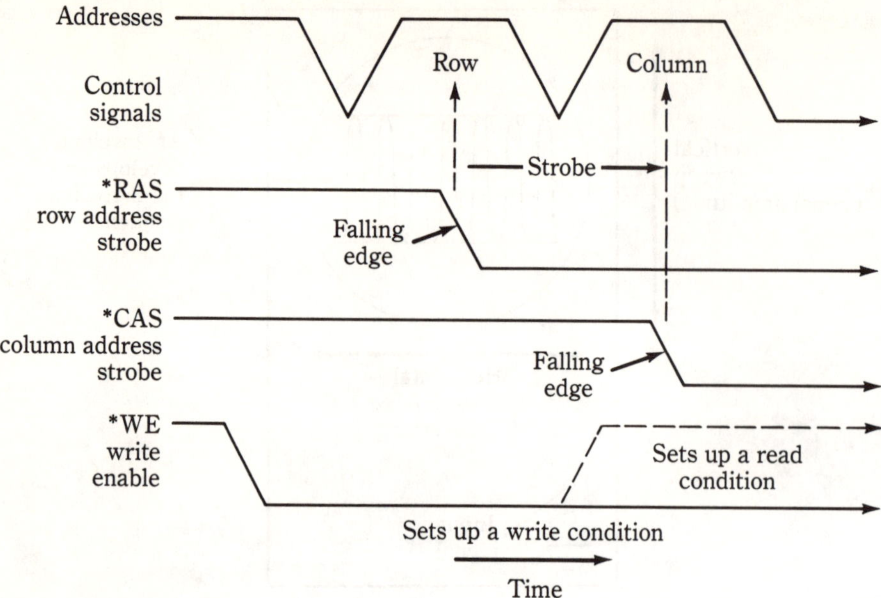

10-13 A timing diagram for 4164 control signals. The falling edges of the RAS and CAS signals are timed to strobe the row and column addresses. WE will either set up a read or write condition.

Frequency counters

A *frequency counter* can be used to measure the actual frequency of the clock or the frequency of circuits that are driven by the clock. This procedure can be done with a magnetic pick-up loop or with a direct physical connection. The advantage of using a magnetic loop is that loading effects on the circuits are minimized or eliminated. Capacitive coupling can also be used to reduce loading effects. The loop can quickly be moved close to the clock-generating crystal and it can be used to measure the crystal frequency. A defective crystal or frequency-determining circuit can be found with this method.

Logic state measurement

Individual system timing and system logic levels might appear to be correct when observing a single bit, line, or pair of lines, but in some cases a number of lines might need to be observed at the same instant in time. In this case, logic analyzers (sometimes called *digital-domain analyzers*) are used. These instruments allow the simultaneous observation of up to 32 lines. They can generally display these bits in binary, octal, hexadecimal, or in the form of conventional oscilloscope traces. The display can be triggered when a given combination of bits occurs.

State analyzers can store a number of clock cycles and they can display several sets of signals before and after the trigger set. Each set of signals in time is known as a *state*. The available analyzers are designed to provide two types of information. Some provide mostly timing information and others provide mostly logic state information. The timing information analyzers are configured like multichannel oscilloscopes. These devices are most useful where logic spikes, noise, or logic-level problems are to be investigated.

Signature analyzers *Signature analyzers* are based on storing repetitive sequences of signal values in a recirculating shift register. The values are clocked into a display each time around. The sequence of values will generally have a unique signature, unless similar points or lines are being measured.

Each node in a system will have its own signature when it is working properly. It will also have a special signature for each possible problem. By using fault-tree methods, which are developed by using the signature analyzer, faulty equipment can be debugged quickly. It will not find software problems or the cause of intermittent failures in a system. A typical unit is the HP 5004A Signature Analyzer.

Testing problems

An example of improper testing is passing too much current through a sensitive IC. This can cause damage, such as an open. Applying too much voltage to a device can cause arcing and eventual breakdown because every device has its limits. Another problem is the loading effect on a single output line on an IC. A parameter drift can cause the system to read or write improper data values on an intermittent basis, which might depend on temperature.

Other subtle errors include timing problems of a particular part. Suppose that the address for a particular memory part must be stable for 30 ns. If the address gated to this memory part must be stable for 30 ns before the data and write pulses arrive, but it isn't, the system timing will be incorrect. Some problems require specialized equipment for quickly completing the troubleshooting effort, but a VOM and oscilloscope can be used for most problems if time is not as critical.

Problems with intermittents must be checked. The system can be operated at different temperatures to localize sensitive components. A can of freeze spray and a heat lamp can sometimes be used to locate temperature sensitive problems by heating and cooling the suspected parts.

Comparison tests

With *comparison tests*, a device or board under test, is compared to a known good device or good board. They share the same common input, and outputs are compared. This is a hardware method, and the required tools have been covered. The underlying principle of this testing technique is to compare an existing board, component, or system, to a properly functioning unit.

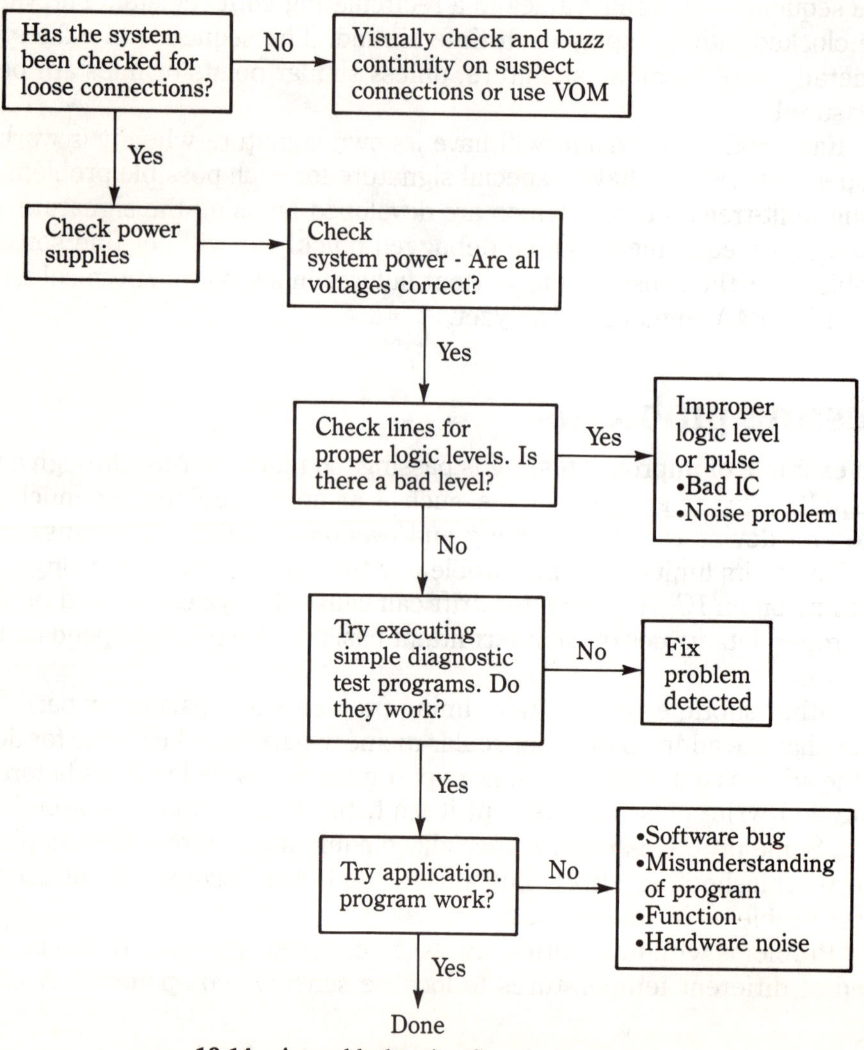

10-14 A troubleshooting flowchart.

The problem is to know how a proper unit functions and how to implement a reasonable procedure for performing the comparison in a systematic manner. Other problems include making the measurements themselves and recording a time history of these measurements for the comparison. The basic test instruments and techniques needed for performing such comparisons have already been described.

Components, software, and noise can sometimes cause problems. Figure 10-14 describes some basic methods to approach typical related problems. Future hardware tools will be oriented toward the more specialized types of analyzer. A large number of logic state, trace and test capabilities, as well as the ability to display the various states of the computer's operations, will be features of the new test units. Figures 10-15 and 10-16 show two examples of specialized testers.

PC board repair

Today's PC boards are manufactured in a highly automated factory. The PC board starts as a laminated fiberglass or plastic fiber board with a copper foil layer on both sides. A circuit connection pattern is designed for the particular part layout. This pattern is used to control an etching solution, which removes the copper that is not needed for the desired connections.

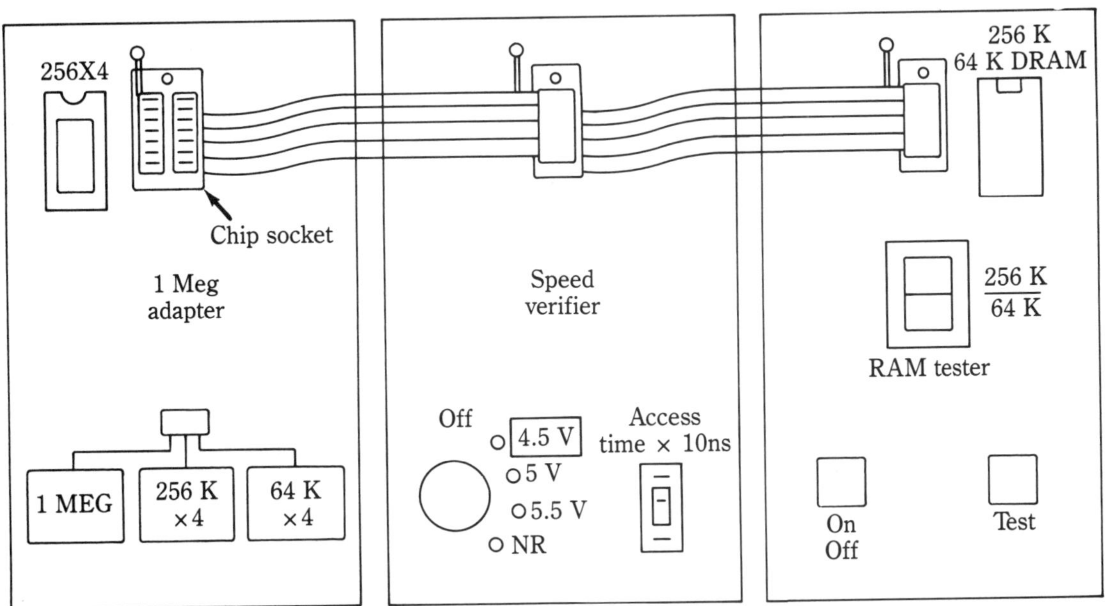

10-15 A portable DRAM chip tester. It has an 8088 microprocessor that writes, reads, and refreshes each memory cell at least four times. It has current limiters that protect the chip and prevent damage if the chip is inserted backwards. The speed verifier measures the chip's access time and can be used to find a slow chip that could be causing a problem. An auto loop test can be used to find intermittent problems.

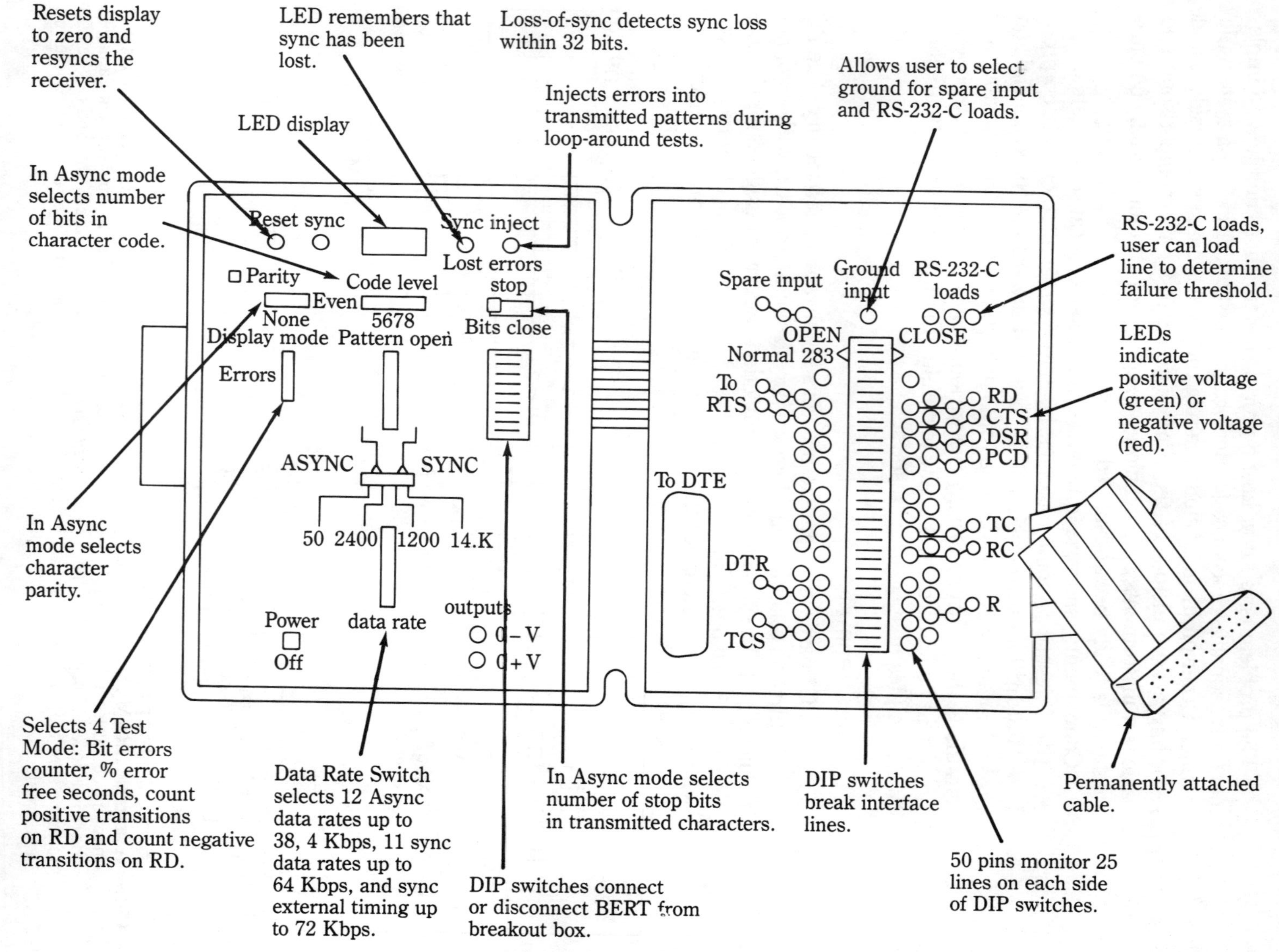

10-16   An RS-232 tester.

Some components, such as DIPs, require holes through the board so that the pins can be soldered to the copper foil tracks. Surface-mount devices (SMDs) use solder pads so that the SMD legs can be soldered to the pads. Factory robotics can produce completed PC boards with very small pin-to-pin spacings. The specialized equipment used can solder small pins quickly. If a chip fails, then you must desolder the package and resolder a new one in place. Unless you have experience with close-tolerance ICs, the replacement of an IC can be a difficult job. However, it is not important for your replacement to physically look like the original manufactured connections. It is much more important to complete all of the connections properly without disturbing nearby connections and components.

Chip packages

The PC board will hold the IC chips that compose the bulk components. However, there are usually other support components, such as capacitors, switches and jumpers. The larger of these are relatively easy to desolder, replace, and resolder—especially for those components with only a few connections (such as capacitors). IC chips are more difficult to replace unless they are socketed. These chips usually have many close pins.

DIPs Most older PCs used ICs with a *Dual-In-Line Package (DIP)*. The pins on the DIP package are placed in holes in the circuit board. Then, the pins are soldered to the circuit tracks on the board. The pins are numbered counterclockwise, from the top (Fig. 10-17). The marks might be a half circle or dot indentation or a painted dot. Plastic DIPs are usually found in PCs. The pins are 0.1 inches apart. The plastic DIP usually has tin-plated pins, so 60/40 solder works well.

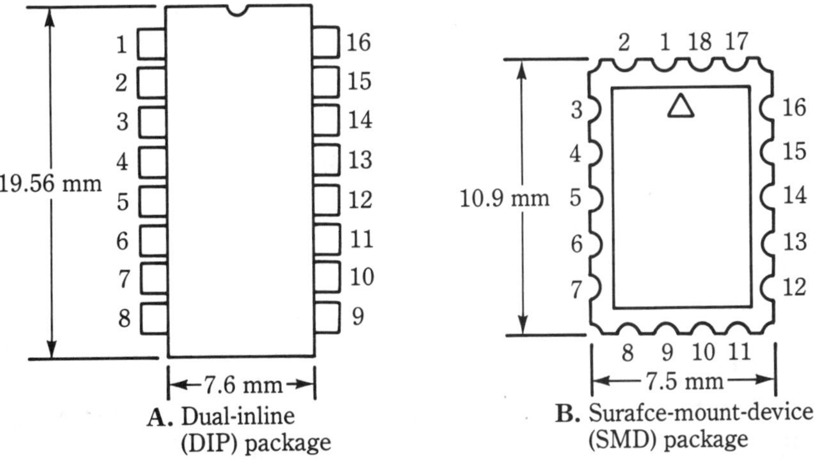

10-17 IC chip packages (top view).

SMDs   *Surface-Mount-Devices (SMDs)* use solder pads. Chips can be mounted on both sides of the board. The SMD package is smaller because four sides can have pins. The SMD can be made 40% to 60% smaller in surface area than a DIP that contains the same chip. One type of SMD is called the *Chip-Carrier-Package (CCP)*. These devices use pins that are bent over and resemble feet. These feet are designed to be soldered to pads.

When the boards are manufactured, the feet are positioned over the pads and the board is heated, the solder melts and the feet become attached to the pads. The connection provides both a physical and an electrical bond. The surface-mount technology is both cheaper and faster to manufacture than DIP technology. Two of the SMD-foot styles used include the gull-wing and J-shape (Fig. 10-18 and 10-19). An SMD board will cost about 50% of a DIP board, but it is harder to repair. The distance between pins is tighter and the solder pads are harder to get to. However, it is possible to test and replace SMDs with the proper tools and techniques.

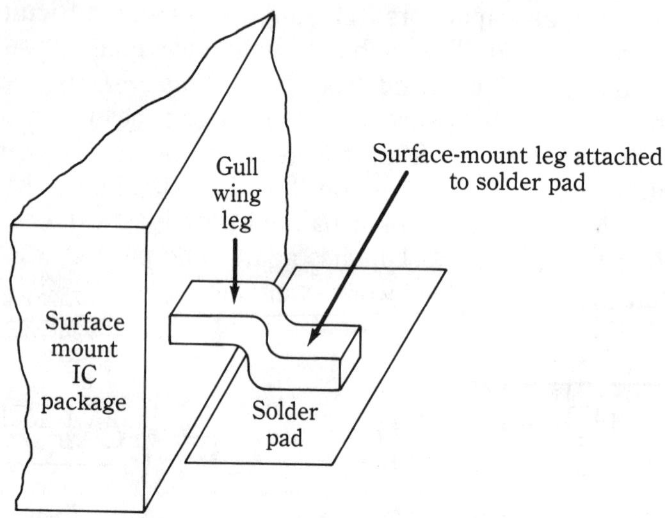

10-18   Gull wing legs on surface-mount packages are representative of the different foot sizes and shapes.

Another type of SMD is the *Chip-On-Board (COB)*. These assemblies are not replaceable, except with factory equipment. The COB chip is wired and bonded directly to the board using a type of foil for connections. The chips and leads are all part of the board assembly. A plastic sealant is molded over the chips and leads for protection. Once the assembly is complete, it is difficult to remove a chip without damaging it.

Chip replacement   IC chips (Fig. 10-20) are harder to troubleshoot

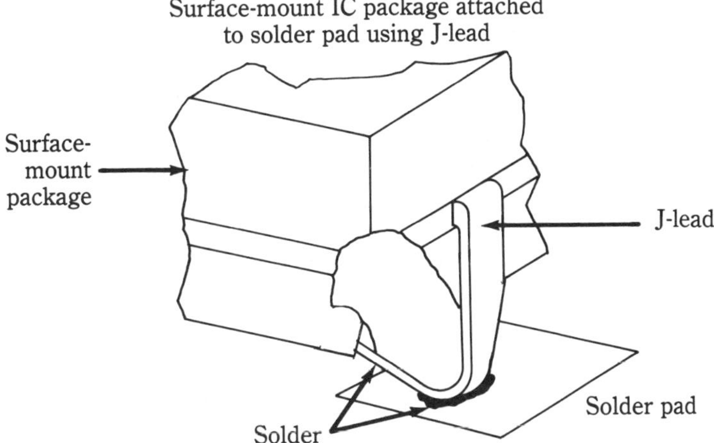

10-19 Another leg shape for an SMD is the J-lead. The solder tends to accumulate in the hook of the leg. This provides a stronger solder joint.

10-20 A PC board, the IC chips are labeled with U, the capacitors are labeled C and are used for filtering.

and repair than the discrete components on the PC board. The larger components (such as vacuum transistors, diodes, capacitors, and resistors) are larger and easier to test and replace. When these components are shrunk to microscopic size and put on a silicon chip, they can have the same types of electrical shorts, opens, and leaks. When one of these chip components fails, the complete chip must be replaced.

If the package is socketed (Fig. 10-21), the replacement is simple. You must pull the bad chip from its socket and install a new one. Even a DIP

10-21 The 8088 microprocessor is socketed and replacement chips are readily available for quick substitution.

with a low pin count that is soldered through holes in the PC board is not too difficult. This type of chip can be tested on a pin-by-pin basis with a logic probe, VOM, or oscilloscope.

Soldering To replace a small DIP, it is best to use a low-wattage iron with a solder sucker (Fig. 10-22). The solder sucker has a small rubber bulb that is used to take up melted solder. This type of iron is designed to desolder chips; for resoldering you will need a regular low-wattage iron.

When the DIP is desoldered, the iron is heated and the bulb is squeezed while the tip of the hot iron is placed on the bottom of the board

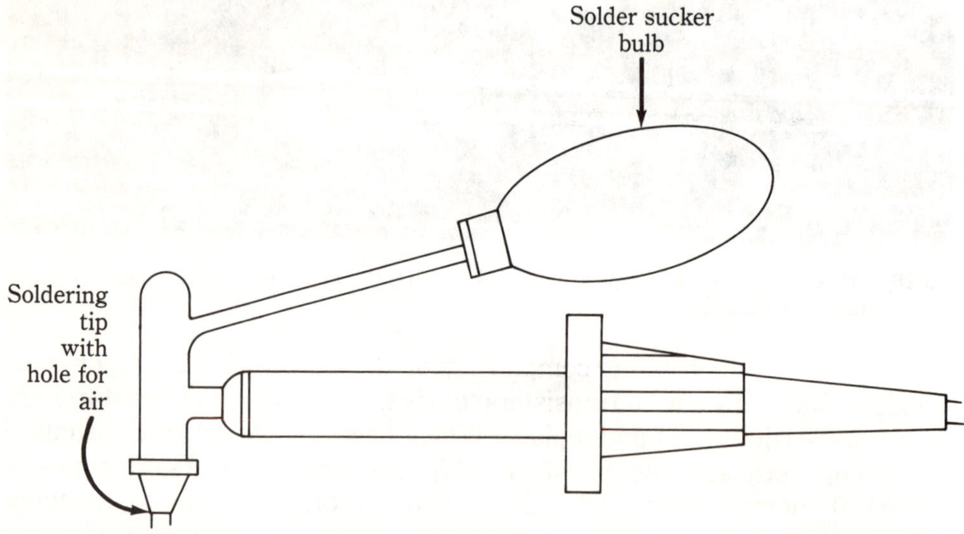

10-22 A rubber bulb is available with a special hollow soldering tip for desoldering DIP packages. When the bulb is released, some of the melted solder will be vacuumed into the hole in the iron.

under the first plated through-pin. It helps to have a bright light on the bottom of the board. The bulb is held closed while the solder melts. When the solder is liquid, the bulb is released. The solder at the heated pin is sucked into the bulb. The solder is removed from the bulb by squeezing it. This technique is repeated until all the pins are free and the chip can be removed. If some solder is still in the holes, it can be cleared using a toothpick to open the holes.

The new chip must be installed with the marker in the correct orientation. The chips will go in backwards also. A regular iron of 30 W or less should be used for resoldering. Small-diameter solder should be used because only a spot of solder is needed for each pin. The solder must not drip because it could form shorts across circuit tracks.

The changing of low-pin-count DIPs does not take too long, but the higher pin count chips can become tedious. Equipment can also be desoldered with vacuum pumps and hollow tip irons. These prevent damage because some pins require repeated heating and sucking efforts to free the pin. Some picking of the solder might also be required. Picking solder can damage the PC board. A vacuum desoldering system will usually prevent these problems.

SMD replacement Replacing an SMD is more difficult because it is soldered to only one side of the circuit board. The pads on the circuit board are slightly larger than the foot for the SMD pin. These pads are sometimes called *footprints*. During the manufacturing process, each pad has a layer of solder paste applied, using a stencil or screen. You can use a hand syringe to apply solder paste during a chip replacement. The paste aids in the soldering process by allowing a smooth flow of solder as it holds the chip in place.

During manufacture, the heating is done using an oven. If chips need to be replaced, special soldering irons are used to heat all the pins on a chip at the same time. These irons also have grippers to hold the chip. A cleaning solvent is also used to remove solder flux residues.

The SMD desoldering can be done using pieces of solder braid or wick with a fine-tipped low-wattage iron. The solder braids are dipped in rosin and placed across the pins on one of the four sides of the chip. When the braid is heated, it will tend to melt the solder holding the pins. The melted solder will be attracted to the braid as a result of capillary action. Rubbing the braid over the pins also helps. When the braid has enough of the solder, it is removed and a new section of braid is used.

When most of the solder has been removed, the pins can be heated with the iron and separated from the pads with a pick. This procedure must be done one pin at a time until the chip can be lifted from the board.

To replace an SMD, apply the solder paste with a hand syringe on the pads. Then, place the new chip on the pads and solder the corner pins first. This will hold the chip while you solder the other pins.

Static electricity   Electrostatic discharge (ESD) is a concern whenever chips are handled. The problem is the small size of the MOS transistors used in many ICs. The insulator that protects these is very thin because of the method of construction. Static discharge can break down these insulators and damage the small devices. In most high-density chips (such as RAMs), the insulator protects very small current paths on the silicon chip. Thousands of these paths are on the silicon chip and damage to any one of them will cause a functional failure. Precautions are necessary to protect these chips from static electricity.

When the RAM chips had only a few thousand transistors, the spacing between the leads of the transistors was about five times as wide as it is today. The lead spacing has been reduced and the leads themselves are much smaller. This metallization is vulnerable to static electric currents.

Because these chips are sensitive to ESD, care must be taken during chip replacement. Handling techniques have been developed over time. The human body is capable of providing several hundred volts of static electricity. When the air is humid, this potential is lower and might only be about 100 V because of leakage. When the air is dryer, the leakage is lower and the potential will build up as you move around. It is possible to build up a static charge of almost 1,000 V under the right conditions. If this charge is passed on to a high-density MOS device, some damage is possible if the energy is large enough. Most devices have some type of protection on their input leads, but the protection can be lost if the energy of the static charge is greater than the burnout energy of the protection devices. The energy that is leftover will then burnout functional devices inside the chip.

When the chip is connected to other circuits on the PC board, its pins are connected to ground paths and other low impedance paths. The major danger exists when it is disconnected and being handled.

Grounding techniques   Before you handle a chip, take precautions to lower any static charge on your body. Connect your body to an earth ground, such as a grounded computer chassis. The work table should also be connected to ground.

A number of products are available for static protection. The wrist strap goes around your wrist and carries away the electrostatic charge before it builds up (Fig. 10-23). These lightweight wrist straps have a coiled cord, which acts as the grounding cable and connects to earth ground. It is best to use the grounding bracelet on the same hand that is used to hold the probe or soldering iron. The closer the strap is to the hand that works on the chips, the safer the chips will be.

Because you are now grounded to earth, you have to be especially care-

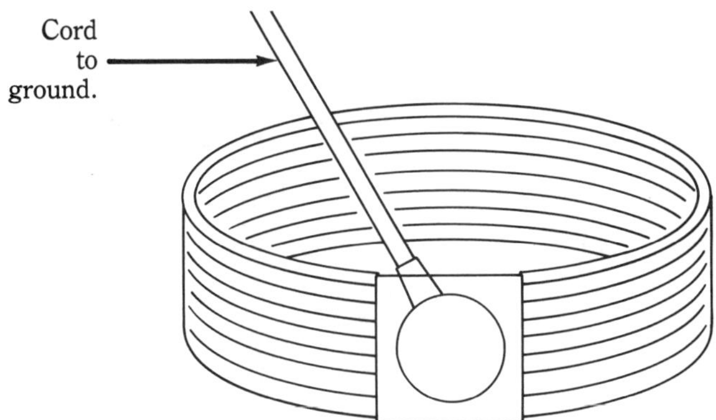

10-23 Static-control wrist straps fit around the wrist and have a grounding cord. Some units use a 1 MΩ resistor to prevent the current from exceeding 0.5 mA for voltages to 220 Vac.

ful not to touch any electrical lines. If that would happen, you would provide a short circuit path to ground! Two things are done to reduce this danger. The outside of the wrist strap is insulated and a 1-MΩ resister is connected in series with the ground line at the wrist-strap connection. This resister prevents the current through the ground line from exceeding 0.5 mA for voltages up to 220 V.

Also, some table and floor mats (Fig. 10-24) are made of a semiconductive vinyl. The semiconductive material provides discharging for static effects, but prevents shorting the circuit-board pins. The floor mat works best for leather-soled shoes. Other types of soles will be insulated from the mat.

The following guidelines should be used while working on PCs.

1. A device should never be inserted or removed from circuits unless all power to the circuits is removed, it is best to remove the power plug so that there can be no question of electrical power removal.

2. Chips should be kept in conductive foam pads. These will keep the pins shorted together.

3. The chip should only be handled by the hand that has the ground strap.

4. Tools that are used to touch the chip should be grounded just before they make contact. This includes chip pullers and inserters, pliers, and solder picks.

5. The soldering iron should have its tip grounded. The power plug should be removed when solder is touched to the iron and when the iron touches the pins of the chip. This action prevents any possibility of damage from line power to the chip.

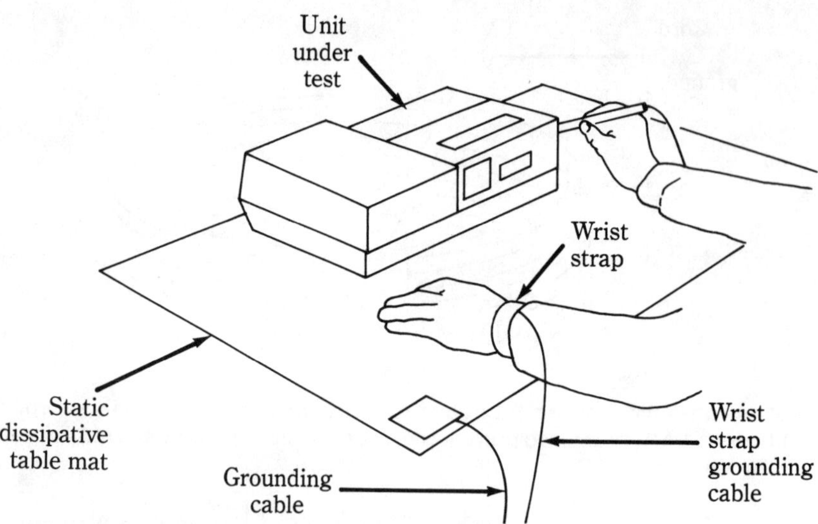

10-24 Static electricity can be shorted to ground using a static mat and a wrist strap to drain the static charges to ground.

Never handle an IC unless you are properly grounded—especially when the ambient humidity is high. A static charge, such as the one generated by walking on carpeting on a dry day, can destroy many MOS chips. Do not install a board in the computer unless power is off and after you have waited at least 15 seconds for all charges to be dissipated. Finally, do not trust specified voltages and currents; always measure them.

Service facilities

Testing PC boards and replacing defective components can be difficult and can require special equipment. Technical service firms that specialize in the repair of the various computer parts are available. These facilities usually have an inventory of good circuit boards that can be swapped if a replacement board is available, or repaired, if one is not.

They are equipped with the required service tools in addition to the stock of good PC boards for the computers that they service. This stock can range from printer boards with a few chips or motherboards with hundreds of chips. The specialized equipment and training allows these facilities to quickly troubleshoot and repair PC boards. They are able to desolder and then resolder large pin-count chips in DIP and SMD packages.

Another type of service that is available is field service. When a computer system breaks down, a field technician is dispatched to the computer site to analyze the trouble. The technician is usually able to isolate the problem to a single PC board. Once the suspect PC board is identified, the technician removes the suspect board and replaces it with a good board. If the trouble was in the suspected board, the computer is repaired and the technician goes on to the next service call. Later, a technician will check out the board with the required servicing equipment. The bad component is found and replaced. The system is then tested and given a final ok.

If you can determine which board or section of the computer is faulty, you are essentially doing the work of a field technician. You could remove the board or disk drive and take or send it to a service facility. They might be able to do the repair while you wait or perhaps service it in the next day or two. Some will give you an allowance for your defective unit and furnish a rebuilt unit. This procedure is often used with disk drives. Following is a list of service firms and their specialities.

Company name	**Repairs**
ACI 550 E. Thornton Parkway Suite 100 Denver, CO 80229 (800) 231-0743	Floppy drives, monitors, and printheads
AEG Olympia, Inc. 1255 Viceroy Dr. Dallas, TX 75247 (214) 630-4608	Monitors
BL Memories 17070 Royal View Rd. Hacienda Heights, CA 91745 (818) 913-1851	Disk drives
CAP Industries, Inc. 600 Ansin Blvd. Hallandale, FL 33009	Boards and printers
Capital Computer Solutions, Inc. 50210 W. Pontiac Trail Wixom, MI 48393 (313) 624-3260	Keyboards and printers
CTS Services, Inc. 31 Hayward St. Franklin, MA 02038 (508) 528-7720	Monitors

Decision Data   Printers
One Progress Ave.
Horsham, PA 19044
(800) 633-2863

Depot II   Monitors
2968 W. Ina Rd., #167
Tucson, AZ 85741
(800) 345-9331

Independent Computer Support   Monitors, printers, and tape
   Services   drives
400 Devon Park Dr.
Wayne, PA 19087
(215) 687-0900

Intron Corp.   Monitors
7420 Fullerton Rd., Suite 114
Springfield, VA 22153
(703) 569-1500

Maxdata Technologies, Inc.   Floppy disks and tape drives
8100 Remmet Ave., #9
Canoga Park, CA 91304
(818) 702-8836

MicroLogic Systems, Inc.   Printers
5111 Troup Hwy, #105
Tyler, TX 75707
(903) 561-0007

Midwest Computer Support   Hard drives, monitors, and
1946 N. 13th St.   printersToledo, OH 43624
Toledo, OH 43624
(419) 259-2600

OMNI CEO, Inc.   Keyboards
70 Industrial Ave., East
Lowell, MA 01852-9923
(508) 937-5004

PTS Electronics Corp.   Monitors
5233 S. Hwy. 37
Bloomington, IN 47401
(800) 333-7871

Quality High-Tech Services, Inc.   Monitors and printers
11865 Forestgate Dr.
Dallas, TX 75243
(214) 231-6696

Reset   Disk drives and printers
49 Strathearn Pl.
Simi Valley, CA 93065
(805) 584-4900

Stingray   Printers
607 Swan Dr.
P.O. Box 558
Smyma, TN 37167
(800) 467-0242

Technical Equipment Services   Keyboards
83 Harwood Ave.
Littleton, MA 01460

Texas Computer Brokers   Monitors and printers
1305 Summit Station 10
Plano, TX 75014
(214) 881-0777

Tech Zam   Hard drives
7745 Alabama Ave., Unit #8
Canoga Park, CA 91304
(818) 887-3046

URS Information Systems, Inc.   Monitors and printers
44 Concord St.
Wingmington, MA 01887
(508) 657-6100

Zenith Data Systems   Monitors and printers
611 Development Blvd.
Amery, WI 54001
(715) 268-8106

Most service outlets try to have a quick turn around time so that you can get your system running quickly. With a little knowledge and some basic tools, you can usually find and replace the faulty components without much trouble.

In-circuit component testers   In-circuit component testers are general-purpose troubleshooting test instruments, that are designed to evaluate and visually compare digital, analog, and hybrid semiconductor devices and reactive components in or out of the circuit with the power off. They can be used to detect leakage problems and bonding problems, shorts, opens and other failure modes. In many cases, these problems can cause intermittent failures.

The operating principles used are similar to those used in a semiconductor curve tracer. A current-limited sine-wave voltage is injected across the two points of the device under test. The resulting signature is displayed as a current and voltage trace on the built-in CRT display (Fig. 10-25). The display indicates the dynamic conditions of the semiconductor junction.

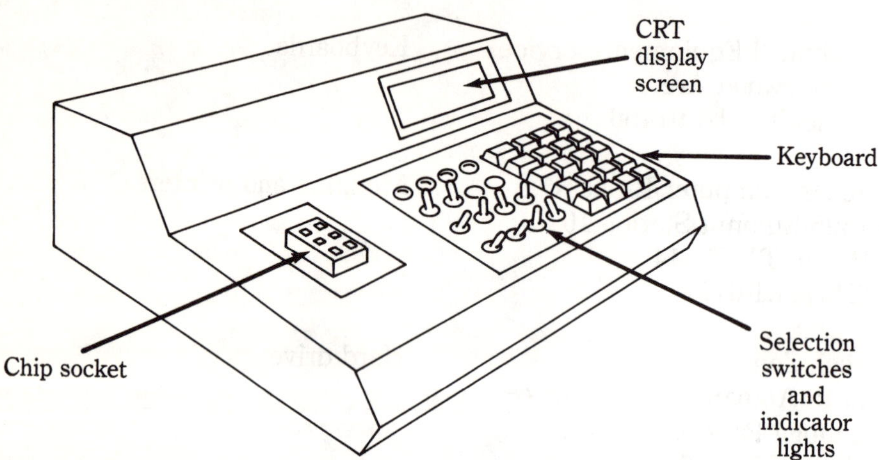

10-25   An in-circuit tester can be programmed with a device interface. It has component and chip sockets, a keyboard, and a control panel.

A well-defined junction appears as a straight line, which indicates a normal semiconductor. Poorly-defined junctions show up as curved lines and indicate excessive leakage. These displays represent the condition of the semiconductor and can be used to find defective devices, as well as marginal components. A comparison mode can be used to alternately display CRT signatures of both a unit under test and a known good board or component. This arrangement allows the user to identify defective boards and troubleshoot at the component level. When a defective component has been identified and removed, the tester can then be used to verify if the replacement component is good.

The following components can be tested:

Diodes General purpose, Zener, tunnel, varactor, and high voltage.

Transistors Npn and pnp bipolar, Darlington, JFET, MOSFET, and unijunction.

Thyristors SCR, SGS, GCS, Triac, Diac.

Optoelectronic devices LEDs, LED displays, phototransistors, and optocouplers.

Integrated circuits Digital; CMOS, NMOS, PMOS, and TTL.
Analog; op amps, voltage regulators, and timers.

Component switching An interface unit is also available for switching circuit boards and components. A set of IC clips is used to route the signals from both the board being tested and a known good board through an automatic switch. The rate at which the signals are compared on the display is controlled by the interface unit.

The switching unit can also be used with general-purpose test equipment for power-on troubleshooting. This unit can be used to make voltage, signal level, resistance, or other measurements of powered circuits and components. IC sockets on the unit allow A/B comparisons of 40-pin DIP packages. Thus pin-for-pin comparisons can be made to replace ICs.

Power supply testers Power supply testers are designed to monitor the voltage of a suspect dc power supply. It can aid the troubleshooting process by isolating a problem to either the power supply or the system under power. It can be used to detect and store out-of-range conditions and provide a test vehicle to see whether or not a power supply has stayed within specifications over a period of time. This information can then be checked against any intermittent failures that might have occurred in the system under power. These testers replace the need for chart recorders or digital storage scopes.

Power problems PC downtime can be caused by a number of factors. The reliability of hardware and the quality of software are certainly key to keeping a PC functioning and available. Another important, yet often neglected, factor is the quality and reliability of the computer's electrical power supply. Although the quality of the hardware and software are controlled to a large extent by the manufacturing process and correct usage of the products, the quality of the electrical supply depends on many factors that are often beyond the PC user's control.

Although high-quality electric power might be generated by the utility, it can be corrupted by special circumstances, such as lightning or grid switching, during high-demand peak periods. These factors interrupt the continuous flow of power so that a computer might not always meet the electrical requirements of the system.

Additional power contamination might be created by influences in the building. When other equipment is turned on, the starting in-rush power requirements can temporarily cause transient voltages and surges resulting in data errors and equipment damage. Most studies show that power disturbances occur on the average of two times a week for a typical commercial facility and most disturbances are generated within the building.

The following types of disturbances have been found to cause problems by both IBM and Bell Labs.

1. **Sags**   These are cycle-to-cycle decreases in the power-line voltage below 80 percent of the nominal value. Sags usually last less than several seconds. Sags occur frequently at the wall socket level and account for the majority of total power-line disturbances. These disturbances are a major cause of data loss.

2. **Surges**   These are cycle-to-cycle increases in the power-line voltage above 110 percent of the nominal value. Surges last less than several seconds. These cause most of the hardware damage in computers.

3. **Outage**   This type of power failure results in a zero-voltage condition. They are about 15 percent of the total number of power-line disturbances that occur at the wall-socket level.

4. **Oscillations**   These fluctuations are also known as *noise*. They usually decay within a cycle of line voltage and have a frequency range from 400 Hz to 5 kHz.

5. **Spikes**   These are also known as *impulses* and show up as overvoltages that are superimposed on the line voltage. They can last between 0.5 and 100 μs.

Power transients can force too much power into the computer or deprive the computer of the necessary power. The first type includes surges and spikes while the second includes sags, brownouts, and blackouts. Because spikes are rapid excursions of voltage with a large amplitude, they can propagate through the system and cause sensitive components to break down. See Fig. 10-26 for typical power line problems.

All disturbances can cause malfunctions in computers. Power disturbances can affect a system differently, depending on their duration and which part of the system was being used when the disturbance occurred. Sags can result in two types of problems in computers, depending on their duration. If the sag lasts longer than one or two cycles, it can cause the

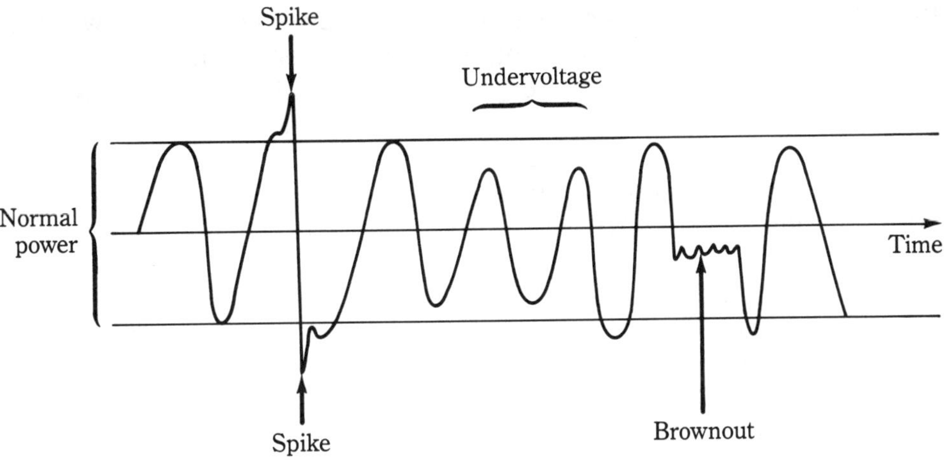

10-26   Powerline problems.

computer power supply to detect a low voltage on its output, which shuts down the computer. The computer must then be rebooted.

If the sag lasts for a cycle and its duration is approximately equal to the holdup time of the power supply in the computer, the problem can be more critical. The power-supply voltage of the computer will decrease near the end of sag, then increase. This transient condition can reverse 1s and 0s in memory. These changes will be transferred to disk storage as bugs or data errors. They can cause program hang-ups. Power blackouts can create the same types of problems as sags.

A power surge is an overvoltage or increase in the ac line voltage. A spike is more of an instantaneous or short-term overvoltage. It lasts from 0.05 to 100 μs and acts like a large, but faster surge. Insurance company data shows that 40 percent of transient problems are surge-related. Surges stress computer components, particularly in the power supply and can cause premature component failure.

A transient dip in the voltage is usually called a *sag*, but it is an under-voltage condition. A long sag becomes a brownout. Undervoltage problems cause more damage than surges, but the surge that follows a sag can cause serious damage. As long as the power goes out quickly enough, the computer will not be damaged. When the power returns to normal, it does so in a series of surges, and produces an effect called *hammering*. Hammering can cause the hard disk head to fall down onto the surface of the disk and then lift up and drop again with each surge.

Electrical noise can enter the computer through the power cable. This can be interference from fluorescent lights and other equipment. Noise can cause fluctuations in the voltage and lose or corrupt data. If the amplitude of oscillations is less than 50 percent of the nominal voltage over a period of time, the power supply can break down. If it does not break down, the oscillations will appear on the output of the power supply and have the same effects as sags on the power-supply lines to integrated circuits.

A number of devices between the service entrance and the workstation affect the power. Air conditioners can cause surges on power lines. Fluorescent lights generate noise that, if it gets through to the machine, can cause erratic performance. Other devices that can cause problems are copiers and printers.

All computers have some type of filtering capacitor, which acts to reduce transients. The computer's internal logic circuits require a clean, continuous source of power; these filter capacitors and the power-supply shutdown are designed to deliver it. However, any capacitor has a finite storage capacity (the capacitance). The transient on the ac power line might swamp the capacitor if it has enough energy.

There are various ways to protect devices ranging from surge suppressors (Figs. 10-27A and 10-27B) to Intelligent Power Systems (IPS). *Surge suppressors* are probably the most common and least effective power-protection devices. They reduce the voltage of a surge, using a device (such as a varistor) to limit the maximum voltage. Thus, voltages of less than 200 to 300 V might get into the computer. Varistors have a long response time that can allow short spikes to pass through. Varistors are used in about 90 percent of the surge suppressors.

Surge suppressors also use gas tubes or inductive chokes in series with the line. Gas tubes can handle large amounts of energy and can provide some protection for lightning effects. Series choking devices allow the normal ac line power through, but limit the effects from surges.

The problem with surge suppressors is that they have no power reserve to apply in the event of an undervoltage. This type of power problem requires a standby or uninterruptible power system. A *standby power system (SPS)* is also called an *offline system*. It contains a battery that will support the computer in the event of a power sag, brownout, or blackout.

The SPS is plugged into the wall outlet and the machine is plugged into the SPS. When the power drops below a certain level, the SPS switches from ac power to battery back-up. An important part of SPS performance is the *switching time*, the time required for the system to switch from line to battery power. If it is too long, the data generally will notice it (even though the hardware might not). This is especially true on a network where information is traveling over some distance. The maximum allowable switching time is about one ms. Most SPSs have switching times from one to four ms.

An *uninterruptible power system (UPS)* is known as an *online system*. Although an SPS lets the normal line power through until it senses an irregularity, a UPS provides the power from its own battery, which is con-

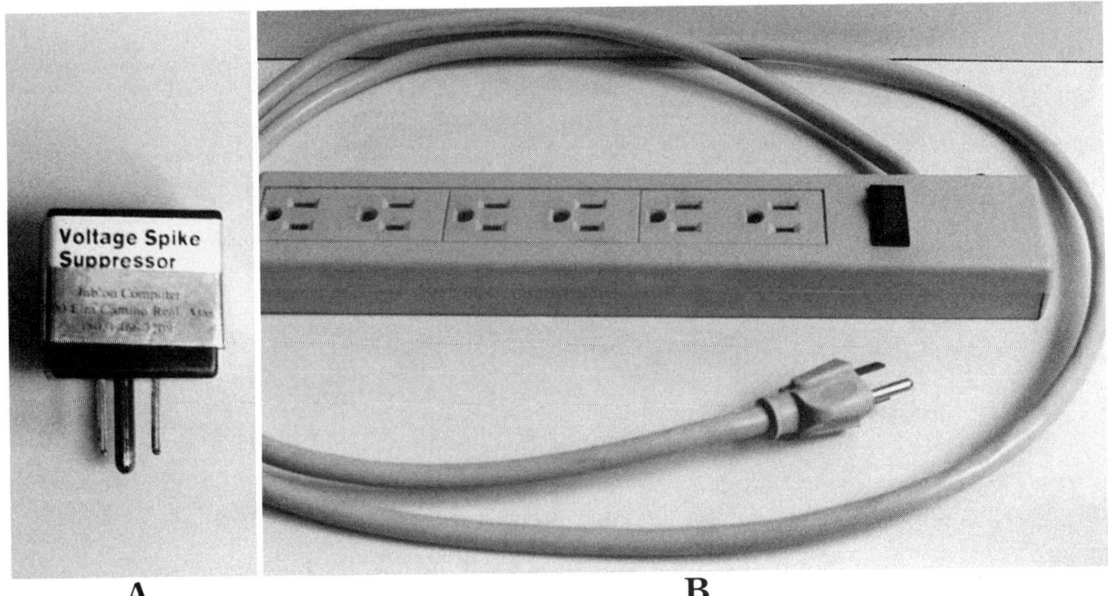

A   **B**

10-27 Two types of surge suppressors. (A) A single-outlet surge or spike suppressor. (B) A multiple-outlet surge suppressor with switch.

tinuously charged from utility power. There is no switching time and line conditioning is built into the system. When a blackout occurs, the UPS provides backup long enough to allow a systematic shutdown of the computer.

A disadvantage of a UPS is that they can generate heat, which reduces the lifetime of the internal components. The battery also needs to be replaced periodically. The usual approach to the heating problem is to oversize the components so that they generate less heat.

The *intelligent power system (IPS)* is like a UPS, but it has software that sends a warning message that the computer is going down in a certain amount of time. It then goes into an orderly shutdown of the system, saving and closing files without losing any data. When the power comes back on, the software brings up the system and reopens the files to where the system was when the power went down without losing any data.

A major advantage about an IPS is that a system or network that is protected by an IPS can be left unattended. An UPS can provide an orderly shutdown, but someone must be available to perform the shutdown before the battery runs out. An IPS will shut down the network automatically.

Index